Janice Winsley
Non 4/02

D0428049

hold me close,
let me go

ALSO BY ADAIR LARA

History of Petaluma, A California River Town

Welcome to Earth, Mom

Slowing Down in a Speeded-Up World

At Adair's House

The Best of Adair Lara

ADAIR LARA

hold me close,
let me go

a mother,

a daughter,

and an

adolescence

survived

BROADWAY BOOKS

NEW YORK

BROADWAY

A hardcover edition of this book was published in 2001 by Broadway Books.

HOLD ME CLOSE, LET ME GO. Copyright © 2001 by Adair Lara. All rights reserved. No part of this book may be reproduced or transmitted in any form or by any means, electronic or mechanical, including photocopying, recording, or by any information storage and retrieval system, without written permission from the publisher. For information, address Broadway Books, a division of Random House, Inc., 1540 Broadway, New York, NY 10036.

Broadway Books titles may be purchased for business or promotional use or for special sales. For information, please write to: Special Markets Department, Random House, Inc., 1540 Broadway, New York, NY 10036.

PRINTED IN THE UNITED STATES OF AMERICA

BROADWAY BOOKS and its logo, a letter B bisected on the diagonal, are trademarks of Broadway Books, a division of Random House, Inc.

Visit our website at www.broadwaybooks.com

First trade paperback edition published 2002

Designed by Jo Anne Metsch

While all the incidents in this book are true, some of the names and personal characteristics of several of the peripheral characters have been changed in order to protect their privacy.

The Library of Congress has cataloged the hardcover edition as follows:

Lara, Adair.
Hold me close, let me go: a mother, a daughter, and an adolescence survived /
by Adair Lara.
p. cm.
1. Lara, Adair. 2. Mothers—California—Biography. 3. Parent and teenager—
California—Case studies. 4. Mothers and daughters—California—Case
studies. 5. Problem youth—Family relationships—California—Case studies. I. Title.
HQ759.L364 2001
306.874'3—dc21
00-062171

ISBN 0-7679-0508-3

1   3   5   7   9   10   8   6   4   2

For Morgan, Patrick, Bill, and Jim
for trusting me with this story

Pick Me Up
Hold Me Close
Put Me Down
Let Me Go

*—the story of raising a child,
according to an old adage*

acknowledgments

People often think of a writer as going into solitary rooms where he or she hunches over a machine surrounded by balled-up paper for two years or so and emerges with a finished book. For me it was like that, except there were many people crowded into that room with me. First, there was Morgan herself. She was not thrilled at any time about the notion of a book about her wild teenage self. It's a self most of us like to put quietly behind us rather than having it etched permanently into the record and then sold to strangers in stores. But she let me write this book about our experience. I can't think of a larger act of trust in my whole life.

And in that room with me was Bill, who is such a thorough and selfless editor that he first lived through every day of those difficult years, then consented to read about it again and again, always telling me to keep going.

And then there were the women: Ginny McReynolds, who was my writing partner when Morgan was a teenager; Neshama Franklin; Annie Lamott, who read a terrible first draft and told me to keep going; Donna Levin, who read terrible second and third drafts and gave me the title; my sister Adrian Isola, who read sections throughout; and my friends Cynthia Gorney and Tracy Johnston, who both generously read the manuscript at an early stage, using time they surely could have used for something else. And then my writing club, Wendy Lichtman, Rebecca Koffman, and especially Janis Newman, whose critiques made the book much better than it would have been otherwise. And if it isn't crowded enough already in my little writing room, in there with the rest of us were the readers of the *San Francisco Chronicle*, who read my columns about Morgan over the years, following her progress and cheering her on until she got through high school and then college.

And when I emerged from that room, there were more people: my agent Fred Hill, and Harriet Bell, and my wonderful editor, Gerry Howard, with his generous understanding of the book and its aims.

hold me close, let me go

LEANED against the doorjamb, sticking my head into Morgan's room stiffly. "Where you going?" I asked, hoping to sound casual.

"Holly's," she said, her eyes on the pile of jeans, underwear, and bras she was piling into the red Nike bag that lay open on the floor. Holly was a school friend who lived a few doors down from us.

Morgan's hair was Manic Panic red, the only bright spot of color on a gray August Tuesday. She folded several pairs of cutoff jeans, then a white T-shirt with torn-off sleeves, on the front of which she had scrawled in black marker, "Why yes, I am Wonder Woman."

She was not running away.

I was throwing her out.

I watched her pack, then, unable to watch anymore, walked blindly out of the house. I stood on the sidewalk and looked back up at the house, a large yellow Victorian capped by a tower. At my feet, in the cement, were the names Morgan and Patrick, scrawled there when the kids were six and seven. I walked three miles over the steep Castro Street hill to 24th Street and back. I must have taken Cody, our sheltie, with me, but I don't remember. I must have waited at red lights, walked by the Walgreen's, Noah's Bagels, and the Bank of America, but I don't remember that either.

When I got back an hour later, she was gone. She'd left a note on the table next to her cereal bowl, empty except for the last few Lucky Charms, yellow moons, pink hearts, and green clovers drowned in rice milk. "Mom, I love you. Bill wants you to call. I love you very much. Morgan."

I felt the bones in my neck turning to concrete. I folded the note and put it in my pocket and went into her room. It smelled of wet towels and the peach bubble bath she always used. On her bulletin board she had thumbtacked a picture of me reading to a small crowd at a bookstore. In it I was wearing my green speech suit. My head looked tiny, like the top of a PEZ dispenser. Postcards were tacked to the walls haphazardly—we'd given up talking to her about making holes in the wall—and her snowboard leaned against the dresser that she insisted on keeping in the closet, the white closet doors gaping wide.

On the table beside the bed lay a snapshot of her I'd taken at a school play only months before. I picked it up and carried it over to the window. She stood at center stage with two other girls, taking a curtain call. All three were dazed and smiling at the applause, but Morgan managed to hold the spotlight, smiling radiantly. Even in that blurred photo, you can tell that Morgan helped herself to the best features of her parents—my slightly slanted brown eyes, set wide apart like her dad's, with a lot of green in them. Jim's blond hair, thick like mine. My small nose and his high cheekbones.

The phone rang. I fished through the pile of jeans and tank tops next to the bed until I found the white cordless phone.

"Adair? It's Judy." Judy was Holly's mother. "Are you all right?"

"No," I said.

"Morgan is here at my house. Would it be okay with you if I kept her for a couple of days?"

"Yes, of course," I said, feeling relief flood me. "Did she tell you what happened?"

"Yes, she did. Morgan feels she doesn't need the recovery pro-gram." Judy spoke in a neutral tone, but it was clear to me what she was really thinking: What kind of mother throws out her own six-teen-year-old daughter?

I didn't blame her. The same thought tortured me. It had taken us just three years of shouting, slammed doors, tears, phone calls, and notes sliding under doors to get to this most terrible of days.

chapter 1

MORGAN was still asleep, though it was almost eleven. The light from her west-facing window washed the top half of her face and her tumbled hair, the same brownish-blond as her brother Patrick's. One pink foot stuck out. I sat on the edge of the bed and shook it.

"Mom, I was sleeping." She smiled lazily at me.

"Is it true that last night you and Tara went into Dolores Park?"

"Mom, what are you talking about?" Morgan, caught off guard, sat up, trying for an expression of injured innocence.

"Did you?"

"What park?"

"Dolores. Where the drug dealers hang out."

"Well, yes, but we were totally safe." She said it with a little shrug.

"What about the beer?" I said in a tight voice. "Tara said something about a six-pack."

"It was just sitting in a bag in a parking lot. I didn't drink any of the beer. It was sour. I just sprayed it on the ground. God, Mom.

You're overreacting, just the way Daddy always does." She slumped down, then, in a sudden change of mood, grinned at me. "It was worth it. It was the most fun I ever had in my life. The only problem was getting caught."

"Fun? You could have been raped or murdered, two young girls out on the streets. Don't you remember those two girls on Potrero Hill who were just standing on a corner when a gang of boys took them off to a shed and raped them five or six times each? They were only thirteen, like you and Tara."

"I'll be fourteen in two months, and anyway my friends wouldn't let anything happen to me," Morgan said confidently. "If anybody tried to hurt us, we'd kick them in the you know where."

I was getting nowhere, so I stood up. Having a thirteen-year-old was like having your own personal brick wall. The phone rang. I found it under a pile of junk on Morgan's floor.

"Hello?"

"Hello!" said a familiar gravelly voice.

"*Dad?*"

"In the flesh."

"Where are you?"

"In the valley, in my hidey hole."

"Your hidey hole?" My head was still full of Morgan. It had been years since I'd seen my father or heard his voice. I swallowed. "How long have you been back?"

"Couple of months. I was wondering if you could find it in your heart to come out here today to see your poor old dad."

"I can't. I'm on deadline." I wrote a column for the *San Francisco Chronicle* on Tuesdays and Thursdays. "And the kids start school to-morrow."

"I know you're busy, but I need you to come out here. Jesus Christ, I haven't laid eyes on you in five years. For all I know, you're taller."

"Dad, I told you . . ."

"Besides, it's an emergency."

"An emergency?" I couldn't help the frosty tone of my voice. "Are you in jail?"

"No, I'm not in jail. Tell you when you get here."

"Hey, let me talk to my grandpa!" Morgan yelled.

"Shush! I can't hear him!"

My dad had said something, but I missed it. "I'm sorry, Dad, I was talking to Morgan. Listen, I'm not coming out there."

"Come on," he urged. "You can tell me what a rotten father I've been."

"You *have* been a rotten father."

"Come on. You'll be back by early afternoon."

"Maybe next weekend."

I could hear Dad sigh. "Why are all you kids so angry?" he asked. "I gave you everything you ever asked for." He paused. "Except, of course, for the basic necessities. Those I left to your saintly mother." He paused, and I heard him sigh again. "All right, see you when I see you."

The phone clicked in my ear.

"I thought Grandpa was in the desert. Is he back? Where is he?" Morgan was up, pulling a pair of corduroy overalls over the T-shirt she had slept in.

"I'm not sure. In Marin County somewhere. I'm going out to see him."

"I want to come!"

"I'm sorry," I said in the snappish new way I had of talking to her. "You are grounded for the rest of your life." She had been sneaking out of the house for months now, and I always grounded her, for what little good it seemed to do.

I left her and tried to return to my column. But the sound of jack-hammering outside the window kept distracting me, and I was restless and unable to concentrate. Outside a man lifted a piece of cardboard out of a stack someone had left on the corner. I watched as he shaped it back into a box, then flattened it again and walked off with it.

I called my twin sister, Adrian, reaching her at the Ukiah County Courthouse, where she was the civil clerk. She wasn't surprised to hear from me. We talked to each other three or four times a day.

"Hey, hag."

"Hag yourself."

"Guess what."

"What?"

"Dad's back."

"He is? Where is he?"

"In his hidey hole, he said, which I guess means somewhere out in the San Geronimo Valley. He just called, wants me to go see him. Says it's an emergency."

"Are you going?"

"No. I have my hands full here. Guess what Morgan's done now. Sneaked out last night with one of her little friends and went out roaming the streets."

"How did you catch her?"

"Tara spilled the beans to her mother this morning, and her mom called me."

"And now Dad's back."

"Yeah."

"Well, good luck."

I hung up, went into the kitchen, and grabbed my purse and keys. Since I had to finish a column, my husband, Bill, had gone off early for a hike on Mount Tamalpais with friends. Bill was not Morgan's dad but my second husband (well, technically my third), who had arrived on the scene when Morgan was eleven and Patrick ten. Today Patrick was playing basketball down at the rec center.

Where had Dad said he was?

I drove north across the Golden Gate Bridge, and followed Highway 101, Mount Tamalpais looming on my left. I took the exit to Sir Francis Drake Boulevard, which runs north and then west through central Marin County and out to the ocean. The air was warmer, and I rolled down the window.

After Fairfax, the foothill called White's Hill reared in front of me, warning me and everyone else that we were leaving the land of lawns, sidewalks, and brunch and entering San Geronimo Valley, in the last pocket of hills before the rolling grasslands that lead to the coast.

The road flattened out on the other side. Coming into the valley with its golden hills felt like driving into my own childhood, into those scenes that lay in the back of my mind like short videotapes, jerky and slow, like the Super 8 movies my mother used to take of us.

When I was little, Dad was the sound of hammering, the stray scent of tobacco and sawdust, the roar of a truck starting up, a man holding an anvil over his head for the camera. "I couldn't stand myself then," he told me once, "but I had all those lovely muscles." He was on the edge of my world, as I was on his: "You were always twisted around something in the foreground," he told me in a letter, "part of your mother's entourage." We were living in this valley then, a large unruly Irish-American family struggling along on the wages of a journeyman carpenter who only worked in good weather. Dad stayed until I was ten, when he was carried away on a high-cresting wave of Schlitz. Mom tried for years after he left to get the seven of us to call him Gene and hate him for deserting us, but we still sometimes slipped out, in ones and twos, to wherever he was, to drink his instant coffee and watch him strum the guitar that he never did learn to play.

When he was sixty-five, after he had realized his shoulders were shot and was wondering what he would do when he could no longer work at all, Dad discovered he was eligible for social security.

A man who up until that minute had worked for every dime, he sat turning that first check over and over in his hands.

The possibility that he might be eligible for social security had not occurred to him. A man who has never voted, seldom made enough money to pay taxes, a man whose driver's license was revoked after he dreamily drove a car over a cliff and then walked away unhurt for about the fifteenth time--this is not a man who figures that the laws he has devoted his life to thwarting are going to underwrite the comforts of his old age.

That's when he left for the desert. "I waited until my dotage to break loose," he wrote me, "underwritten by Reagan's few dollars. It's enough to make a cat cry. It puts a terrible strain on better late than never."

He'd been out in the Mojave Desert for five years, living in his truck. Cruising down the road, with his dog Fred riding shotgun.

I woke from my reveries as I flashed by my old Mexican stucco school, now a community center. Dad had said he was in his hidey hole. What did that mean?

I reached Forest Knolls, the middle of the three little valley towns stretched along Sir Francis Drake Boulevard, and parked in front of the Lodge, a whitewashed stucco building with a few pickups parked at odd angles in front of it. I stepped into the gloom and waited for my eyes to adjust, but I could already tell he wasn't here, at his old stool at the bar, drinking a Coors under the dusty beer mobiles.

A young woman who stood behind the counter, watching the TV screen, swung around when the door creaked shut behind me. "You're a Daly, aren't you?" she said as I was turning to go. "One of the twins?"

"Yes, I'm Adair," I said. "Adrian's living up north in Ukiah." I had recognized her too. "You're Susan. One of the Dugans."

When I was growing up here, San Geronimo Valley was filled with big families--the Dugans, the Neilsens, the Weavers, the Dalys--each yard filled with kids racing around long past dusk, their white T-shirts blurring in the dim light. In each family, even ours, the kids looked so much alike that you could spot them anywhere. The Dugans were dark, with pug noses and huge eyes. We were paler, with thick hair, small noses, and brown eyes.

"I heard you moved to the city," Susan said.

"Yes, I've been there twenty years now." I had come over to the bar, and moved my sleeve so she could wipe down the corner. Her family had added some modern features to the bar over the years–a laser disc jukebox and a large screen TV, and a sign advertising margaritas. "I'm looking for my dad. Have you seen him?"

"No, not for years. Not since he took off for the desert. His tools are still stored down in our basement."

After I left the Lodge I tried a grassy hill up the road, where Dad had lived in his truck for a while near the house of his best friend, John Ericson, another feckless father of a large family. All I found was an empty Camel pack in the grass that had grown back. I crushed it in my hand.

I decided that he must be back at the ranch. The Richardson ranch sprawls between the old twisting back road and the hills of Woodacre. The Richardsons used to let Dad park his truck there for a dollar a day while he built porches and fixed screen doors to keep himself in bananas and tobacco and used paperbacks.

I drove around the circular driveway twice, past barns, sheds, and corrals full of horses flicking their tails in the heat, before I noticed, deep in a corner near some blackberry bushes, his truck with that lazy curl of smoke coming from the vent cut through its roof. His old sign was tacked to the limb of an oak tree: CARPENTERING. SHODDY WORK, HIGH PRICES. INQUIRE WITHIN. I smiled despite myself and stopped the car. I got out, sniffing appreciatively at the smell of alfalfa coming from the barn.

"Is that you there, Adair?" Iris Richardson was hurrying toward me across the circular driveway, her thin figure lost in a sweatshirt and jeans rolled up at the ankles. Iris owned the ranch.

"I'm looking for my dad," I said.

"I haven't seen him," Iris said, "but when you find him you can tell the son of a bitch for me he has until dark to remove his vehicle from this ranch. He tore up my entire kitchen floor, then he went to town for the new tiles. That was yesterday at noon, and I haven't seen him since. I can't go into my own kitchen for fear of falling into the basement."

"I said I'll fix it, and I will," said Dad's voice, and there he was, walking up the dirt driveway, carrying a bag that said "Fairfax Hardware" on it in red letters. He wore jeans and a gray sweatshirt, and his graying curls were squashed under a filthy black Giants cap. His face was deeply lined, and his whole body seemed shrunken, smaller. His white-and-black mongrel, Fred, trotted ahead of him eagerly.

I waited for him, feeling as if I was consciously standing my ground.

"Dare!" he said, stopping a few feet away. "Good to see you."

"Hi, Dad. What's this about an emergency?"

"Come into the house," he said, bending back a branch so I could enter his truck. "I'll tell you all about it."

"What about me?" demanded Iris, her voice shrill. "Aren't you even going to explain why you disappeared, leaving me without a kitchen floor? You promised it would take four hours!"

"And it will," Dad said. "Now let me talk with my daughter a minute, can you? It's not every day she comes out to see her old father."

"We'll see about this!" said Iris, storming off, her feet kicking up dust clouds as she strode back to the farmhouse.

"Come in, tell me what's shaking," Dad said again. He patted the side of the van. It was a 1949 green panel bakery van. You could still read BORDENAVE in faint white letters on the side. Fred nosed my ankle, and I reached down to scratch his ears.

"What do you think of it? I pulled it free of the weeds growing up through its floorboards. Now we adventure together."

"Does it run?"

"Sure does. It's not much on hills—not much on level ground either really," he said, patting it again, then catching himself doing it, and smiling ruefully. "Goes like hell downhill, though, and that's where I'm heading, according to most reports." He opened the door, motioning me to climb in ahead of him. "And lookee here. Spare tire, wood burning stove, air mattress. I even figured out how to hold down the heat by a judicious use of draft controls. By God, it's a functional success, whatever they may say at the sanity hearing."

A cot was made up with an army blanket, and Dad had fashioned a desk out of planks and placed it under the van's back window.

"My picture window," Dad said, gesturing at it. The window framed a placid view of a field, with a stream in the foreground and a black horse grazing in the distance, like an English painting. "Do the other kids' dads have a view like this?"

"Iris said she'd throw you off the property," I said, sitting on the cot.

"She might do it, too." Dad had dropped onto a rickety swivel chair in front of his desk. "I told her I'd fix that floor, and then I just put down my tools and walked off."

"Why do you do things like that?"

"It just seemed pointless, all of a sudden. But it's all right, I'll find a way to mollify her. She's a good soul."

He clapped his hands on his knees. "Now what can I offer you? I have some very nice bananas today." He pulled one off a bunch sitting on a cardboard box of clothes and tossed it to me.

He watched me peel it and take a bite. "You look good," he said. "You kids get your looks from your mother. I always thought my gifts to you would only begin to appear when the comeliness inherited from your mother begins to tarnish."

"You look good, too, Dad," I lied. His thick hair had dulled to a dusty gray brown since I had seen him last.

"Still cutting a wide swath in the big city?"

"I'm doing all right."

"Married?"

"Yes, Bill and I got married a year ago."

"What's your title these days?"

"I'm a columnist, Pop. You know that."

"Yes, I know that." He paused and looked at me. "I say something wrong?"

"Why'd you come back home, Dad?" I said abruptly. "I thought you were happy in the Mojave."

"I'm just here for a breather. I'll be right back out there in a matter of weeks."

"You mentioned an emergency."

"I think I have that yuppie disease, what's it called? That fatigue syndrome. And I get this kind of near-blackout now and then. It feels as if someone stepped on the hose carrying blood to my head. Also, I have a lump."

"On top of your fatigue syndrome and what do you call it, the garden hose thing?"

"Yes, Smartie, on top of those. Here, feel it yourself."

He pointed to a spot on the left side of his neck, just under his chin. I touched it gingerly. His skin was dry and papery and warm. I felt odd touching him and dropped my hand. "There's nothing there."

"Nothing?"

"Nothing."

"Are you sure?"

"Pretty sure, Dad."

"Well, I'll be damned. That's a relief, I don't mind telling you." He fingered his chin with eager fingers.

"I remember you writing about fatigue syndrome, Dad." I hadn't believed for a second that he had such a thing. I thought he was just depressed out there in all that emptiness and didn't realize it.

"I wrote to you about pretty much everything, didn't I? How come you wrote me such lousy letters back? Aren't you supposed to be a writer?"

"They weren't lousy."

"Oh, Christ, Dare."

I was silent. I watched a fly settle on the blackberry bush outside the window. I stood up. "I can't stay. I have work to do. And you seem to be fine."

"Oh, hell, Dare, don't go," he said. "Have another banana? Or– let's see"–he peered into a cardboard box near his feet–"how about a Butterfingers? You used to like those."

"I liked Big Hunks. Adrian liked Butterfingers. But okay, toss it over." He threw it and I caught it. I always liked candy. I got that from him. I took a bite. "Doesn't sound as if Iris is all that thrilled to have you back. Where are you going to live?"

"Well, I don't know," Dad said, diverted. "I don't suppose your mother would take me back?"

"No, Pop."

"How about you, can I come and live with you? A little place at the hearth for your broken-down old father?"

I tried to see Dad in my kitchen, scribbling away in a cloud of cig- arette smoke as Bill and I read the paper over our coffee. "Sorry, Pop. There're the kids and . . ."

"I might have an apartment lined up anyway."

"Really? How did you manage that?"

"Never you mind. Besides, I may not stick around at all," Dad said briskly, slapping his hands on both knees. "Places to go, people to let down." He turned back to me.

"How are your kids?"

"Patrick's fine. Morgan's been difficult."

"Morgan?"

"My daughter, Dad. I was talking to her when you called, re- member?"

"I know who Morgan is. It's just that every time you say that name I get confused. It never occurred to me you'd name your kid after the family dog. Never knew that red-eyed old mongrel meant that much to you. What do you mean, difficult?"

"Sneaks out, cuts class, lies, yells, has awful new friends." The candy had become a wad of cotton in my mouth. "She's a bad girl,"

I said. "And I made her. If a factory is judged by its product, I'm a
bad mother."

"I'm not qualified to advise anyone on parenthood," Dad said. He
poked a stick at the stove crammed with newspapers, then struck
a match. "I do know that being someone's parent–or someone's
child–is something most people fail at, at one time or another. We
were all ordinary people before we became parents."

We heard a screech outside the truck.

Dad leaned out of the truck to take a look and then was back. He
seemed determined to ignore the commotion outside the truck, so I
did too.

"Sounds as if this girl of yours has spirit," he said cheerfully.

"Oh, yes, she has spirit." As I spoke I remembered what had come
into my head when I heard Morgan had been out on the streets–an
image of her standing on a dark corner, small in a yellow glow of
lamplight, then a strong hand closing on the flesh of her arm,
pulling her into a waiting car.

"Maybe she'll grow up to be an escape artist like her grandpa."

"She's not like you," I said shortly.

"I like you combative," he said. "Tells me I may not have frittered
away my genes after all."

He tapped some tobacco from his pouch onto a cigarette paper,
rolled it, and then licked the paper.

"I don't have much hope about your brothers and sisters," he said,
"but I'd like to see something of you, now I'm back," he said. "I want
you to get to know me. I have some oddments crammed in my head
I would not mind sharing with you."

Just as he lit the rollie with a battered black Bic lighter, something
heavy banged the truck from outside. The walls swayed, and the
English painting fell away from Dad's picture window, leaving only
blue sky. "What the hell?" he shouted, hurrying outside.

I followed and saw a white tow truck had attached its stiff black
arm to the bumper of Dad's truck, raising it in the air. Iris stood

watching with her arms crossed, a look of satisfaction on her thin face.

"Are you crazy!" Dad yelled. "My daughter was in there!"

"I told you," Iris said. "I told you."

Iris signaled the driver of the tow truck, who cut the motor and got out. Dad unhitched the hook from his front bumper and threw it into the nearby blackberry bushes.

"I want you off this property, Gene," Iris said. "Right now."

"How am I supposed to do that? Take a look at what you've done to my truck!"

We all looked. The two front wheels topped a log that had been hidden by the blackberry bushes.

"If you look closer, you'll see the axle's smashed," Dad told her. "You know in the Old West shooting a man's horse was a hanging offense."

Iris's blond hair straggled across a face red with rage. "You get off this property now, Gene," she screamed. She picked up a child's toy broom that had been lying in the dirt and brandished it.

chapter 2

DON'T suppose I could get a lift into town with you?" Dad said.

"A lift where?" I stalled, unhappy at the idea of Dad in my car.

"Just into the city. There's a fleabag hotel on Bush Street where I can usually get a room."

I pointed at Fred. "What about the dog?"

"He comes with me. Would you have me leave him?"

You've done it before, and with your family, I wanted to tell him sourly.

"Okay, I'll take you to Bush Street," I told him, giving in.

I opened the door of the Toyota. Dad snapped his fingers at Fred, who sprang into the backseat and started to drool. We got in, and I put the car in gear and headed toward town.

"How much did this whizbang run you?" Dad said, eyeing the useless but showy tachometer on the Toyota's dashboard.

"It wasn't that much," I said.

He smiled. "Not for you, I guess. You and Bill, all snug in the middle class."

He looked out the window at the passing stores as we came into

Fairfax, the first of the towns that flow one into the other until you reach the soaring headlands that lead to the bridge. "You were such a forlorn, twisty-legged little thing as a child, with your taped-up glasses and those absurd bangs. My guess is that you haven't changed all that much, despite all this"–he waved his arm at the car's dashboard–"glitz."

"You can buy a Toyota without giving up your soul, Dad."

"Can you?"

"Yes." I was uncomfortable with Dad so close. He smelled of tobacco and motor oil and, oddly enough, toothpaste. Fred was in the back, panting softly. I cracked the window for him.

"How's your mother?"

"She's good, Dad. When did you see her last?"

"She drove out to see me about ten years ago when I was living on the ranch. I'll never forget her looming up at the trailer door, swinging that big purse of hers. She still lug around all those quarters? Scared the bejesus out of me. 'I just wanted to have a look at you,' she said, 'heard you'd stopped drinking.' 'Nope,' I said. And then she drove off again. What does she look like now? If I'm seventy, she must be–well, she's six years younger. What does that make her?"

"Do the math, Dad."

He was silent a moment, then said, impatiently, "You do the math, college graduate."

"She's sixty-four."

Dad said nothing. When I glanced over next, he had rolled a cigarette on the worn cloth of his jeans and was reaching for the cigarette lighter on the car, which had never been used before.

"Please don't," I said.

"You're not going to let me smoke in your car?"

"I'd appreciate it if you wouldn't."

"I'll just smoke one."

"I'll pull over then." I put my blinker on. He looked at me, and then shook his head. He stuck the cigarette behind his ear. "No, forget it."

Soon we were on Highway 101, heading for San Francisco. Fred put his paws on the back of my seat and whined in my ear, his breath stinky.

"I believe I'd like to see your mother," Dad said suddenly. "I had a lot of time to think while I was in the desert. It's never too late to make amends."

"You're kidding, right?" I said. I looked over at him through my dark glasses. "Did you forget you left her to raise seven children on her own?"

Dad sighed. "You were in fat, rich Marin County. I knew the family would make out okay–there were ladies aplenty in the welfare office, bone tired of sailing paper airplanes, only too happy to throw out a welcome mat to your mother."

"We needed you, Dad. More than we needed money. Did you know that after you left, Sean used to spend his afternoons gluing together model cars, getting every detail right? Then he'd put the model on a stump in the yard and blast it to pieces with his BB gun."

"And you?"

"I wasn't like Sean. He followed you everywhere, remember? He was always all greasy from helping you down in your workshop. And he was fourteen, so it hit him hardest, your going, leaving him in a houseful of girls."

"You're forgetting Shannon."

"He was eight."

As we came up over the Sausalito hill, San Francisco had disappeared, and the bridge with it. The fog was so thick that cars with their lights on seemed to be coming at us from a ghostly highway in the sky.

I drove Dad to the hotel on Bush Street, but it had gone out of business. I double-parked, while he surveyed the bagel shop that now stood there. "Well, just put me on a bus back to the county," he said. "Iris will have cooled down by now."

As soon as he said that, I relaxed. If Dad was willing to take himself off, then of course I wanted him to stay. "Why don't you come and see where I live, first?" I offered. "Then I'll drop you on Van Ness to catch the bus."

"Sure," he said. "Why not?"

It occurred to me, driving toward the house, that my dad had never been to my house, or to any of the houses I'd lived in since I'd grown up. It was almost as if he was a visitor from the past: he wasn't part of this new life I'd made in the city. I realized that I was, despite myself, looking forward to showing him my house—and my kids, whom he had seen only once or twice when they were smaller.

We lived on the south end of Scott Street, right in the middle of the city, in a neighborhood called the Duboce Triangle. I parked in the driveway, opened the back door of the car to let the dog out, and led Dad around to the front of the house. He glanced incuriously up at our house. Then he saw the street signs telling us we were at the corner of Scott and Waller Streets. "Oh, my God," he said. "You've landed four blocks from where I grew up, at Scott and McAllister."

I liked this idea. I had always felt at home in this neighborhood, and now Dad was saying that by falling in love with my kids' dad all those years ago, and coming to live with him in this house on this San Francisco street, I had managed to find my way home. I led Dad up the stairs.

"Hi, Grandpa!" Morgan exclaimed over my shoulder. She had heard my key in the lock and come running to the door. Fred had begun sniffing at one of Bill's cactuses in a white ceramic pot.

Dad was visibly charmed. "I don't believe anybody has ever called me that before."

"Called you what?" I said.

"Grandpa."

How strange that was. Dad had at least eleven grandchildren.

Patrick came in the room wearing shiny black Nike shorts and carrying a basketball. His blond hair was sticking up. He was twelve, and about to start the seventh grade. "I have another grandpa," he said. He stared at Dad as if determined to memorize his features. "But he's dead."

"Well, I'm not dead," said Dad. "I'm the reason you have the blood of Irish kings in your veins." He sat down on our red corduroy couch.

"Mother's more Irish than you are," I put in, coming over to perch on the end of the couch. "She says you're half French."

"That is a vicious untruth," Dad said. He turned to Morgan, who had returned to sitting on the floor amid a pile of torn-up magazines. "I hear you've been giving your mom hell," he said to her.

Morgan cut out Drew Barrymore's face. Her friends all tell her she looks like the movie actress, and in fact she does. She wore makeup over her perfect thirteen-year-old skin, and brown lipstick. "It's not true," she said, her glance sliding to me. "I've been really nice to Mom. She just hasn't been noticing." She smiled nicely at her grandpa and got up to give him a hug.

"This is your hellchild?" Dad said over her shoulder, raising his eyebrows.

"I'm not a hellchild," Morgan said. "Where have you been, Grandpa?"

"In the desert."

"Doing what?"

"Thinking, mostly."

I heard the back door open. It was Jim, letting himself in with his key. Jim is my ex-husband, his sixty-one years evident only in thick blond hair that had finally turned gray, and a slight thickening at the waist under his blue Choral Society sweatshirt.

"Hi, Daddy," Morgan said, and Patrick went over to hug his dad.

"Hello, Jim," Dad said.

Jim looked over, startled. He hadn't seen Dad since he had found him nervously chain-smoking in a corner at our wedding, and asked him if he would help arrange the flowers, if he wasn't doing anything. No one had ever asked Dad to arrange flowers before. It surprised him and won his respect.

"Hello, Gene," Jim said, recovering from his surprise. "Good to see you again." They shook hands. After a pause, Jim turned to me.

"If Bill's making turkey, I have some peppers and green beans that'll go with it."

I looked at him, puzzled. "Bill's not making a turkey. He's not even here."

"He's not? He left me a message asking me if I had a turkey baster."

"Oh!" I said, remembering. "He overwatered his cactus. He wanted the baster to draw off some of the extra water."

"Oh, that was it," Jim said. He turned to leave, then turned back. "I found that batch of unmated socks you threw into the garbage can outside."

"You did?"

"I took it upstairs. Turns out I had most of the mates."

I watched Dad taking this in. "Jim lives upstairs," I said. "Bill and I bought this flat from him, as tenants in common."

"Well, you certainly have a lot in common," Dad commented, his glance taking in not only the room but the kids.

"Yes, we do," I agreed. Jim lived upstairs, in the top two floors of the house. His flat had dark antiques, oil paintings, and oriental rugs. We lived on the floor below, in a smaller flat. Our taste ran to bright colors—our kitchen table was red Formica—and light-colored wood. Outside our back porch was a set of wooden stairs that led up to Jim's back porch. Underneath our flat was a one-bedroom rental apartment.

When we got married, Bill and I had looked for a house to buy but couldn't afford one. Meanwhile, the problems of swapping the kids back and forth had mounted—they were always claiming the math book they needed was at Dad's house. So Bill and I bought the downstairs flat in Jim's Victorian from him. Patrick had his main bedroom upstairs at his dad's and a bed on our porch, and Morgan had her main bedroom downstairs with us but also had a room at her dad's.

Bill came into the room, sweaty and rosy-faced from a hike, with our sheltie, Cody, a little dog who looks exactly like a miniature Lassie, at his heels.

He took his baseball cap off and mopped his forehead with his handkerchief. It was then he noticed that a stranger was standing in his living room. And worse, a strange dog.

"Hi, sweetie," I said, crossing the room to kiss him. "This is my dad, Gene Daly."

"Oh, my God," Bill said. "What a surprise!" He smiled and crossed the room to hold out his hand. "Bill LeBlond."

"So you're the new husband," Dad said to Bill, shaking hands. "Marry enthusiastically and often, my kids do, God love them." He glanced at me. "How many does this make for you, Dare?"

"Three, Pop."

"Three! Good for you. Three's the charm, huh?" He turned to Bill. "How about you, Bill?"

"My second," Bill said. He smiled at me again. "And last." His eyes went to Fred, who was sniffing Cody. Cody barked at Fred, then took off down the hall, and Fred, tail wagging, obliged by chasing him. "Maybe I could put your dog on the back porch for now?" Bill said when the pair reappeared and whipped around the couch.

"He would just claw your door down. He thinks I'm his mother," Dad said, grabbing Fred as he went by and holding on to his collar. "I'm a little old for motherhood, but what the hell." He patted the dog and looked up at Bill. "Where are your parents?"

"They live about forty miles north of here, in Santa Rosa."

"Are they rich?"

"No. My father was a salesman for a pie company. My mother was a nurse."

On his way to put away his backpack, Bill pushed Patrick off his chair without looking at him. Patrick spun around on the floor and grabbed Bill's foot, bringing Bill and the backpack slamming to the floor. "Who says you're leaving, weakling?"

Ten minutes later the pair of them had stopped wrestling and were lying in the hall, red-faced and panting, still trading insults.

"Do they do that every night?" Dad asked.

"Pretty much," I said.

The five of us talked for a while more, then I said to my father, "Bill and I have to run to Safeway for some taco makings. Why don't you just stay over, and I'll drive you home in the morning?"

"Stay over?"

"Sure, why not?"

"Thank you. It'll give me a chance to get to know my grandkids," Dad said.

"All right, Pop," I said, grabbing my purse. "We'll be right back. You're baby-sitting."

"You mean we're grandpa-sitting," Morgan said.

"Whatever."

Minutes later, Bill and I were walking down to the supermarket, Cody at our heels. "Was it weird for you, having him pop up?" Bill asked me.

"Yes, but you get used to that. He's a jack-in-the-box."

"What's he up to? Does your mom know he's back?"

"I don't know—and no, Mom doesn't know."

WHEN we got back, Dad and Patrick were watching *Mutiny on the Bounty* on TV, the one with Marlon Brando as Mr. Christian. Bill went in to start the tacos. He's a cookbook editor but didn't bother trying any exotic recipes out on the kids. I watched as the thirsty crew threw all of Captain Bligh's plants overboard.

"Where's Morgan?" I asked Patrick.

"I don't know where she is, Mom," Patrick said. "The phone rang, but it was right in the middle of the show."

The red message light was on, and when I pressed the button I heard Morgan's voice. "I'm baby-sitting at Jane's," she said.

I called our friend Jane, who picked up the phone on the first ring. "Morgan?" she said, sounding baffled. "I haven't seen Morgan for weeks."

I put the phone back in its cradle and hit the button on the answering machine to listen to Morgan's message again. "Jane called and asked me to baby-sit. Please don't call here because I'm putting the kids to bed and it might wake them up."

I sat on the couch, balling my fist against the red corduroy. Though Morgan had been doing things like this for a year now, I still felt as if it had never happened to me, or to anyone, before. Bill came in to ask Patrick to grate some cheese for him, and I threw myself at my husband the way a hurt child throws herself at her mother's skirts. "I just finished grounding her again this morning!" I said. He took me in his arms. "Why would someone who is supposed to be crazy about me want to make me so unhappy?" I said.

"I don't know." Bill patted my hair softly. "She's not doing it to you, sweetie." When I tipped my head back to look at him, though, he was staring bleakly past my shoulder.

That evening, as I waited for Morgan to come home, I listened to Bill angrily banging pots and pans out in the kitchen and tried to watch the movie. Dad had gone out to the back steps to smoke a cigarette, and I was sitting next to Patrick. For the first time I identified with Captain Bligh. I could feel his impatience, his desire to do the right thing--and his impulse to strike out and punish when his unruly "children" thwarted him.

I sniffled. "Are you okay, Mom?" Patrick asked, looking up from the TV. He scooted over and reached to put his arm around me.

"I'm okay, sweetie," I said. "Just worried about your sister."

But I wasn't okay. I was crying, Bill was angry, Patrick was worried, and Morgan was gone. Oh, God, yes, and *Dad* was here.

I took a deep breath. I would stop being like this, right now. I went to the bathroom, washed my face with cold water, and returned to the living room.

Dad was looking at my book, a collection of columns from my

first four years as a columnist for the *Chronicle*. It had just been published. "Here, let me give you a copy," I said, taking one from a row in the bookshelf. I held it in my hand for a second, pleased by the weight, and then handed it to him.

Dad took it, leafed through it for a second, put it down. He looked at me. "I'm sure this impresses the hell out of a lot of people," he said, "but it doesn't impress me. You put something the size and shape of a book on the market all right, but we both know it isn't the real thing."

I stared at him. It was as if I had handed him my heart, quivering and red on my palm, and he'd glanced at it and said, "Is that all?"

I was just standing there, frozen. It was an effort to take the next breath. "I know that's hard to hear, but I want to be able to talk to you this way," Dad continued. He tapped some tobacco from his pouch onto a cigarette paper, rolled it, and then licked the paper.

I found my breath. "Dad, Morgan's taken off again, so there's going to be a scene when she gets back. If you don't mind, I'll just take you to the bus stop. In fact, I'll take you to the bus stop even if you do mind."

Dad sighed. He put my book back on the shelf. "What about Fred?" he said. "They won't let him on the bus."

We both looked at Fred, asleep at Dad's feet. "Call a cab," I said flatly.

"Just drop us on Van Ness," Dad said.

The turn signal clicked loudly in the silent car as I pulled over to let him and the dog out at the bus stop. He could always hail a cab from there. "Who will tell you these things, if not your father?" Dad said as he got out.

"No one," I said, and reached over to pull the door shut after him. I edged back into the traffic.

As I drove home, I remembered the first time he left, when I was ten. I had been sitting on my heels splitting kindling on a stump down by the corner of our house in Lagunitas, a spot where I could keep an eye on the road. Dad always came home promptly at four, coming up the path below the house in his white overalls, the hammer swinging from the loop at his side. The kid who raced down the path and reached him first would get the warm leftovers from his hot, sour-smelling black lunchbox—a pink or white Hostess Sno Ball, or a stack of Lorna Doones wrapped in wax paper.

That day four o'clock came and went, and his black Dodge pickup never appeared. My pile of splintery sticks of kindling rose higher than my knees, and still I sat with my hatchet. When he still didn't come, I went into the kitchen cupboard and saw that the Hershey bar Mother had bought for his lunch was still lying on the torn blue-and-white checked shelf paper.

I found Mother out hanging up clothes on the line in the yard. She shook out one of Shannon's pairs of blue jeans and pinned them next to one of my sister Connie's yellow print dresses. She reached down for more clothespins, forgetting she already had two in her mouth. She always told us she thought about each of us as she was pinning up our clothes. "Where's Daddy?" I asked.

She spoke from around the clothespins. She was shaking out a wadded T-shirt that could have belonged to Adrian or me. I hoped it was mine. "Don't worry about him, he'll come home when he's ready," she said, casting a distracted look at me.

I thought of the nursery rhyme in which the sheep get mislaid, and the rhyme says, "Leave them alone / And they'll come home / wagging their tails behind them." I stared up at mother, who seemed impossibly tall, impossibly far away, her dark head full of ringlets silhouetted against blue sky—as far away as my dad was.

Plunged into an uneasiness new to me, I went back to splitting kindling, stopping to listen every time I heard a truck go by on the road below.

It seemed to be a secret, where Dad was. There were lots of secrets now, things other people knew that I didn't.

A month later it was the beginning of summer and he was still gone. We had moved up the road to a rental cottage, with everything stored in cardboard boxes along the damp walls. The cottage itself sat in a kind of gully below the road, in a nest of bramble bushes, as if it had slid downhill. Bats whirred in the basement at night, until the exterminator came and took five hundred of them away in a barrel. I got mad when I wasn't allowed to see the corpses. We slept in our musty beds, and ate baloney sandwiches on Wonder bread, dripping with mayonnaise.

One day Aunt Frances, Dad's sister, came to visit, negotiating our dirt-and-wood steps in her tan pumps and linen dress. I was hanging belly-down on the swing, wearing shorts and nothing else, watching her as she looked around.

"Hi, Adair," she called. She could make a simple greeting sound worried. She stared for an abstracted moment at my bare brown chest. "You're ten now, aren't you?" she asked, and I answered proudly, "Ten and a half."

"How old are you?" I asked.

"Forty," she answered. "Old as the hills." I knew she was one year older than Dad.

A few minutes later I wandered into the kitchen and listened to her talking to Mother, who was standing at the counter cutting up carrots for beef stew.

"Have you heard from him?" Aunt Frances was asking. She sat on a kitchen chair, both hands clasping the purse on her lap.

"Not a word," said Mother. An orange circle of carrot rolled off the counter unnoticed. "Has he written to you?"

"He sent me a card from Cabo San Lucas. I looked that up. It's in Mexico, on the Baja peninsula," Aunt Frances admitted after an uncertain pause. "I think he's trying to find himself."

"He's not the only one. I know a lot of people who are trying to find him," said Mother shortly. She picked up a pack of L&M's from the table and took the matches that had been slipped inside the cellophane packaging. She lit a cigarette and took a puff. When she took it away from her lips it was smudged dark pink.

Aunt Frances looked sad, as she always did when Dad was being criticized. "He's confused," she said. "All these kids. He had it rough, you know, when he was little, after our mother died and we were passed from relative to relative. Did I ever tell you that our aunt once beat him just for taking a bite out of the middle of a banana?"

"Many times," Mother said.

I was standing against the doorjamb with my arms in back of me, against the cool wood, trying not to be noticed.

I stared at my bare feet, black-rimmed along the edges, and tanned the color of tobacco on top. My arms prickled with fear.

ONE afternoon a few days later my older sister Mickey and I cut across the ridge on the forest trail that led to what we called "the Dam." It was a deep green pool formed in a circle of rock at the foot of a spillway that came down from Kent Lake, a reservoir above.

We played for a long time on the logs that floated in the pond, trying to balance on them like lumberjacks, then lay on the rocks at the swimming hole, shivering as the breeze and the hot sun vacuumed the water droplets from our skin. We were starving, but had forgotten to bring anything for lunch. Across the way, a man and woman were cutting a huge watermelon into slices for their kids.

"Mommy's going to have a baby," announced Mickey, who was twelve. She was leaning back on her elbows now, staring over at the watermelon, and her golden hair spilled over her tanned shoulders.

"No, she isn't," I answered, stung by the enormity of the news.

"I heard them talking."

"Who?"

"Them. Mother and Aunt Frances. Aunt Frances said how far along is it, and Mom said two months."

"Maybe they were talking about something else."

A shadow fell across us, and a man's gentle voice said, "You kids hungry?" It was the father from across the way, bringing us each a long, thin slice of watermelon.

I reached for it eagerly and bit into the sweet red flesh. I wondered how the man had figured out, from way across the rocks, how hungry I was, and how I had been longing for that watermelon. I suddenly missed my father, yearned to smell his familiar smell of tobacco and wood shavings, hear his light tread as he headed to the bathroom at dawn. I ate the watermelon hungrily, feeling the juice running over my jaw, but it wasn't enough. It wasn't nearly enough.

THEN, as mysteriously as he had gone, Dad was back at the end of the summer. Sunburned, wearing a white cotton shirt open at the neck, he just appeared in the kitchen one day, with a cardboard box full of trinkets from Mexico, his eyes darting from one end of the room to the other. Mother dropped the butter knife with which she'd been slathering government-issue mayo on Wonder bread and left the kitchen when he came in, saying, "Daddy's home, kids."

We hung back, wary of the box. It wasn't like Dad to bring us anything. It was like getting presents from a visitor. We all got sombreros. Shannon got a toy ukulele, and Sean, at fourteen the oldest of the six of us, got a silver belt that he immediately looped through the threads of his jeans, his eyes shining. I got a black-and-white owl clock whose eyes moved back and forth as it ticked, shifting nervously from wall to wall, as Dad's had when he came in.

WHEN I got home after dropping Dad off, I got out my address book and called around to Morgan's friends. No one had seen her.

Where was she? I imagined her standing in the light of the doughnut shop down on the corner of 24th and Church, talking to the kids who hung out there. Kids who didn't seem to have homes or parents.

At nine-thirty the phone rang.

"Mom?"

"I'm listening," I said, stonily. Upset Mom had disappeared with the sound of Morgan's voice. She was safe. Pissed Mom could take over.

"I'm at Tara's, and I don't think you should be mad."

"Just come home," I said. And, for the first time in my life, I hung up on her.

The phone rang again. "Mom?" said her small, uncertain voice.

"Just come right home," I said, and hung up again. I sank into a chair, feeling the tension in my forearms. By the time Morgan came home an hour later, sliding around the door, small face wary under the hood of her burgundy jacket, Bill had gone to bed. Patrick was on the couch, sleeping with one arm flung out to the floor. No matter what I did to make his bedroom inviting–bought new comforters, slipped in foam pads to make the mattress soft–he always ended up sleeping on the couch.

"Where's Grandpa?" Morgan said.

I didn't feel like explaining right then. "He decided not to stay over," I said. "Where have you been?"

I played the answering machine back for her. She listened without expression. When the machine clicked off, she said blithely, "I'm sorry, Mom, I really am. We weren't doing anything wrong. We were just walking around. It won't happen again, I swear to God."

That night I lay in bed and stared up at the dark ceiling, listening to the sound of Morgan's boots hitting the floor in the other room, then her voice whispering on the telephone.

chapter 3

I DROVE Morgan to her first day of high school the next morning, the two of us barely talking. Two months shy of fourteen, she had unrolled the window and hung out a nonchalant elbow, so that the cold breeze came around and hit me in the back of the neck. You had to look close to see how nervously she was beating time to the music on her bare knee with her other hand.

"Did Grandpa go back to the valley?" she asked.

"I don't know. Probably."

"I liked him. He was cool."

"He liked you, too," I said. "Said he'd rather have troublemakers in the family than lemonade stand proprietors."

"I'm not a troublemaker, Mom. Stop!" Morgan had spotted crowds of kids streaming along Eucalyptus Drive as we approached Lowell High School, a collection of low beige buildings set below the roadway less than a mile from the Pacific Ocean. "Drop me here, please, Mom." We were three blocks from the school.

She got out, and then reached in the backseat for her pack. A blue

Honda had stopped in front of me, and a skinny Asian girl lost in oversize overalls bolted from the passenger door. Her mother hurried after her with a backpack.

"Your homework schedule for high school, by the way, is five to seven every weeknight, starting this afternoon," I told Morgan through the window.

"No, Mom, no way," she said in a level tone. "I'm going to be nice, but I'm not going to do that." She walked off.

"Yes, you are!" I shouted after her, but she didn't turn around.

I rolled up the window and drove back over the hill over Portola, slowing as always to admire the skyline view of San Francisco from the top of the hill, a line of tall white buildings shimmering above the green bay.

Despite all her class cutting and other hijinks in middle school, Morgan's test scores had got her into Lowell, San Francisco's prestigious academic public high school. Ninety-nine percent of Lowell graduates went on to college.

But not everybody graduated. "Your freshman son or daughter will be doing homework for four hours every night, and will be lucky to get D's," the principal had said in the auditorium the week before. We parents had blanched. I saw one mother wrapped in a peacoat jot a note down on her "Welcome, Lowell Parents!" sheet. The man next to me ran a hand through his thinning hair and seemed almost to rock with anxiety beside me. I wanted to rock, too. I had read somewhere that even if it meant standing over her chair while she did it, you had to make sure your high school student did her homework. I didn't see myself doing that for the four hours the principal had stipulated, but I could manage two.

I spent the rest of the day staring at the blue screen of my computer. Student essays from the writing class I taught on Thursday nights, press invitations, telephone messages, and newspaper clippings littered my desk. I stared at a note from a reader that I had thumbtacked to my bookshelf: "I wish you would explain the purpose of your column. When you are not occupying that space, others write of similar personal experiences and I just do not understand what place they have in a newspaper."

This was one of these days when I didn't either. I was tinkering with an idea about latchkey adults for the column and was just rejecting it in despair when the phone rang. "I called to remind you that I'm not coming home at five," Morgan said in my ear when I answered it.

"Yes, you are," I said. And she did. I heard her key in the lock, and then she came through my office. Her backpack bulged with books.

"Why should I have to do homework when you say I do?" she yelled, by way of greeting. Then she went into her room and started her assignments. By six she was in the kitchen, filling out an order to the Columbia Record Company and talking to a friend on the phone.

Her two hours weren't up. "Morgan, it's still your homework time," I said. "You have to go back to your desk."

She exploded. The tiny paste-on stamps of CD covers went flying. "You don't even know if I *have* homework. You've never gone to my school!"

"I spent four years in a high school!"

"What does that have to do with me?" Morgan asked.

The next night, Morgan was working at the kitchen table amid the clutter and noise. Bill was making spaghetti at the stove. Patrick sat at the table unscrewing the wheels from his skateboard while telling me how his first days in the seventh grade had gone. (His homework schedule was only an hour and had already ended.)

I wanted her to do her homework at her desk in her room, where she wouldn't be distracted by the TV or our conversations. I grabbed her red notebook. "No, Mom!" she yelled, grabbing it back. Huddling over it, all shoulders, she stayed where she was, writing her English homework with pink marker, three or four words to a piece of binder paper, while listening to a rerun of *Roseanne* on TV.

"Morgan, I want you to work at your desk." I switched off the TV. "Those are the rules."

"I'm doing my homework, Mom," she said. "Isn't that the point?" She picked up the remote and clicked the TV back on.

I retreated to my bedroom and started to fold the laundry I had earlier dumped out on the bed. Both kids were wearing such huge clothes now that just two pairs of pants and a sweatshirt made a pile that threatened to topple over. I folded quickly and sloppily, feeling sorry for myself.

I was not used to conflict. I once burst into tears when a man ordered me to take my bike out of his grocery store. Yelling and screaming was as new to me as it was to Bill, who had taken to covering his ears in his living room chair when Morgan and I were arguing. I never yelled, not even in childbirth, not even as a child. I was always a good girl, avoiding confrontation, a classic child of an alcoholic, distressed by loud voices.

But I would yell if that's what it took. I shook out Morgan's clown-size overalls and folded them into a square. I saw her, forty years old, in a stained white blouse, hair lank across her forehead, carrying five plates through a swinging metal door in a restaurant because no one had made her do her homework in high school.

I hadn't plucked the image out of thin air: my mother had been forced to go to work as a waitress after Dad left. She came home tired, pulling her white blouse out of her black nylon skirt, and left slabs of leftover tea cake and bags of French bread on the counter.

She seemed uncomfortable with us once we hit our teens and had new adult bodies and problems. We went to Sir Francis Drake High School, one after the other, but nothing was ever said about college. She was just trying to get us to adulthood.

I knew from my own family that high school divided kids into two groups: those who would eventually wear long coats and carry briefcases, and the working class, who'd wear short jackets or jeans or uniforms. I was working class, so was Bill, and so was Jim, who'd grown up on a farm in South Dakota. But we'd made our way into the briefcase-carrying class by going to college—Bill and I had been the first in our families to do so—and I was determined that the kids would, too.

On Saturday morning, Morgan was standing in front of the old-fashioned pedestal sink in the bathroom, squinting with one eye while applying blue eye shadow to the other. Makeup and brushes littered the sink.

She was dolling up for some sort of block party with Holly.

"You have to do five hours of homework today, to make up for coming in late on Wednesday and Thursday nights," I said. "Anyway, you're still grounded for that baby-sitting stunt the other night."

"It's my homework, not yours! I'll do it when I want to do it!" she screamed at me. The tiny stick of eye shadow waved in the air like a baton. "I'll run away if you're going to be like this!"

I grabbed some toilet paper and wiped the sink with it. "Every day I read in the paper about kids whose parents drink vodka at break-fast, or use the rent money to buy crack, or slap their kids around," I said, throwing the gob of toilet paper away. "You are surrounded by adults who love you. And you're going to run away because you have *homework*?"

"Stop it, Mom, stop it! I hate it when you're like this!" She had a paw print of black mascara above her right eye. "I promised Holly I would go to this party with her!" She bolted from the bathroom.

I followed. On the back porch, I grabbed her roughly by the arm and shoved her down on the bed we kept on the porch for Patrick.

"Stop it, stop it, stop it!" I yelled. Before I could stop myself, I hit her on the arm.

"Morgan?" We hadn't realized Jim was standing in the doorway that led to the yard, melon and peaches and grapes peeking from the top of the bags he was holding.

"I don't like you, Dad," Morgan told him through the open door. "I was talking to Mom." He trudged on upstairs, his tread heavy. Later, outside the door, I found he had left a bag of mandarin oranges, Morgan's favorites.

Shocked at myself, I could still feel the soft give of her flesh against my knuckles. But Morgan hadn't seemed to notice. I heard the front door close and knew that Bill had once again left the house, retreating to a coffeehouse down the street, where he read the paper from front to back rather than be around the yelling.

Gritting my teeth, trying to calm down, I sat on the bed next to Morgan and stared down at my hands.

"It's clear that my plan is intolerable to you," I said. "How about a compromise? You do your homework your way, and in three weeks I'll check with your teachers to see how you're doing."

"Why, Mom?" she asked. "Why do you care so much whether I do my homework or not?"

"Neither of my parents finished high school," I said. "Neither did my brother Shannon or my sister Robin. It's a hard way to start your life, with that failure in front of you."

Morgan tugged at a hole in her jeans, making it larger. I watched her worry the white threads. She said nothing.

"From here on in, it counts," I insisted. "The colleges you apply to will look at your entire high school transcript, including the classes you're taking this first semester."

"I'm going to college, Mom. When did I say I wasn't going to college?"

"I want you to take the life I'm offering you," I persisted, "a good education followed by a good job."

I had read that parental expectations counted the most, when it came to motivating kids. My brothers and sisters and I, all bright kids, had not been expected to go to college, and so most of us didn't. Besides me, only my older sister Connie had gone to college. Though she was forty, my twin, Adrian, was in college now, going at night, one class at a time, while working as the civil clerk at the county courthouse in the daytime. Textbooks—biology, history, pre-calculus—covered the backseat of her truck whenever she came over.

"All I want is to be happy," Morgan said now in a hopeless voice.

"It's all I want for you, too," I said. She hugged me, and I tightened my arms around her. We stayed that way for a long time.

I could not back off. To let up on her homework would be a form of leaving, and I was determined never to leave her. I knew too much about what that felt like.

COMING home from the paper a week or so later, my head full of a book I'd been reading, I jumped down from the N Judah streetcar at Duboce Park, near our house, and nearly collided with two teenage girls who had paused to light cigarettes as soon as they got off.

One of them was Morgan.

"Morgan!" I said. She wheeled around, her backpack a blur of blue. She wore plastic mirrored sunglasses. I saw myself in them, my collar pulled askew by my briefcase, pale, my short blond hair disheveled. I grabbed her cigarette and ground it under my heel, then picked up the butt. With her was Holly, dressed all in black, as she always was. I'd seen her quietly let her own cigarette drop. "See you later, Morgan," she said, and walked off quickly, her boots clicking.

"I was just trying it out," Morgan said to me, as the other passengers parted around us, heading up the sidewalk or across the green park.

"Tell me the truth, Morgan," I said. We had turned to walk toward the house, but I stopped her on the sidewalk and looked at her. "Do you smoke?"

She didn't drop her eyes. "Yes," she said.

"Since how long?"

"Since last summer."

A year, then. This, from a girl who had started a "Just Say No" club at school when she was eleven.

I felt sick. "You used to hate it yourself when people smoked. You thought it was stupid."

"I know, Mom," she said.

"You *don't* know!" I said heatedly. "You never knew your dad's brother Herb. He smoked all his life and died of lung cancer." I remembered green-eyed Herb, the handsome one in his family, watching football surrounded by his daughters, shifting his hips in response to a persistent ache that would turn out to be cancer. Dead at fifty-eight.

"I just did a column on this," I said to her. "Only five percent of teenagers who smoke believe they'll still be smoking in five years. Seven years later, two thirds of them are." Morgan had her head down, waiting out this boring lecture.

"And of those who smoke by age seventeen, half will still be smoking at age thirty-six. *Half!* And of those, half will die of a smoking-related disease." The statistics had lodged in my head.

I might have been the sound of the wind in the trees. We had passed the rec center, and Morgan was eyeing our yellow house at the end of the block as if salvation lay within it.

"I'm going to quit, I promise," she said impatiently. "You don't have to keep talking about it."

"What do the other kids think of your smoking?" I asked. The September sun burned the back of my neck.

"The ones who don't smoke tell me I should quit. The other ones bum cigarettes."

We walked in silence. The old Chinese man who lived on the corner was sweeping the walk with the edge of his newspaper, as he did every morning.

No wonder Morgan wasn't worried. She knew no one in my family has died of smoking, and my family's been on fire for years. When we go across the bridge to visit my mother in the county, we enter a friendly club, people who go through each other's purses looking for smokes, bum matches, and argue about who stole whose Merit Lights.

"I don't want you to smoke," I said again, feeling hopeless. I knew she would go on lighting sticks of tobacco and drawing the nicotine deep into lungs that were in her body, not mine. I couldn't do a damned thing about it.

After that, every time I smelled tobacco on her clothes and asked her about smoking, she claimed she had quit. Jim and I went on finding packs of Newports in the pocket of her BP gas station jacket. "Those aren't mine," she'd say hotly. It reminded me of how we used to find candy wrappers in her pockets after school. "Kids drop wrappers on the playground," she'd explain piously. "I pick them up to throw them away."

Several nights later I sat in my office, arms aching from the tension stored in them as I listened to Morgan laughing at *The Simpsons* with her new braying laugh. It didn't sound quite real, her new laugh. It sounded forced, as if she was trying to convince herself that she was amused, that everything was fine. I stalked into the kitchen and said, "You must have homework."

"You promised you wouldn't bug me about that," Morgan protested. "You always break our deals!" We argued for a while before stomping off to our separate rooms. "I want my old mom back!" Morgan shrieked from behind her closed door.

I sat on my bed, staring at a framed photo on the wall of the kids and me at a footrace Adrian was running in, years ago. I'm crouching down, holding the two little kids by the legs, all three of us wearing the white caps they'd been handing out and grinning at the camera.

I wanted Morgan's old mom back, too. I had been so confident, so easy with them before.

Jim and I divorced when Patrick was four and Morgan was five. I moved into a downstairs apartment, then into a couple of other places around the city. Now I was living downstairs from him, with my new husband. I suppose a shrink would hazard a guess that our boundaries were becoming fluid. Jim sent bowls of soup downstairs, cake servers, and eggs, and stored his wine in our extra refrigerator. He came down to show me funny things in the Clark, South

Dakota, paper that he subscribes to by mail from his hometown. He came in to use my fax, to ask me to read over something he's written for a book flap (he's a publisher of local books), to discuss the state of the roof (Bill and I now owned 34 percent of the building), or to show us how to unstop the bathroom sink with a kitchen plunger.

He walked in unannounced, always calling "Hello!" but then using his key to let himself in. We all had master keys that unlocked every door in the house. Sometimes Bill, imagining himself alone, reading the paper in the early morning, was surprised to hear Jim in Morgan's bedroom arguing with her about what time she had to be ready for school.

When I went upstairs, I didn't need a key, since he never locked his back door. I sprinted up to steal apples from his kitchen (we called it the "Jimstore," as in "We're out of rice. Can you get some up at the Jimstore?"), to play Ping-Pong with Patrick, or to browse through the shelves of books.

Even Mike, my old bad-tempered black-and-white cat, yowled outside Jim's door when he wanted to be let in downstairs.

No matter how often I went up there, it was always, fleetingly, like stepping into my own past. Jim and I raised the kids for the first five years of their lives there. He never changed anything, so the pictures on the walls were all of the kids when they were under five, because I put them there. My hats were in the downstairs closet, the kids' baby albums in the living room shelves, my college texts in the attic, my old coats in boxes upstairs, my former husband working the crossword at the kitchen table.

When we talked, we stayed, always, in the present. A wife and husband learn intimacy together: an ex-husband and his ex-wife must unlearn it. We talked about Morgan's grades and Patrick's shoes, but not about our history, his and mine.

Before I met Bill and moved back into the building, Jim and I shared the kids equally, half a week each, and everybody got along. I remember walking down the street holding a blond child with each hand, smiling back at old ladies who smiled at me. You could find the three of us together in front of the TV, eating dripping Popsicles while watching *Police Academy* 6. I bribed them to memorize Robert Frost poems. Evenings we got through homework, and then danced together to Michael Jackson in the kitchen, blasting it out through the windows to Patrick's escaped turtles in the backyard. At night Morgan would pretend to fall asleep on the couch so that she had to be dragged, useless legs catching on everything, a smile on her supposedly sleeping face. Once I had told the teacher the kids were sick when the three of us had really taken our bikes on the ferry to Marin.

Morgan seemed fine then. Morgan *was* fine. A typical outfit for her at age eight was boots, black parachute pants under one of my All American Girl sweatshirts, charm necklace, hair raked off to one side à la Tina Turner, carrying her lunch and wadded-up homework in a pink aerobics bag. In the second grade she was at a loss to understand why Mr. Sichel wanted to be the only one who got to talk in class. She had firm plans to marry her cousin Ryan, could spell "hypothesis," and wanted to skip "oh, three or four" grades because the work was too cinchy. She had three Cabbage Patch dolls who were present for every meal, and were, as Morgan indignantly reminded me five or six times a day, not to be referred to as "dolls."

I was relaxed then. I was almost nonchalant. I knew I was a pretty good mom because I liked myself when I was with them—because when I was with my kids, my world felt right, felt complete.

But when Morgan entered the eighth grade, I became a new kind of mom. I was vigilant, watchful, suspicious. Morgan was Annie in the musical, always trying to get out to the streets, and I was Miss Hanigan, creeping after her. It was clear to me that Morgan felt the lure of the street. Until she got older, and got some sense, I would have to keep her safe, and in school.

The danger was real. Two girls Morgan's age really had been raped and killed by a gang of boys in the city, as I had told her, and Morgan had blithely admitted to having hung out on that very same corner where the girls had stood.

What did I do to keep her in? I grounded her.

Grounding was what I knew how to do. My mother had grounded my brothers and sisters and me, or tried to. We would come in late, or cut school, or throw something in the neighbor's yard and get the neighbors mad at Mom, and she'd say, "You're restricted!" But after her first fury had passed, it was hard for her to remember that we were being punished. "What are you doing hanging around the house for on such a nice day?" she'd ask me after she had grounded me for walking the streets with my boyfriend Johnny after curfew.

The year before Bill and I had bought travel locks, the kind to give hotel guests protection against intruders with keys. We didn't lock her in her room, of course (though it was tempting), but at bedtime we'd creep from front door to back door, after Morgan had gone to bed, and affix these flimsy tin locks to the doorjamb. The locks became a new secret language between her and me. She never mentioned seeing them. It was as if they didn't exist. The locks said, "I don't trust you." Her silence about them said, "I never try to sneak out, so I never see your stupid locks."

Morgan needed a wise TV mommy, one who could laugh at her foibles, exert loving but strict discipline, and dish out wisdom. What she had instead was me. While she'd been changing into a restless thrill-seeker, I should have been preparing myself somehow, getting wiser or stronger or more intuitive. Instead I had lost ground, grown soggy and weak, undermined by love and fear.

chapter 4

I F I needed more proof that grounding did not work, I got it on a Saturday night a couple of weeks later. Patrick was at a friend's, and Bill and Morgan and I had lingered over a nice dinner–Bill had cooked pizza with feta cheese especially for her. We talked around the table, and she helped clear the dishes.

As Morgan carried plates to the sink, chattering about how it felt to be one of the managers of the wrestling team, Bill and I looked at each other and smiled. I bent down to put a pot away in one of the lower cupboards. I was thinking of asking Morgan to watch *My Cousin Vinny* with me, a movie we both loved. When I straightened up I said, "Morgan, do you want to watch . . ." and trailed off, looking around for her. Bill was grinding the coffee for breakfast–something he did in the evening so he wouldn't wake the kids early in the morning.

Morgan had disappeared. Puzzled, I looked in her bedroom, then the bathroom, then in the rest of the flat.

"She can't have left," I said to Bill, feeling dazed. "We were just having fun. And she knows she's grounded."

Bill stiffened. He stopped fiddling with the coffee filter and stared at me. "Maybe she's up at Jim's?"

But she wasn't. She wasn't anywhere in the house. She had walked out again. I felt as if she had hit me.

"Let's get her back here," I said to Bill.

Bill drove, and I directed him up Haight Street. Instinct told me she would have gone in this direction. When we got to Haight and Divisadero, we scanned the lighted bus stop with its transparent plastic walls. No Morgan. But at the next stop there she was, sitting on one of those little orange fold-down seats, smoking a cigarette.

Bill blasted the horn. Morgan's head jerked and she came toward us with a smirk that said, okay, I'm busted.

"Get in," I said, unrolling my window as she reached the car. Fury made my voice tremble. I leaned my seat forward, and she climbed in the back.

We drove downhill toward home.

"You're grounded for a month," I said without turning around.

"I don't see what the big deal is," Morgan said, and when I turned around in my seat, she had that smirk on her face again. "You guys flip out over everything."

Bill slammed on the brakes. He jerked the wheel and drew the car into a bus zone, threw it in park, and then he was over the backseat. He seized her by the front of her jacket. "You horrible little bitch!" he yelled. "Who do you think you are?" He shook her so hard she snapped backward and then forward in the seat.

I flung myself on him. "Bill! Don't!" I yelled, grabbing his arms and pulling them off Morgan, and then Morgan was screaming. Bill released her and we drove the last block home to the sound of Morgan's frenzied sobbing. I reached a hand backward to her knee to comfort her. I felt as if we were all moving in slow motion, or underwater. I felt as if we had come to the end of everything. Bill's face in the wavering streetlight was a mask of misery, but I didn't touch him. In that moment, I thought I might never touch him again.

When we got home, Morgan jumped out and ran for the gate.

"Morgan!" Bill said.

Morgan stopped and looked back at him. "I don't know what to say about what just happened," he said in a tense voice. "But I want you to know you don't have to worry about it ever happening again. I give you my word."

Morgan said nothing. She turned and unlocked the gate, and then we heard her footsteps on the back steps as she fled up to her dad's.

Bill and I said nothing to each other as we went into the kitchen, where all the lights were still blazing, and the plastic lidful of coffee beans still stood on the counter. I watched as he grabbed his jacket from the hook, and then heard the front close softly behind him, a sad, distant click.

I was alone in the house. I sat in a chair, staring out the window at the night.

"You can have her for a few days," I told Jim when he came down to hear what had happened. Jim nodded, looking sad.

I didn't trust myself around her. I was so angry, and so hurt. She was a raw, hurting place in my mind.

Much later Bill came back, chilled and tired. "I walked all the way to the ocean and back," he said. "I was sure that I'd really done it this time, that you'd never let me near you again."

I put my arms around him, feeling his cold cheek against mine. "Oh, baby, I was angry, too," I said. "I understand." Bill had never done anything like that before. When he said he never would again, I believed him.

"She brings out the worst in me," he said miserably against my ear. "It's not that I can't stand her. She's just a kid. It's that I can't stand myself when I'm around her."

"I HAVE to interview an old person for my school project. How about if I talked to Grandpa?" Patrick asked.

Weeks had gone by. I had not seen my dad since I dropped him on Van Ness, though I'd heard that a friend had helped him get into an SSI-assisted apartment in Fairfax, having arranged it for him when he was still down in the desert.

"Luke is on the blink," Dad said without preamble when I phoned him, as if he had been the one to place the call. "He's emitting loud chirps every minute or two."

"Luke?"

"My parakeet."

"What happened to Fred?"

"He's at the ranch, spreading delight. No dogs allowed here."

"Iris is taking care of your dog for you?"

"Sure. To what do I owe the honor of this call?"

"Patrick wants to know if he can interview you for a homework project," I said, adding cruelly, "he's supposed to talk to an old person."

"I see one in the mirror every morning. Come on over."

The three of us drove out on Saturday. "But she's grounded," Bill objected when he saw Morgan was going too.

"Doesn't apply to going places with family," I explained.

"Shotgun!" Morgan cried, claiming the front seat next to me. Grumbling, Patrick climbed in the back. On the drive over, she sat gluing legs from magazines onto a paper towel—a card for a new friend, Edan.

I drove past a sign that said BENNETT HOUSE and parked. "Hey, this is a nice place," Patrick said with surprise.

I was surprised myself, looking at the nice plantings, and the well-cared-for pastel three-story building with its back to a grassy hill.

"Leave your legs in the car, all right?" I pleaded with Morgan. Patrick got out carrying his dad's old Panasonic tape recorder, the cord trailing on the cement. To the right was what appeared to be a communal garden. An old woman in an apron was on her knees, weeding.

I found "Daly" on the list of names next to the lobby door and hit the buzzer.

"Yeah?"

"It's us, Dad."

He buzzed the door open, and we took the elevator to the third floor. We stepped off the elevator–wide enough for a gurney, I noticed–and filed past groups of pastel furniture and a large black treadmill, the price tag still dangling from it.

Dad was waiting in the hall for us, slightly bent over, a thin old guy wearing a checked cap, a short-sleeved summer shirt, and checked pants. Smiling, not even trying to hide how glad he was to see us, he led us into a large room with a desk, a cot, and a couple of secondhand couches. He dragged an old office chair over for me to sit on, and moved a pile of books and a bag of Halloween Hershey bars out of the way so Morgan and Patrick could sit on the beat-up couch. I crossed the room and glanced down the wide back window at a schoolyard below the hill. "How do you like it?" Dad asked me, watching me. "Your tax dollars at work. Got most of the furniture at the Salvation Army."

"How much is this costing you?" I said, looking up at the vaulted white ceiling.

"It's six hundred fifty, but I pay only a hundred fifty of it. I'm supported by the state. An old draft horse who always shirked in the traces but is being supported anyway."

"Did you ever get your van fixed?" I said, remembering the broken axle. I sat down on the couch, shoving books and papers aside to make room.

"Yep. Iris felt so bad when she calmed down that she insisted on paying for the repair."

"We saw only old ladies in that big room downstairs," Morgan observed, looking around curiously.

"There are lots of them," Dad agreed cheerfully. "They stare at me when I go by. They remind me of old hens sitting in a hole."

"Well, Dad, that's your dating pool," I pointed out.

"Yeah," he said with an impish grin.

"Why is your nose all banged up, Grandpa?" Patrick asked.

"Got drunk and fell on the sidewalk," Dad said, touching his nose carefully. "They took me to the emergency, sent me home with a riveting bit of reading matter." He picked a brochure off the littered end table next to him and handed it to me. Big white letters on the front said, "You Are an Alcoholic. You Must Go to AA."

There was a silence. "You know your mom shot me down," he said to me. "I suppose that gave you a kick."

"She said she got some letters from you," I said.

"Yep." Dad gestured at two letters lying on the couch beside Morgan, both addressed to my mom in Dad's small neat handwriting, both marked "Return to Sender." The couch seemed to serve Dad as a desk. He sighed and looked at me through a cloud of smoke. "Good old Lee. What every bum hopes to find in a boxcar. And then wishes he'd taken the bus instead."

"Tough luck, Pop," I said. "Maybe Thomas Wolfe was right–you can't go home again."

I noticed three cellophane boxes of chocolate bunnies on a chair. Dad saw me looking at them. "Your brother Shannon called, said he might bring his kids by. Your kids might as well take them."

"Maybe he's still planning to come by."

"Maybe," Dad said, keeping his expression neutral. Then he added, "You might refrain from mentioning this to him. That would give your brother quite a picture, me sobbing over my three chocolate bunnies."

I heard a chirp. "I hear Luke," I said. "But I can't see him."

"I took him down to Bell Market parking lot in my cupped hands and let him go. He wouldn't stop that goddamned chirping. Now he seems to be behind the furnace housing."

"Behind the furnace housing?" I said, confused. "You mean he's trapped in the wall?"

"Yes. He's dying in there, and I can't get him out, so I'm having a beer." He had a can of Budweiser at his elbow. A small wicker basket at his feet held two empties. "There must be some lost soul in this fucking world who doesn't blame me."

We all listened a minute to the irregular chirp of the bird in the wall.

"I wouldn't blame you, Grandpa," Morgan broke in, "except for one thing."

"What's that?" Dad asked.

"That isn't a bird in the wall. It's your smoke alarm."

"My what?"

"Your smoke alarm. It needs a new battery."

Dad looked amazed. I felt like an idiot myself, not having figured that out. "The smoke alarm?" he repeated.

"Sure. Here, I'll show you." She dragged a chair over to a spot in Dad's entryway, climbed up and pressed a button on the small white disk on the ceiling. The chirping stopped.

"Well, I'll be damned," Dad said. "I'll be goddamned."

"You let the bird go for nothing," Patrick pointed out. He had switched to Dad's narrow daybed, where he was lying down reading his magazine and waggling his feet. "There was probably nothing wrong with it."

"Fucking hell," Dad said, taking a pull on his beer. "I wonder where the little bastard is, then?"

He started to say something more, but instead coughed violently. I watched him, alarmed. All of a sudden he looked drained and pale, his green eyes watery. He rose from his chair, mumbling, "Need some water," and went to the kitchen, an area made separate by a half wall and counter. His walk was more of a totter. He reached out to the wall to steady himself for a second before going on into the kitchen.

When he came back, he put two cigarette papers on his knee and shook tobacco from a weathered red pouch onto them. He rolled it, licked it, and then looked around for his lighter.

Morgan had it. She flicked it open and leaned forward to light his cigarette. "How have you been?" Dad said to her as he inhaled. "Still giving your mom fits?"

"She's still *having* fits," Morgan corrected him.

"And what do you think of your grandpa? Your grandma has poisoned your mom and her siblings against me. She hasn't got to you, presumably."

"I think you're cool, Grandpa. You get to do whatever you want," Morgan said.

I fought to keep my voice calm. "Mr. Cool here quit high school, he walked out on jobs, and he quit his family," I told her. "He even deserted from the army."

"You did, Grandpa?" Morgan said.

"Well . . ."

"Wait a second," I said. I wanted both kids to hear this.

"Patrick!" I hissed.

Patrick looked up from his magazine.

"Your project?"

"Oh, right."

"Grandpa? Can I interview you now?" he called out.

Dad smiled at Patrick. "I'd be charmed," he said.

I plugged in the tape recorder behind the couch and Patrick read his first question off a folded piece of binder paper that he took out of his pocket.

"I'm skipping some of the dumber questions," he assured Dad.

"Don't do that on my account," Dad said eagerly. "I'll answer them all."

"Where and when were you born? What were times like when you were young?" Patrick read off the sheet. "What advice or training did your parents give you that has helped you to lead a better, fuller life? Do you feel there is a difference between city people and country people?"

DAD told them about growing up in San Francisco and becoming a carpenter after the war, about meeting my mom, the grandma they knew so well, at Ocean Beach in 1945.

As he described meeting her, I imagined the scene: he came out of the water, rubbing the salt from his eyes, but didn't yet go rejoin his friends, a crowd of army veterans who hung out below the seawall at the north end of the beach, the section known as Muscle Beach. Dad had exhausted the benefits of the 52/20 clubs, the twenty dollars a week granted to soldiers separated from the service and looking for work, and had a job on a construction site downtown. Jobs were easy to find: postwar San Francisco was booming.

It was Saturday, and the long beach was crowded with people who had come out on the streetcar after a long week at the office, filing insurance claims in downtown offices or serving lunch to Pacific Heights matrons or unloading ships at the dock. A high concrete wall shielded the beach from the Great Highway above, and bright graffiti was scrawled on it everywhere. One sign said, KILROY WAS HERE.

Then he saw her again, a young woman he had noticed on the beach on previous weekends. She was tall, with generously rounded curves and long, flowing black hair that made her look almost Hawaiian. She and her girlfriend were slathering baby oil over themselves in the sand about twenty yards up the beach, their legs splayed out in front of them, ignoring the looks they were getting from the men on the beach. A bottle of lotion was stuck at a rakish angle in the sand, minus its lid. She had lowered her straps of her white-and-red flowered bathing suit and was vigorously slapping on lotion. She wasn't fat, or even close to it. She was abundant, solid, lush. She could have been sitting on the towel for days, she looked so at home on it.

"She was a little above my market value, but I thought to myself, this is a woman I can have," Dad told the kids.

They ran with a Bohemian crowd, and Dad once drove to L.A. to give speeches in the park.

"God, we were kings of the world then!" he said now. "I can still see that little haranguing park, paved with broken Thunderbird bottles. I remember being parked nearby, Lee with a baby on her lap, wads of soiled diapers. Tiny car, covered with dust, us sitting on top of the debris. Sean with lockjaw as usual. A woman peering in the window. 'Oh, the poor thing!' My sister on the phone, saying, 'You animal, send that poor kid and your half-expired baby up here this instant.' " Dad looked at us. "Fabulous," he said. "Youth, youth, as Conrad might say."

His grandkids listened to his story, trying to understand. I sat on the couch, watching the two of them struggling for connections, to feel what they merely knew: this is my grandfather. I am his grand-child.

"How do you feel about life in general today?" droned Patrick when he sensed Dad had stopped answering the previous question. Patrick had the efficient interviewer's trick of not listening, but go-ing right on to the next question. He'd probably grow up to have his own TV show.

"Never mind that," Morgan interrupted after five minutes. "Tell us what happened in the army, Grandpa."

"Yes, Dad, tell them that," I said, leaning back and crossing my arms.

"Did you really desert?" Morgan said.

"That was later," he said, "after I realized that Pearl Harbor meant the war would drag on and on. I slugged an officer and they threw me in the stockade. Same one where they shot the movie *From Here to Eternity.*"

The kids looked blank. "Anyway, I got a hacksaw, went out through a window."

"You hit an *officer?*" I said.

"It's not such a big deal as all that," he answered. "Problem sol-diers are forever socking their officers. The army is chock-a-block with COs slumped behind their desks."

"Then what?" said Patrick. He was straddling Dad's office chair.

"I went over the hill for seven months. I had to wear my uniform because all haolies were soldiers or sailors."

"Howlies?" Morgan said.

"White people."

"Hawaii's an island," Morgan pointed out. "You can't desert on an island."

"So I found out." Dad smiled slightly. "They caught me and sentenced me to ten years of hard labor and a dishonorable discharge." He sucked at his cigarette. "You could say the springtime of my life had gone seriously haywire."

"How long were you in prison?" Morgan was looking at Dad with awe. "Is that where you got your tattoos?" We all looked at the eagle tattoo on Dad's right arm. It used to bulge, when I was a kid. Now it clung to his arm like an expired balloon, faded and sagging.

"I served about four of the ten years in Leavenworth. Managed in the end to evade the dishonorable discharge," Dad answered. After prison, he had gone back into the army as an athletic instructor at Monterey for a year and been given an honorable discharge. Now he paused, looking around at the kids' rapt faces. "But I served every day of that sentence. I'm still serving it. We might call it the life sentence without possibility of parole."

The tape recorder was hissing softly on the couch. The kids were quiet now. Morgan's hands were still for once, and she stared at her grandfather.

"WHAT about the story you just heard?" I asked Morgan on the drive back to the city. "Maybe if your grandpa had finished high school, he would have known how to finish things. Maybe he wouldn't have gone on to quit the army, and his jobs, and his family."

"You're too hard on people, Mom," she said. "Grandpa just wasn't army material. Can we talk about something important instead? Like, am I going to get a car when I'm sixteen?"

I felt as if I had played my biggest card, and she had looked at it and said, "Is that all?" I wanted to shake her, say, "Listen to me! Don't start your life like this!"

chapter 5

WE didn't get out to Marin to see my dad again for a long time after that. The second half of Morgan's freshman school year and the first half of her sophomore year passed in a haze of arguments, stalemates, and outbursts. I remember watching a movie with Bill, and going upstairs to throw Morgan and her friends out of Jim's flat, when Jim was out. I found Holly and Morgan hiding in the downstairs shower, giggling, stoned, and shushing each other.

A black worry was growing in the back of my head. I remember picking her up at friends' houses and having the impression she had been drinking beer. How much was she drinking? I fantasized about getting one of those breathalyzers sold in mail-order magazines. Instead of greeting her with a cheerful hello when she came home, I would pull her over like a highway patrolman and test her. What would that do to her and me? Her link to me was her lifeline.

In January of Morgan's sophomore year–Patrick was now a freshman, also at Lowell High School–the kids and I drove home after a weekend visiting my twin sister in Ukiah. "Just drop me at Noah's house, okay, Mom?" Morgan said from the backseat. Noah was a school friend whose mom lived in Marin.

"Is his mother home?" I asked.

"No, but it's all right."

"It's out of the question," I said. "I'm not dropping you at a boy's house. I've never even met Noah."

"Come on, Mom. Just drop me. It's fine with his parents."

She argued and argued as we sped in the dark car down 101. "I'll never give you permission," I said finally, exasperated. "Never! Not in a thousand years!"

"But Mom, I promised Noah I'd help him with his paper. It's due tomorrow."

I swerved the car over to the side of the road, gliding to a stop and switching off the motor. "I'm not going to drive if you're going to bring up staying at Noah's again," I said, my fists still tight on the steering wheel. Why couldn't she accept even a loss this small, not being dropped off at Noah's? How could she grow up if she couldn't?

"Okay, Mom, sheesh. I was just asking," Morgan said. I pulled back onto the road.

Around nine o'clock, we stopped for a burger at a truck stop west of Petaluma. Morgan went to the bathroom. I was trying to persuade Patrick to give me the last bite of his cheeseburger when she returned to the table. "Noah says it's fine for me to stay at his house, so you can just drop me there," she said brightly, dropping into the red upholstered banquette and reaching for a French fry.

"No," I said in a strangled voice, throwing money on the table for the check, grabbing my coat and leaving the kids to follow. "No."

We drove in silence. Patrick sat slightly hunched forward in the front seat, edging away from his sister. He was reading his magazine, as if he hardly dared to talk to me himself. I had switched on the interior light for him, so we drove in a bubble of light. Morgan stared blandly out the window in the back. She seemed unaware of what I was feeling. The weekend's fun might as well have happened to some other family.

I couldn't seem to make her take in what I was saying anymore. When had I lost that simple motherly skill?

In February I tried drawing up a contract with her. "It's time we started treating you like an adult," I said, and she beamed. An adult is what she wanted to be. "What do you want?" I said. I held my pen over the paper, ready to write.

"I want my own apartment, freedom to ride the buses at night, and not to go to school," Morgan said.

"I want you never to leave the house again, except to go to school, until you're thirty." I said, lowering my pen. "Maybe we can meet in the middle?"

After much noisy discussion, we settled on an eleven-thirty curfew on weekends, no going out on weeknights, and Morgan's word that she would always let me know where she was. Then we hugged. I felt like a model mom, a mom who was paying attention, learning to make adjustments as her kids grew toward adulthood.

The next day Morgan and I were competing for the mirror in the bathroom, Morgan trying to apply mascara and me trying to get my short hair to look less, well, short. She had put brown eye shadow on her eyelids and darkened her light brows with pencil. The makeup seemed to transform her almost into somebody else's child, a slightly hardened, in-the-know, deliberate half-child, half-woman. I was inept with makeup, and Morgan scolded me when I even got near the sink now, as if even the way I walked toward makeup was wrong.

As she painted one eyelid, Morgan brought up the contract. "I think it's too repressive," she said, squinting into the mirror. "For instance," she said, brushing her left eyelash in long, practiced strokes, "if I'm over at Chelsea's house, and about twelve-thirty at night a bunch of us decide we want to go out. Would we have to call you up?"

I stared at her in the mirror. So much for the contract, and the temporary, insane illusion of control it had provided. It was as if Morgan had suddenly been whisked off to a distant plain and was shouting from over there, and I was shouting back.

"You're fourteen," I sputtered, finally. "You can't 'go out' at all. Let alone at twelve-thirty A.M."

"Don't get all mad," she said calmly, starting on the other eye. "I was just asking."

That afternoon I went to the place I always visited when I felt blindsided by life: the bookstore. I entered Clean Well-Lighted Place for Books on Van Ness Street and found myself instantly comforted by the rows and rows of gleaming books. I found shelves teeming with advice on how to raise teenagers: *Uncommon Sense for Parents with Teenagers, The Seven-Year Stretch, The Romance of Risk, Living with Your Teenager, The Secret of a Good Life with Your Teenager.*

I thought if I just knew more, knew better how to handle her, then she would be reasonable and be happy.

I brought home half a dozen volumes and sat with them out on the front steps, doing what I had done all my life when at a loss: reading, thumbing through advice books.

I could not find a book that could tell me how to get a teenager to tune in to her mother, but I found tons of advice that filled me with hope.

Between Parent and Child said you're supposed to mirror your children's feelings back to them. When a kid comes home depressed because he didn't get the baby-sitting job he wanted, the father is supposed to say something like, "You must feel really disappointed."

I cringed, reading this. If I said, "Morgan, I hear that you are angry," she'd say, "Mom, I hear that you've been reading your parenting books again."

But when I tried it, it worked. One Sunday morning Patrick complained that Morgan wouldn't let him borrow the black basketball that had come with her Nike watch. "You always borrow my clothes and my basketball, and you never appreciate it," she screamed at him. "I don't want you to borrow anything of mine again, ever." She grabbed the ball from him and headed for her room.

Instead of saying, "Oh, Morgan, you know you never use the basketball yourself," as I usually would, I said, "Patrick, Morgan needs to know that you appreciate it when she lends you her things."

Both kids seemed to hold their breath for a minute. Then Patrick gave his sister a token shove and went off without the ball, but she smiled at me. And actually put her dirty plate in the sink.

Encouraged, I went back to my books, going through the advice with a yellow highlighter while my work piled up next to my computer. "The more she loves you, the worse the rebellion as she struggles for independence," said one book. "The more she feels loved, the freer she'll feel to be obnoxious."

Morgan must have felt loved to death, I thought.

"It is with girls, not with boys, that parents experience the supreme disruption of adolescence," said a book called *Get Out of My Life, but First Could You Drive Cheryl and Me to the Mall?* "Sweet cooperative daughters turn, often rather suddenly, into hysterical, shrieking monsters."

This, too, was cheerful reading. How could her metamorphosis into a Gorgon-headed changeling be my fault–or her fault–if I could read it in a book?

One book advised me to separate incidents into Her Problems and My Problems. My problems included keeping her safe, providing for her needs, and making sure she felt loved even when we couldn't stand her.

One night I knew she had a Spanish test the next day, but she'd been on the phone for hours. I was snapping pencils at my desk, so I asked her to get off the phone. "I don't like to see you on it," I said.

She said, "That's your problem, Mom. Deal with it."

And she hadn't even read the book!

I learned that good moms are firm. Good moms say, "No, you may not take ten minutes out of your homework period to watch

MTV. No, you cannot stay at school for song girl tryouts even though that's suddenly always been your dream and tryouts are to-day only and you hate me, I'm a peeface."

Between Parent and Teenager said never make blanket statements to your kids, telling them they always do this, or they never do that. I marked the passage for her dad to read. "This is typical of you, Jim," I said in a yellow Post-it. "You always do this."

I put the book through his mail slot (our front doors stood side by side on the small front porch), but he never read it. Like a lot of men, he didn't go in much for instruction books. He taught himself how to restore Victorian houses and later how to make me maternity blouses on his old sewing machine, all without reading directions. (When Patrick was three, a friend of his had a hole in his pants and Patrick said, sympathetically, "You should get your daddy to fix that.")

I'd find the books I gave him lying amid the clutter on his bed-room floor, the Post-its still flying from them. I watched from my kitchen window as Jim pulled out of the garage in his red Volvo every morning, headed for Lowell, with Morgan sitting in the back-seat, staring out the window. She never sat up front with him. I thought of how much easier it would be for him to bear her re-moteness from him, if he had read, as I had, that many adolescent girls distance themselves from their fathers.

Jim was a wonderful father for a little girl. He made cakes with her, took her for walks, laughed at everything she said and did. When we brought Morgan home from the hospital, I lolled on the bed, receiving visitors, with my baby in my arms. Then I handed her to him. "Go bond," I said nonchalantly, and he took the baby. An hour later he brought her back, putting her in my arms with a glazed look on his face. He was a goner.

When the pediatrician said that Morgan might stop merrily drib-bling oatmeal down the legs of her high chair if we let her go hun-gry once or twice, I tried it. Just put her to bed hungry.

Then I got up in the night and found Jim had sneaked downstairs.

The two of them were caught in the bright pool of light cast by the overhead, she crowing happily in her high chair as he tenderly ladled applesauce into her mouth. "Well, she was hungry!" he said when he saw me.

They began to battle when she was about eight. He would call me up and tell me what terrible things she had shouted at him right on the school playground, in front of everybody.

"Let's just make her stop," he said angrily when we discovered she was cutting class to go smoke in "the Pit," an outside area at school where smokers congregated illegally.

"Sure," I said. "And while we're at it, let's just tell her to keep her room clean, and not sneak out, and by the way to please get straight A's."

Jim was a man in love, but love is not enough, when it comes to teenagers. I thought he needed advice at least as much as I did—and I was listening to anyone and everyone. "All you have to teach her, you have already taught her," a woman in the line at the bank told me, patting my arm, when I started gabbling to her about the hell-child I had at home. I tried desperately to remember something, anything that I had taught her, besides an appreciation for red licorice and all the words to "Last Kiss."

I read through March and April of that year. I recognized the wisdom of the many suggestions I was given. I wish I could say that after this period of research I was transformed into Donna Reed. But it wasn't true.

Too much was in the way.

The person—me—who was trying to take in all the advice was a harried, nervous, shivering wreck. Morgan was the tornado, and I was the trailer park in her path.

One day she had hung up on me and come in fifteen minutes late. Wanting to take the advice of the book and not wanting another unpleasant evening, I said nothing. We all had Bill's baked chicken together, and I let her spend two hours on the phone even though I knew she had algebra homework.

I was fine. She was fine. Until the next morning, when I barged into her room as she was getting ready for school. "You left your wet towels on the floor in my room when you were in there swiping my black sweater this morning," I snapped, and then caught myself.

"It's hard to remember everything when you're rushing around in the morning," I tried to go on. But what came out instead was: "And you didn't get your algebra done last night."

Morgan blinked in surprise. Hurt, she left for school again without saying good-bye. I heard the door slam.

I would let something go one day but secretly store the irritation and freak out two days later at something else, like my friend Sallie. She overlooked her sixteen-year-old son's breaking the delicate china plate she had brought all the way from France, but threw an ice tray at him and told him to get out when he had once again used all the ice and left the empty trays in the sink.

Reading should have brought enlightenment. Enlightenment should have brought change. But I hadn't changed. I was hurt and mad and unsure of myself.

Books tell you what teenagers are going to do. What they don't tell you is how you will *feel*. If our home life had been a novel, Morgan would be the man whose feelings had turned cold, and I would be the spurned girlfriend waiting by the phone, the one as much in love as ever.

And I was scared. It was the worst period of my life to ask me to calmly and humorously put parenting advice into practice. To be calm when I wanted to yell. To laugh when my heart was cracking. I was like a friend I knew with a back injury, who would lie face-down on her hospital bed, her gown hiked up in back, and scream if the doctor touched her back, even when he did it with a feather.

All the time now, I found myself screaming at feathers.

Not having control was an awful feeling. When she talked on the phone for hours, and I knew she had a math test the next day, I was not enraged because she was in danger of not knowing any math. I was enraged because she wasn't *minding me*, because she was standing in my house and not doing what I wanted her to do. Behind the rage was cold fear: If I couldn't control her, I couldn't save her.

Sometimes the books advised me to use humor. "Don't give them the reactions they're after," they said. It struck me that my sense of humor had been the first thing to go. Where was the mom who used to drop on all fours? All of a sudden, parenting had become deadly serious.

One night she'd been on the phone for two hours, dressed in ragged cutoffs and a tank top, lying atop her cluttered bed like a shipwrecked passenger on a raft. "I did not tell anybody that sophomores could kiss my ass," I heard her say heatedly. "I do *not* want a hug," she said next. Then: "I like you as a friend," she said. "I want you to respect my boundaries."

I picked up the extension. "If you don't get off the phone, I'm going to sing." I said I would sing "Tie a Yellow Ribbon Round the Old Oak Tree" into it.

And we did, Bill and I warbling off-key into the phone, "Tie a yellow ribbon on the old oak tre-e-ee" while the dog barked crazily. Morgan laughed—and got off the phone.

"I never managed to do it again, though," I told my twin sister, Adrian, when she came to visit for the weekend. We were hanging out in the kitchen, drinking wine. "It sounds so easy to know what to do," I said, twirling my wine glass. "Divide our world into her problems and mine. Practice detachment. Use humor. Oh, and be firm."

"Name one real mother who does that," said Adrian. She got up to stir the pasta sauce she was making for dinner.

"I do it," I said.

"You do? When?"

"When she's not home. I'm the Queen of Calm then."

AND then there was Morgan herself. My books had said that teenagers want to separate from their parents, but she stalked me. All day, her voice poured into my ear in a heated rush. She was always in my office, talking, arguing, and yelling. Sometimes I drove her out of the room telling her that I made twenty-five dollars an hour at my job and I was going to deduct it from her allowance if she didn't let me work.

She'd storm back in. "My algebra book is at Mara's house," she said one time. "I need it to do my homework." Mara lived over the bridge in Corte Madera.

"I have to finish this," I said. "Maybe you could take the bus over there."

"I can't!" she said, and we argued until I got up and went into my bedroom to escape. "Where are you going?" she shouted from outside the door. "We don't have anything resolved!"

In *Get Out of My Life, but First Could You Drive Me and Cheryl to the Mall?* I read, "Teenage boys go in their rooms, girls go in your face."

"Like boys," it said, "adolescent girls find it totally unacceptable to feel attached to, or dependent on, their parents. But girls do not withdraw. Instead they fight."

"Your curfew is eleven-thirty," I told her one day. I had already repeated it dozens of times. "That's fair."

"It's not fair!"

"Just walk away," advised the books. Morgan followed me right into the bathroom. "It's more than just not fair. It's actually wrong," she shouted at me as I lowered my pants.

"Well, I don't feel comfortable with a later curfew."

Tears sprang to Morgan's eyes and her voice rose. "It's selfish to say, 'Well, I don't feel comfortable.' I don't feel comfortable having to be in that early! None of the other kids have to!"

When I finished, and she sat down to pee herself, I made my escape. But my getaways were never clean: I always took her with me. It was more than my own hurt and angry feelings, more than the strength of her will that prevented me from being the firm mother I ought to have been. I had a bigger problem: I could not figure out where I left off and she began. I was always in contact with her, even when she was at school and I was at the paper, staring numbly at my computer. If she left without saying good-bye, I could feel her misery. You can only be as happy as your unhappiest child. I didn't know who said that, but it was true.

For the year after she was born, I couldn't take a shower without hearing the baby's cry in the roar of the shower. I'd shut the stream off again and again to listen for that phantom cry.

When she was one year old, I was still putting her to bed with a bottle. The doctor said all that milk was bad for her teeth and sucking might cause orthodontia problems later. So, periodically, I'd make a sweep through the house, gathering up all the bottles and throwing them in the trash. When I'd put her to bed without one, she'd wail bitterly, the crib rattling, fists flailing, thinking herself all alone, her bottle forgotten.

But she wasn't alone: I was huddled ten feet away on the couch, listening. Her cry went right through my flesh to the bone, but I couldn't get off the couch and walk out of earshot. If she had to suffer, I had to suffer.

She was bigger now, but otherwise nothing much had changed. One weekend Morgan, grounded as usual, had spent three hours washing the front steps, cleaning the kitchen, and making blueberry muffins. I soon learned why our stovetop was shining clean: she wanted to go to a party on Friday.

"But she can't," Bill said when I reported this to him. He was unknotting his tie and pulling off his shirt, changing into a T-shirt and jeans for our walk. "Have you forgotten that she waltzed out of here when she was already grounded? You have to stick to your guns."

"It's the big party of the year!" she screamed when I said she couldn't go. "All the kids are going! If I don't go I'll probably never see those kids again!" I raised my eyebrows, and she added, "Except at school, which doesn't count."

I was a rock. I was Ulysses tying himself to the mast so as not to be able to respond to the siren's call. "I'm sorry," I said. "You're grounded, and that's that."

Even as I said that I ached, thinking of her not getting to go to the party. I saw the lighted windows, heard the music, felt the excitement.

I wasn't thinking about being a parent, consistent and firm. I wasn't thinking about what she had done to deserve missing the party, her boots clicking down the dimly lit street when she was supposed to be under her comforter sound asleep. Instead I was remembering myself back in high school, slumped against the green-painted low brick mantel in the living room, crying in anguish because my mother had said I couldn't go to a party. I forget why I couldn't go, but it must have been for a very good reason.

I had to go. A boy I liked would be there. I can't remember now what his name was, but in my memory that boy moves in radiance, his skinny pegged pants, his surfer shirt, the blue ink drawings on his binder, right down to the smashed tuna fish sandwiches he always had for lunch. He had blond hair falling in his face, and he would be there, at Debbie Haslon's party. I wailed louder, remembering. Mother, polishing her waitress shoes on the couch, letting Robin, the baby, help with the toes, said "No, no, no!" and finally gave in. As I knew she would. As she always did.

As I always did.

I was Morgan's mom, wanting to be firm, but I was also Morgan, wanting desperately to go to that party. I watched her face as she, switching tactics again, began to fold the laundry, making big messy piles on the coffee table—Bill, Patrick, me, and her. "If you come straight home every day after school this week, you can go to the party for a little while," I said.

She jumped up and hugged me, sending a drift of Bill's Jockey V-neck T-shirts cascading to the floor. "Thanks, Mom."

I returned to Bill, who had put an apron on and was stirring spaghetti sauce for dinner.

"Don't tell me," he said.

• • •

It wasn't my fault. "No one is leaving this house until it's spotless!" my mother would announce on a Saturday morning when I was little. She'd be standing there in a rolled-up man's blue shirt and a jeans skirt, her Hawaiian-looking black hair still powdery from the morning's pancakes. "I don't care if it takes all day!" She'd be mad over something–maybe we had let a neighbor boy get into her photo albums, or had cut each other's hair--and you could see it in her eye, her determination to get tough with us this time.

But before long a warm ray of sunshine streaming through the open window would catch her attention, and she'd let the soapy, oatmeal-encrusted bowl she'd been scrubbing slide under the water. Pretty soon she was searching for beach towels and telling us kids to get our suits on. "Don't worry about the house," she'd say, absently. "We'll do it later."

I'd let the broom fall with a loud bang and run for my suit, leaving a pile of sweepings in the middle of the floor. My sister Mickey would drop the washrag she'd been scrubbing the tub with and run to get her suit off the line. My brothers, Sean and Shannon, would toss a final milk carton into the rusting incinerator in the backyard, poke it down into the fire, then run to their room to root through the mess on their floor for their suits, still damp from the last swim. Adrian and Connie would stop scooping toys into a broken plastic laundry hamper. While Mom wrapped peanut butter and jelly sandwiches in waxed paper, the four of us girls would put on our matching striped bathing suits. The house would get clean later, or it wouldn't.

I don't remember if Mother gave in as helplessly to my brothers as she did to the girls, but I knew that for me it was different with Patrick. At thirteen, he was himself a full-fledged teenager. His most typical comment in conversation was *"What are you talking about?"* delivered with great emphasis, whenever an adult finished speaking.

"Mom, you have to get out of here," he said when I went upstairs to watch him and his friend Jason fry mozzarella and ham sandwiches. He said it again when he was in Morgan's room, talking to her about all the teenage things he now kept from me.

Yet he still seemed tuned in to me. When I came into the house, he asked me where I'd been. I was still allowed to sit on his legs as he sprawled on the couch. Once I was hurrying out, getting my coat, and Patrick was sitting sideways in Bill's chair, reading *Manchild in the Promised Land.*

"Are you mad at me, Mom?" he asked. He thought that earlier, upstairs, I had greeted him perfunctorily, and he'd been worrying about it. "No!" I exclaimed, heading over to ruffle his hair. He dodged, but smiled.

With him, I could effectively apply the advice from my books. When he told me his math teacher had locked him out for being late, I remembered: "Never tell a teenager anything unless you think it will improve your relationship with him."

I said, "Oh, sweetie, that must have felt awful, getting locked out of your class."

"Yes, it did," Patrick said. "I have to start getting up earlier."

With Morgan, I was incapable of anything like this. If she had told me she was locked out of her math class, it would have made me feel that everything was hopeless. I would have blurted out something like: "Well, start getting up earlier."

With Patrick, it was just getting locked out.

I felt that he and I were alike in deep ways and superficial ways: he was left-handed and had been cross-eyed as a baby, as had I. And he lived in his head, as I did.

Yet I knew where I ended and he began. I could cause him pain, for his own good, without feeling it in my own bones.

Patrick's preposterous claims never moved me the way Morgan's did. "Okay, mister," I said, when he demanded a drum set one Sunday night. I reminded him that two days before he had had his heart set on an electric guitar. "Sort it out for yourself," I said gently, but firmly. "When you come back down to earth, we'll talk."

Morgan never seemed to come back to earth. But sometimes, just when I thought she was lost to me, she would send me a signal, like a smoke signal from a distant plain that said, "It's all right. I'm still here!"

One morning in May, for example, I kept trying to give her some red gym shorts she seemed to be forgetting as she was leaving for school. "Those are Patrick's," she kept saying, but, not paying attention, I stuffed them in her backpack anyway.

That night I found them in my tennis shoes in the closet.

I put them on her lamp and then switched it on, so it glowed pink.

They turned up a day later stretched across a picture above my bed.

I pinned them up in her window, like an odd pair of curtains. Neither of us said a word about the shorts. We just played our game, silently.

Later that month we had a trying week. Morgan had not turned in any math assignments. When she wrote us a letter to explain why she was doing badly in math, Jim said it made him wonder how she could be passing English.

So I wasn't in the mood when she kept asking me why I never wore my *Chronicle* sweatshirt anymore. I said, "What do you care? You know you can't borrow it." Crossly, I picked up the apple juice boxes and half-empty cereal bowls that marked her passage through the house, then jerked my *Chronicle* sweatshirt off the hanger, and put it over my head. My arm wouldn't go through the sleeve.

There, rolled up in the arm, were the red shorts.

On the following Sunday I heard Morgan say, "It's Mother's Day! Aren't you going to spend it with your mother?" to someone on the phone, her voice drifting through her closed door. This, from a girl who the night before had said to the same phone, "No, I'm home all by myself tonight. Well, my mom's home."

When I walked into the kitchen, ready to go wild over my cards and school-made flower vases, the table was bare.

I stomped in to find Morgan luxuriating on her disordered bed in her blue Joe Boxer jammies. "Clean up this mess," I snapped, by way of good morning. I went outside to sit on the front porch, and stared at the discolored roses on the bushes in the front garden. The dog licked my hand.

"Where are you, Mom?" Morgan called.

"Out here," I answered, my voice thin and bitter. Two years ago I had been awakened at six A.M. when the kids brought in an angel food cake covered in purple frosting and made me eat a slice on the spot, before I even got up.

Morgan came out to the porch and sat down beside me, wearing my white tank top. I'd have to pitchfork through the piles on her floor to get it back.

"Did you do your room?" I said in my mean voice.

She ignored that. "Look," she said. She showed me a plaster replica in a shoe box. It was of the red shorts.

"See where it broke?" she said. "I've been trying to glue them back all week." She had been, too. Bill found his tube of glue, open and dried out, on the basement floor.

"And I have a painting of the shorts at school," she went on. "I couldn't bring it home because we had class outside and I couldn't get back in."

"That would have been good," I said, still sulkily, but liking it, the idea of a ceramic of the red shorts and the painting. I smiled and hugged her, and she hugged me back.

It took so little to make me bounce back. I was one of the plastic stand-up clown punching bags we had as a kid. Punch me down, and I came back up, smiling gamely. I was a mom.

I was still smiling when I got in the car to go grocery shopping.

And found the red shorts stretched out on the steering wheel.

chapter 6

MORGAN and a new boyfriend named Paul, a classmate from Lowell, were sitting close together on the living room couch, waiting for his mom to come pick him up. He was a tall, half-Asian kid who had a habit of drumming his fingers on his knees. He'd been to the house once or twice before. "Well, I'm going to bed," I told them. Something about the way they were sitting was making me nervous.

Next morning she asked me three times if I had seen her orange condom, then I heard her asking directory assistance for the number of the Condomania store. I didn't ask her what that was all about. I didn't do anything. By then I had logged years as the mother of an acting-out teenager, and I was tired. Sometimes I didn't notice things that were happening right in front of me. Or I did notice them, but did nothing. I was having a hard time dealing with the stuff I did know about, without looking for more.

Weeks later Morgan and I were at a sushi restaurant on Post Street. She was a vegetarian now, except on the nights her dad made his special Julia Child hamburgers.

A kind of moat ran around the interior of the oval counter where the diners sat. Sushi dishes floated by on little boats, and you grabbed whichever you wanted. They totted up your bill by counting the empty dishes in front of you.

Morgan grabbed a boatful of California rolls. She picked one up with her chopsticks, dipped it in her wasabi sauce and put it in her mouth, then said, "Promise me you won't get mad."

I had grabbed a piece of tuna with my chopsticks, and now I let it drop back onto my plate. "I promise," I said.

"I'm not a virgin," she said.

I sat there blankly, looking at her. "Say something, Mom," she nudged me. She looked at me meekly, but with a trace of pride. I could read her expression: I'm a woman now, Mom. I have a life separate from yours. The other diners were chattering and grabbing boats. I took a drink of my sake. "Are you having sex with Paul?"

"Yes."

I wasn't shocked. I wasn't even surprised. That familiar, odd feeling had seized me. I was both of us: the upset, blustering mother, and the teenager busting with her exciting secret.

But I winced at the images that were coming up of her in a tousled bed with a boy, with some stupid boy. I knew from my advice books that I was supposed to say, "And what did you learn from that?" Turn her revelation into a valuable learning experience.

"You don't think you're too young?" I asked. "You've just turned fifteen. You're even younger than your classmates. That's pretty young to be able to handle the emotional complexities of sleeping with someone. I really wish you would wait, sweetie."

"The way you did?"

Okay, she had landed that one. I said, "We have children so we can get it right the second time."

"How old were you?" she asked. "When, you know."

"Older than you," I said. Thinking: barely.

"With Mike Lara?"

"No, Mike was later. He and I got married when I turned eighteen, in my senior year of high school."

I was startled, hearing myself speak. Was that me, who got married while still in high school?

"I made a lot of mistakes," I said to Morgan now. Her eyes were bright. She grabbed another boat loaded with colorful rice squares and set it in front of me as I spoke. "I guess, like every mom, I keep hoping you can avoid making some of the ones I made. Are you using those condoms you decorate your room with?

"Yes, Mom! Of course! I'm not an idiot."

"I'm glad you felt you could tell me about this," I said. It was a line from one of my books.

"You know it's not necessarily a negative thing, Mom," Morgan said. "Paul and I love each other. We're going to get married when we grow up, probably. Promise me you won't act any different toward him, now that you know."

"I promise," I said. "Did you expect me to start muttering and crossing myself every time he comes into sight?"

She laughed. I tried to think of more questions to ask. I was pretty sure that her school had taught her a lot about safe sex--I seemed to remember a program that was so explicit that some of the parents called the principal to object.

I didn't want to say the wrong thing. I stole a sideways look at her in her black tank top and jeans, the crude scorpion a friend had tattooed on her ankle in blue ink, her toenails painted red. Morgan radiated sex. She always wore halter-tops that made her flesh seem to sort of spill out everywhere. I felt skimpy and self-conscious in comparison. She'd always loved her body and didn't seem to care much who saw it. I was always telling her to for Pete's sake shut the door when she was getting dressed.

"What happens if you get pregnant?" I asked.

She had that all worked out. "There's this school I heard about in Arizona you could send me to if that happens. It's for pregnant teenagers. They have pool tables."

"Listen to me," I said. I reached out and put my hand on her arm so she couldn't raise her bite of rice to her mouth. "No way, if you get pregnant, will I send you to school anywhere," I said. "Get pregnant, accidentally or on purpose, and you are on your own." I released her arm.

I spoke lightly, but inside me was frozen tundra, a winter landscape with bare trees and howling wolves. Inside I was heartsick with fear and love. She had slept with Paul? I thought he was just another one of her friends. Maybe he *was* just another one of her friends. Inside I was planning to throw up my job and move the whole family to Dublin for a year, where she would trudge through the dawn chill to attend convent school.

When we went on with our meal, we talked of other things.

The next weekend, as we were on a bike ride, I told Bill that Morgan was no longer a virgin. I looked back, and he had stopped right in the middle of the road, with traffic whizzing by him.

"Oh, God, what next?" he said when I rode back. "I wish you hadn't told me that." He set his bike on its kickstand in the gutter, and took off his helmet.

"Why are you so upset?" I asked, feeling shocked and strange. "She was going to start having sex eventually."

"I was hoping she'd wait until after we die," he said, and then added, "You're her mother, it's different for you." Meaning, I think, that I was a woman.

We pedaled on. Bill caught up with me again. "Aren't you upset that she started so young?" he said.

"Of course I am," I told him, and dropped back behind when cars honked at us.

But he was right; it was different for me.

As we pedaled on, I was remembering myself back in high school. My sisters and I weren't wild. But we had sort of drifted into raising each other, and ourselves, since Mother was often at work. We ate out of the fridge when we were hungry, wrote our own absence notes for school, earned the money we needed in after-school jobs.

Johnny was short and stocky, with straight brown hair, and wore pegged black pants and woolen Pendleton shirts that smelled in the rain, overpowering even his Jade East. Under that was the sweaty boy smell that I loved. We had met when we were fourteen. He worked as a boxboy at the grocery store where I bought my apples and red licorice. Once at his house his mother had walked in and found us listening to "Penny Lane" on his record player, with Johnny wearing only his shirt and his white briefs.

Johnny had been coming over after eleven, when his shift stacking cans at the market ended. He'd come through the sliding glass patio door I left unlocked for him, then pad softly up the stairs to my room, his sneakers in his hand.

He had to pass my sister Mickey's door. "Johnny! Is that you? You go home, Johnny," came her sharp voice. Mickey, eighteen, unmarried, already had a baby in a crib at the end of her bed. But sometimes she didn't hear him. My mother was asleep in her room.

Johnny and I were so shy that it took hours of fumbling but fevered embraces in my narrow bed to remove even a few clothes, and this consisted more of a kind of rubbing away of garments, like socks disappearing into a shoe, than of frank disrobing. By the time we were fifteen we could make a kiss last ten minutes, until every cell in our bodies was throbbing. Terrified of getting pregnant, I would catch his exploring hand again and again, to make us go back to that fevered kissing.

A truck thundered by close to my ear. I pedaled up next to Bill again. "Please don't tell Jim," he implored me. Another car swooshed by, and his words came faintly. "For his sake. He's her father. He'll feel that she has lost something valuable."

A couple of weeks later, as he was coming up from the basement, Jim passed Morgan's bedroom window and spotted her and Paul. They were just lying on the bed, looking at pictures in *Seventeen* magazine, but something about the scene clicked for him. Looking grim and defeated, he came into the kitchen, where I was marking student essays. "I know they're having sex," he said.

I put down my yellow highlighter and turned on the teakettle. "Let me make you some tea," I said.

As we sat over our steaming cups, I told him what Morgan had told me. His mouth twisted. "Why do you allow that?" he asked. "You're her mother. Can't you stop her?"

"No," I said. "She does what she wants."

"*Why* does she want what she wants? Why does she want to sneak out and cut class and have sex too young? Do you still think that divorce does no harm?"

"What? What does divorce have to do with this?" I felt blindsided, though it was not a new conversation.

WHEN we told them we were splitting up, Jim and I had sat both kids on the couch in the unfinished attic, which we used as a TV room and library. "Daddy and I are getting divorced," I said. "This has nothing to do with you two. We both love you very much, and we will both go on being your parents."

"Please stop talking," Patrick pleaded. He was four, chubby-faced, blond as butter. "Please." He cried, and then asked for cookies. I ran downstairs to get him some, but he turned his face away when I handed him the plate.

"I told you not to do this," Morgan, five, said.

"I know, baby," I said, tears sliding down my face. She knew kids at school with divorced parents–a lot of them–and had asked me never to do that. Later she kicked me, and told me how mad she was at me for moving to the downstairs apartment. The next day Patrick complained that his tummy, ears, throat, jaws, and forehead hurt. Soon they were both sick with fevers, and I was giving them orange baby aspirin amid the boxes in my new apartment. Morgan woke up crying from a dream in which she and her daddy and Patrick were all standing in the surf, drowning, calling out to me, while I walked by on the beach, not hearing.

It was my first shocking taste of that curious callousness of a mother. I would have died for them, but I would not, for their sake, go on living with a good man whom I no longer loved.

Patrick spoke fiercely of wanting to tear out the ceiling that divided my apartment from his dad's. Jim was so angry and depressed that he once slammed my door so hard the glass in it broke. He wanted the words "I HATE THIS DIVORCE," entered into our agreement. Later on he joined a singing group and found that Mozart and Bach were strong medicine, at least for an hour or two.

It was one of the worst times of my life, too. I used to go to an aerobics class across the street to sweat off the grief and the worry, hurling myself into the moves while my bare feet grew black from the floor, wanting the tiredness that would follow. Morgan used to come with me and stand right in the front row, in her cool pink-and-black Esprit outfit, and do the routines, staring at herself in the mirror, the instructor grinning at her and making jokes about letting her teach the class. I'd watch her in the mirror as she flung her small self into the music, leaping and twirling, and feel less lonely.

"Oh, the kids are doing fine," I was fond of saying to Jim, and to myself, after the divorce. I said this although Patrick told his dad it made him sick to see me kissing my new boyfriend, and that he pretended I was kissing his dad instead. I said it though Morgan had stomachaches in school, and trouble concentrating. At one point we even took her to a counselor.

I remember once my new boyfriend, Nick, came over late, about ten. The kids and I had by then moved to an apartment in another part of town, and Nick lived next door with his little girl, Katie. Patrick was sleeping overnight at a friend's house, and Morgan was in her room. I had told her a story and put her to sleep. Nick and I were on the couch, kissing like teenagers who have nowhere private to go. Then we heard Morgan screaming from the bedroom. I rushed in, and when she calmed down, I brought her into the living room and she told Nick the story she had just told me, about a road in her head on which stood the men I had dated since the divorce.

Nick was at the end, and Jim stood in the very middle, staring hard right down the road, looking bereft.

When Morgan was in the sixth grade, the kids and I went on an Easter week trip to Los Angeles with Nick and his daughter. Forever afterward, Morgan referred to him as "Mr. Organize, Mr. Good-bye Pee, and Mr. Katie Needs Some Food It's Time to Stop." I once asked Patrick to stay with Nick while I went to the store, and when he refused, said, "You still don't like him?" He looked up from his Legos and said, "Welcome to earth, Mom."

Through it all of course, they had their dad. He was always there, greeting them after school, making them fresh-squeezed orange juice in the morning.

"You think everybody goes through a divorce, and everybody ends up just fine," Jim said now, clicking his spoon in his tea. His wide blue eyes were serious. "Yet we both know hundreds of people who have been permanently scarred by divorce–and I would venture to say you are among them." Jim himself was the youngest of eight brothers and sisters, and none of them, nor his parents, had ever been divorced.

It was funny, but I seldom thought of what had happened to my parents as divorce. It had seemed to be so much more than that.

"You think Morgan is the way she is now because of the divorce?" I said. I fidgeted with my cup, moving it back and forth on the table.

"Are you willing to rule it out?"

"Maybe she was born this way. Maybe she'd sneak out and cut classes and have sex too young no matter whom she lived with, or whether her parents got divorced, or whom her mother got remarried to. Anyway," I finished, hopelessly, "what am I supposed to do about that now? Go back in time and not divorce you?"

"I don't know," Jim said, rinsing his cup in the sink. He got up and went back upstairs and I sat there awhile, listening to his familiar tread above me.

I had known him all my adult life. When I arrived at my English class on my first day of junior college, eighteen years old, dressed in jeans and a hot pink sweatshirt, there he was behind the teacher's desk. He was blond, with a Slavic tilt to the back of his head and muscular thighs that spread across the chair. He insisted on addressing us by our last names, and took forever with the class list, asking everybody how they pronounced their names, and what they meant in the original language. In almost every case, he knew more about the name—and seemed to care more—than the student did himself. "What kind of name is that, Miss Lara?" he asked me.

"I don't know," I said. "Italian, I think. My husband is Italian." I was still married to Mike Lara, the boy I'd married in my senior year of high school, though the marriage would end soon enough. "So I am actually Mrs. Lara."

"I address all female students as Miss," he said. "Your name sounds Spanish to me." And of course it was. Mike's grandfather had been a Spaniard.

It was my first college class. I had different-colored binder paper for each class. I chose green for English, and wrote my first paper in draft after draft, until each word, each comma, had been separately agonized over. I imagined him at home in his book-lined study, his dangling hand ruffling a cat's ears, frowning through a batch of essays. Then he would come to mine and swing forward, his feet in blue socks hitting the Oriental rug. "At last! A student who can *write!*"

When I got it back, I eagerly scanned the comments. Above the first paragraph, in which I had said that the story revolved around Regency Park in London, he had scrawled in a large strong hand: "I hate revolving fiction, don't you?" I smiled despite myself. He added, "I think you are going to be a good writer. And I am repelled by this chartreuse paper."

By the end of junior college, my teenage marriage had ended. When I think of that brief time, I remember French fries snapping in a pan and a pair of Michael's very thin gold slacks that I had only to touch to want him, then and there, wherever we were. We had a dachshund puppy, Tyrone P. Jackson, who refused to even consider peeing outside, and a red Triumph motorcycle that Michael drove at thirty miles an hour even on the freeway. I learned to cook the four dishes Michael would eat: the steelhead trout he caught himself, hamburger, steak, and spaghetti. Once I tried to slip in a meat loaf but he said, "What's that?" and went out to play golf, leaving the lump of meat on his plate.

WHEN I met Jim, I started spending nights in San Francisco in the large Victorian he was restoring on nights and weekends–the same one Bill and I live in now, in the lower flat. He was teaching himself carpentry and Sheetrocking, peeling back decades of cheap white-wash to the red-and-green molding beneath. I was dazzled by him and didn't care that he was a lot older than I was. In his world people bought antiques, and read the *New York Times*, and used margarine only for cooking. He made me read Jane Austen, showed me how to fold a letter neatly into its envelope, and encouraged me to pick out cloth coats instead of ski parkas. Best of all, he lived in San Francisco, twenty-five miles south of my suburban working-class existence.

We got married when I was twenty-four and he was forty-five. The ceremony was held under a cypress tree in San Rafael, in a circle of his friends and my relatives, while a minister who had been one of his students stumbled through the sonnet Jim had chosen, "Let Me Not to the Marriage of True Minds Admit Impediments." The minister left out words and even an entire line, so that I felt Jim's broad hand clench in mine–or maybe it was just nervousness. My mother stood behind us and beamed at the back of Jim's head. She thought I had caught the brass ring. Dad was there too, resurrected for the occasion in a greenish Bargain Box sports jacket–his first–and a borrowed tie. I had remembered I had a dad somewhere, and tracked him to the station wagon he was then living in, out in the San Geronimo Valley, and asked him to give me away. Mother was not pleased to overhear him accepting congratulations from strangers for having raised so many fine kids. He told me later, "I'd been planning to make a shambles of your wedding, Dare, but I was having too much fun."

One day after Jim and I had been married several months, I came home from class to find my blouses all facing the same way on the clothes rack, their sleeves dropping at identical angles. Below them, shoes I hadn't seen for months were lined up on an aluminum rack, the laces of the tennis shoes looped inside. It had amused me then, but later I wondered what had gone through Jim's mind as he untangled the tops I hung three to a hanger, and crawled among the tennis balls, stray socks, belts, and clumps of dust to find the shoes all over the floor.

One Christmas, as I was wrapping presents and listening to Credence Clearwater, Jim came in and snapped off the radio. "I have only a limited number of years left on earth," he said, "and I've decided not to spend any of them listening to that awful music." He walked out, and after a moment I flipped the radio back on. I had only a limited number of years left, too, and I wanted to spend them listening to the music I liked.

After seven years I had started having daydreams that Jim was dead. It was always the same: a highway patrolman came to the door, rain dripping from his hat, his face shaded, and said, "There was nothing anyone could do. It was a ten-car pileup. He died instantly." One day, at a stoplight, I realized Jim didn't have to die: I could leave him.

I had to switch the radio off to let this idea fill my mind. I can leave him. All day those words rang in my head—as we stood together with Patrick in the blue light of the pediatrician's office, and later as we sat on a porch at a friend's chicken barbecue and admired the cows that hung their heads over the sagging redwood fence. My passion for him had seeped away somehow, the way juice dribbles out of an unnoticed hairline crack in a glass. What remained behind was a solid feeling of love and respect for him, as the father of my kids and for himself.

After a long, difficult process of separation, I moved to an apartment downstairs. Time passed, during which we shared the kids in joint custody and I lived in other apartments around the city.

NEXT weekend Jim gave me a "Sex and the Teenager" pamphlet by Ann Landers to give Morgan. She shoved it back at me. "I don't want it if it's from Dad," she said crossly. "I'm not sexually active anymore anyway. Paul and I broke up."

chapter 7

KEPT my jacket on in the dean's office. Jim sat on the chair next to me, a Kleenex balled in his fist. The dean, a stern black man named Wilson, sat behind his desk, the light glinting off his granny glasses above a plaid sweater vest.

The biology teacher was there, too. He tapped a pencil against the knee of his gray slacks. "Morgan is predictable," he said to the dean. "I can predict she will be late, she will be unprepared, she will disrupt the class, she will try to cheat."

I sucked in my breath.

He turned to us. "I was within inches of expelling her, and I still will, for the slightest infraction, in or out of class. If you hadn't come today, I would have recommended her transfer."

Morgan, her face scrubbed clean of makeup, sat on a chair near the door, facing her teachers, the dean, her dad, and me. She looked at everybody calmly. "I can prove I wasn't cheating," she said. "You can test me right now on the answers."

I made myself small on my chair, as if I was the one being accused. She'd been caught with a crib sheet in her hand.

I stared at the speckled pattern on the floor. I was the one who gave her the idea she could talk her way out of anything. I let her wear the black petticoat to school in fourth grade. In the sixth, I let her tell me how little was going on in school that day and how much she could get done on her amphibian report if she stayed at home. I had always congratulated myself for having such adult exchanges with her. I liked her to think that she—a mere child—could, with the power of words, change an adult's mind.

And here was my result: several teachers had come in for this summit on Morgan's behavior in school. I was reminded of a cartoon I had, of an unhappy-looking couple facing a teacher across a table. The caption read: "Your daughter's a pain in the ass."

"I know you're here because you're worried about Morgan. As we all should be," said Miss DeRosa, fixing us with her eyes. She was a graying woman in a white sack dress with freckled hands folded firmly in front of her.

I wanted to throttle the old bat. Jim sat stiffly in his chair, his hands bunching in his pockets. "Your daughter arrives late, without her book or her homework, and is frequently barefoot," the teacher went on. "She led a renegade discussion of *Animal Farm* in my classroom," she continued, tapping her finger on a folder. "A book she has not read."

I fought a smile, felt pride struggling up despite myself. Secretly, I thought that Lowell, with its legions of meek, accomplished students who did A work but had to be prodded into opening their mouths in class, could use a few more Morgans.

"Do you know what she said to me after that class?" Morgan said to the room. " 'Remember, class, the emptiest drum makes the most noise.' "

I swung my gaze to Miss DeRosa, my mouth open. "You said that?"

"I don't remember saying that," she said. "But I suppose I could have." She refolded her hands and stared at me.

"Is that any way to talk to a child?" I said.

"I'm not a child, Mom," Morgan broke in.

"I have caught Morgan cheating in class twice," said her world history teacher, Mrs. Miller, a sweet-faced woman in a pink turtleneck and gray pants. "As you know," she added, "three times means expulsion."

"What do you mean, she cheated?" I asked. "Cheated how?"

"I received an anonymous note saying that Morgan was selling answers to the history test for five dollars. The second time, she and another student had identical test–"

"I wasn't cheating!" Morgan broke in, her voice rising. "I told you that already." I reached over and took hold of her knee, and she let me.

"Well, honey," Jim said in a pleading voice, "if you weren't cheating, then the other student was. Did you allow someone to copy off your paper? Who was it?"

Morgan started to cry. "I won't bust out a friend," she sobbed. "You can't make me."

I was acutely conscious of Morgan on her chair. There were so many of us and just one of her. It was us against her, the adults against the kid, but it also felt like them against our family.

Because I was a parent, sitting there with checks in my purse and car keys and a mortgage, these angry teachers on their wooden chairs thought we were on the same side. But never, never could we be on the same side. This is my child. My child, with her eyes downcast, and her mouth not trembling so it takes a mom to see how upset she is, how scared and alone beneath the anger.

They didn't know my child. They hadn't heard her singing in the shower that morning. They didn't see her at age five, smiling bravely through her shots. If she cheated she must be secretly afraid of this school that we made her go to.

At the same time, I knew that Morgan was making the teachers' jobs that much harder, in this overcrowded institution.

"One more incident like this, and we will have to expel her," the dean said at the end of the meeting. The teachers looked at us pityingly as Jim and I followed Morgan out. "Jesus, do you people have a problem," their looks said.

"What if I dropped out now?" Morgan said conversationally from the backseat as we headed home. Jim was driving the Volvo. Startled, I turned around.

"Not dropped out," Morgan said hastily when she saw my face. "I didn't mean to say it like that. What I mean is, what if I *stopped* high school now and went to cosmetology school? I could take an auto shop class, and learn about astronomy, and then, like, you and Dad can help me with English or something like that, and I could go around and just take classes for the next two years, until I get my GED."

"If you start your life out quitting things," I said angrily, "your life tends to go on that way. I know your grandpa's example didn't impress you, but you can also ask your Aunt Robin."

"What about Robin?"

"She dropped out at the beginning of her sophomore year, and never went to school again."

As I told Morgan about Robin and Mom, familiar guilt feelings awoke.

We were all grown up and off in our own lives. My mom was working full time as a waitress and later as catering manager of the Elks Club. She was never at her best, anyway, with teenagers. Robin was a freshman in high school and the only one still living at home. She had started sneaking off for weekends with her boyfriend Dave, who was four years older. They'd go clear to Sacramento, Robin telling Mom she was staying with a girlfriend. Mom, exhausted, distracted, did not always check.

That year Robin was in two traffic accidents. In the first Dave, drunk, ran a red light. Robin arrived home bandaged with a head injury and a permanently scarred forehead. "Oh, my God," Mom said when she saw the bandages, "I didn't know it was so bad."

Not long after that, Robin and Dave and friends were drinking and driving on White's Hill out in the valley where we grew up when the van Dave was driving flipped over. Robin got nine stitches on the top of her head. Dave, still wearing a neck brace from the earlier accident, was not hurt. Robin lost time from school. When she did go, she felt so isolated and alone that every day she wore a fur coat Dave had given her to school, zipped up to the neck. Once, Mom noticed she was wearing her boyfriend's clothes, and gave her twenty dollars to buy something for herself.

Robin then moved in with Dave, who was working at a gas station, in an apartment on the Miracle Mile in San Rafael, a strip of fast food restaurants, bakeries, laundries, and 7-Elevens. She dropped out of school in the beginning of her sophomore year and began work at a pet store, working at the counter from nine to six. "You're not cut out for school," said Mom. Mom had already raised six children to adulthood alone, and she had no one to turn to, no one to help her with this seventh, this lost child of her middle age.

After that rocky start, it was hard for Robin not to quit things. "She keeps signing up for classes at College of Marin, and then quitting them," I said to Morgan, winding up my story as we reached the house.

"Maybe Grandma's right. Not everybody's cut out for school," was Morgan's only comment as Jim drove into the garage and we got out of the car.

BILL and I went off for the weekend together to Inverness, to a little cabin someone in his office owned. It sat damply in the hollow of a hill, and its rooms were so icy the fire only pushed the cold back. We huddled by the fire and read, and then jumped into the cold bed, yelling, "First naked in the bed!" We made love under the icy comforter, and then found ourselves making a momentous decision.

"I never thought you would want to do this," Bill said. We were talking about getting my Norplant removed. "You said before we got married that you had done that, had your babies. You wanted to find out what else you could do."

"I know," I said. "But I've been thinking about something your brother Rich once said–'Never leave a party where you are having a good time for another event at which you think you'll have a better time.' "

"And?"

"The kids have always been a good time for me." What I meant was that the best of parties was a mere drunken shout across the room, compared to the smell of your own baby's head. I meant that once you have buried your face in a baby's neck, in those soft folds of skin, and smelled that warm scent–after that, for the rest of your life, it becomes something you have to do without, that's all.

Or do again.

"You're the only woman I've ever wanted to do this with," Bill said. He had been married before, but had no kids. I rolled toward him, and we held each other, breathless and stunned at what we had decided.

Sunday we hiked up a trail to the beach, and I read Yeats's "Nineteen Hundred and Nineteen" to him on the way, while he held my elbow so I wouldn't trip on tree branches. At one point he seized my arm and pointed. "Over there!" he whispered, and I looked to see the herd of elk grazing amid the rocks and undergrowth.

As we were driving home on Sunday night, the cars coming toward us switching on their headlights in the thickening dusk, I was back to my customary brooding about Morgan. I remembered how, as she was leaving for school that Friday, Morgan had yelled at me about needing twenty-four dollars, and accused me of making a lot of money and not sharing any of it with her. "I don't like her anymore," I said bleakly to Bill now in the quiet car.

Bill took a hand off the wheel to pat my knee but said nothing. I didn't blame him for wanting to avoid yet another conversation about Morgan, but I needed to talk to him. He was my husband.

"She says she can't stand school and wants to quit," I added bitterly as we coasted down White's Hill, halfway home.

"She's just selfish and lazy," Bill said. He flicked his lights at a passing car to tell it to put its lights on. "She doesn't care about anybody but herself."

"She's not selfish," I said fiercely, and edged away from him, toward the cold window.

He looked over at me in surprise, the breeze from the vent blowing his graying black curls. "What did I do?" he said. "What did I say?"

"Don't tell me she's selfish!"

"But you said so yourself!"

"I'm her mom."

"What *should* I say?" Bill stared at the road. A muscle jumped in his jaw.

"Tell me what a great kid she is. Tell me she'll be fine," I said heatedly.

"She's a great kid," he said without conviction. "She'll be fine." And we rode the rest of the way home in silence.

I worried that the house would be a wreck after Morgan had been alone all weekend, with Patrick staying with his dad and only Jim to check on her. When we walked in the back door, though, Morgan had a surprise for us: she had cleaned up her room and made banana bread without leaving a mess. In the process of rearranging her room (and adding to it a TV from upstairs) she had helped herself to the walnut chest in the hall, stacking the sheets that were in it on the high shelves of my closet.

I felt a surge of hope. Interesting to see what she'll do the instant parents go away, and there's no one around to rebel against: cleans her room, does her homework. She had even moved my big standing photo board full of 8 × 10s of the kids. "It interrupts the flow of ch'i where you put it," she explained.

"It interrupts the flow of me to my books where it is now." I smiled, seeing the board now blocking my shelves.

Morgan grinned and went off to the Grind, a cafe around the corner–to study for a geometry test, or so she announced. I returned to the kitchen, and saw Bill's dark face. "Who does she think she is, taking the chest of drawers into her room?" he said.

"Haven't you noticed the house is clean? You're a hard man to please," I told him as I watched him carrying Morgan's shoes out of the TV room and dumping them in her room, putting her books inside the door, and throwing her jackets on her bed. When he was done, there wasn't a trace of her left in the house, except in her bedroom–and he shut the door to that.

At ten o'clock I took the phone off the hook, something I now did every night to avoid being woken by kids calling late. Morgan rushed into our room to plead for one more call, to Julio, a new boy.

Bill leaped out of bed and put on his robe, leaving with his book to escape the screaming and yelling he was sure would follow. Miffed at him, afraid she'd noticed, I said, "Call Julio tomorrow, sweetie."

Then I went to the living room. "It's okay, she's gone," I said to Bill. He was already sitting in his reading chair, the lamp switched on, bare legs crossed against the night chill. He rose and came to bed, and we lay without touching.

Morgan and Bill didn't speak each other's language. I became their UN interpreter.

"This is just the way he is," I'd tell Morgan when Bill yelled at her about leaving black boot marks on the kitchen floor. "It isn't because he doesn't like you."

Bill scrubbed the black marks of Morgan's boots off the kitchen floor. "I'm sure she says to herself, 'I'll just go ahead and walk all over this floor, leaving all the marks I want, and I won't worry about it because I have good old Bill to clean up for me,' " he muttered as he worked.

"What she's actually thinking," I told him, "is, 'I don't have time for breakfast this morning, so I'll just grab this bagel from the fridge. Where did I leave my key?' Kids are oblivious."

"This is just the way he is," I told Morgan when Bill asked her to take her boots off before walking on the kitchen floor. "He hates dirt and disorder, not you."

ONE day as he was cleaning up a sticky mess she'd left on the kitchen counter, Bill blurted out, "Teenagers are everything I hate, noisy and messy and unpredictable."

Bill had never been noisy, messy, or unpredictable himself, even as a teenager. He was raised by devout Catholic parents in a neat two-story white house in a small town near Worcester, Massachusetts, the oldest son with two younger brothers and one younger sister. Bill himself was being groomed to be a priest, until he read about the Holocaust in his early teens and lost his faith.

Bill's parents are a warm and welcoming couple with endearing Massachusetts accents who live north of us, in Santa Rosa, having followed their children west. A flurry of hugs and smiles greet me whenever I walk in their door, and I could hardly reconcile the couple I knew with the loving but very strict parents who had raised young Bill.

"My parents had us completely cowed," Bill told me once. "We never even thought of rebelling. They lived lives of intense rectitude themselves." Once as a boy he complained to his mom about an off-key singer in the choir and when he got home she made him get on his knees in his Sunday slacks. "Say an Act of Contrition," she said, her rosy Irish face troubled. When he wanted to go to Opening Day at the Red Sox with a gang of friends, his mom wouldn't write him a sickness note for school. "That would be lying," she said.

His dad got up before dawn to start his sales calls, and came home to fix dinner for the kids. "I'm not running a restaurant," he'd growl if anybody dared to refuse something on his plate. Bill's mom worked the three-to-eleven shift as a registered nurse at St. Vincent's Hospital, going from room to room checking the level of IVs, and then coming in late and tired to check on each of her sleeping children in turn.

When Bill was a teenager and got jobs–a box boy at the Hilltop Market, dishwasher in a nursing home, gardener–he turned his paychecks over to his parents. He laughingly told me once that getting his driver's license just increased the number of ways he could be put to work.

Neither of his parents had finished college, and they were determined that all four of their kids would. In eighth grade Bill found an ambitious list of the books children should have read by high school. When he showed it to his father, telling him proudly that he had read three-fourths of the books on it, his dad said, "What about these other books on the list? Why haven't you read them?"

In the end, Bill attended every single day of high school, and then worked his way through Assumption College as the dormitory janitor, cleaning toilets on weekends and all through summer vacation while the other kids smoked pot in their dorms.

HE couldn't believe, now, how much my kids were allowed to get away with. Once Patrick called at ten o'clock, right in the most exciting part of *The Fugitive*, when Tommy Lee Jones is chasing Harrison Ford down flights of steps and shooting at him, about to catch him. "Can you come pick me up, Mom?"

"Can't he wait?" Bill grumbled as I reached for my jacket.

Next day we talked about it. "I'm appalled sometimes at the sense of entitlement your kids feel," he said.

"Wouldn't your dad have picked you up?" I asked, simmering.

"I wouldn't have been out that late at age twelve," he said. "And if I had been, I would have been expected to arrange my own ride."

• • •

ONE morning hurrying into the bathroom to shave before work, he snapped at Morgan in the hall. "I'd appreciate it if you would hang up your wet towels after your shower." She was wrapped in two yellow towels, wet and glowing. I was there, too, on my way to help Patrick find his geography homework.

Morgan said nothing, but just looked at me darkly. Her expression said, "Do you see how he is?"

Bill looked at me too. His expression said, "My feelings count, too, don't they?"

"Please pick up your towels," I said to Morgan. "It's a little thing, but you know it upsets Bill."

"All right, Mom," she said, stalking off down the hall, the glow gone from her cheeks.

I went into the steamy bathroom and did what I had done all along, picking up Morgan's wet towels so Bill wouldn't see them.

Bill was so neat himself that one day in the kitchen he was showing his six-year-old niece that joke where you ask them if they want to play fifty-two-card pickup. I watched her face, looking forward to her delight when the cards flew all over the kitchen. But Bill just showed Claire Rebecca the neatly stacked deck. "And then you throw the cards in the air," he said. Claire Rebecca smiled uncertainly.

Bill was as sensitive to people as he was to his environment, and he knew he hadn't made a connection with Morgan. To make up for the way he felt, he went out of his way to be nice to her, complimenting her on her outfits, bringing home books like *Griffin & Sabine* and posters from the office.

In the mornings he'd go to her room. "What do you think of this tie with this jacket?" he'd say, and he'd always follow her advice. He'd tease her in teen slang, saying, "That's a really ill shirt you're wearing." Morgan was always nice to him, polite, choosing the tie, thanking him nicely for the book, smiling patiently at his clowning. But the look on her face usually told me she was just waiting for an awkward moment to be over, in the way of a child being fussed over by a strange adult.

• • •

Bill and I met in an elevator the year Morgan was going on twelve. I had punched "close" on the elevator door at work when an arm in dark-blue wool shot into the shrinking opening and a tall man in a suit stepped in. I glanced at him sideways as he stabbed at the button. The Sunday paper arrived at our office on Thursday morning and he had one under his arm. He had thick black hair and blue-green eyes under black brows. He looked like a Kennedy cousin. The antique elevator shuddered on its short journey from the second floor to the lobby. "Do you work in the building?" I blurted.

"Yes, I do," the man said. "One floor up, at Chronicle Books. I usually take the stairs, but I saw the elevator door open." We were both heading up 5th Street and had exchanged names and phone numbers by the time I had to turn off to catch the streetcar. He said he'd been reading my column since I started writing it a year and a half before and knew all about me. "I know you and your boyfriend broke up, for example," he said.

We started dating, and he came over a couple of times while Morgan and Patrick were at their dad's. Then one night he came over to meet them. When I heard the buzzer, I turned down the boom box–the kids and I had been dancing to Michael Jackson's "Thriller"–and stopped at the mirror in the hallway to run a brush over my hair. Morgan watched me. "I guess the dancing's over," she said.

I opened the door, and there was Bill. He had a gleaming white toilet lid slung over his dark-blue blazer like a porcelain Greek shield.

Morgan was behind me. I introduced them, and then she and I watched in awe as he went into the bathroom, knelt down on the linoleum bathroom floor in his pressed slacks, and took off the old toilet lid and put on the new one, just like that, with tools he'd brought with him. "I noticed this was broken the other day," he said with a shy smile.

When he was done, he lifted the new lid and even invited me to sit on it, to show it didn't wiggle from side to side anymore. I sat, blushing.

I led him down the hall to the kitchen. "Careful here," I called as he skirted the three mountain bikes the kids and I kept parked in the hall.

Then we heard crying. Patrick, ten, was on the red couch in the living room, his eyes squeezed shut, pounding on the pillows as hard as he could. I knelt, putting my arms around him. As I did, I caught sight of the newt tank over by the sliding glass door. Newts are little water lizards that look as if a toddler drew them with a brown crayon. One of ours had been scooped out and laid on a paper towel. It was very quiet, even for a newt.

I stroked Patrick's hair back from his sweaty forehead. He loved those newts. He fed them, changed their water, fretted when they seemed to be spending too much time staring into the middle distance. "Why did he have to die?" he howled into my blouse.

"I don't know," I said into his hair. "I'm so sorry." It was times like this I wished we had religious platitudes to fall back on, like other families. The newt went to heaven, sweetie. Patrick cried harder, as I tried unobtrusively to shift his head so he would wet my neck rather than my stupid expensive blouse. As usual, he had held nothing back, no little part of him that measured how much love it is safe to mete out to a newt.

"Maybe he was older than we thought," I babbled. "We can get you another newt."

"I don't want any more newts if they're going to die," Patrick said in a strangled voice. His voice was deep for a ten-year-old's. He shifted away from me, then saw Bill and stiffened.

"Be back in a sec," Bill whispered to me. "I have to move the car." I heard the front door open and close. He was gone a long time, but I'd circled the block often enough myself, looking for a parking space to open up.

A half hour later he came back, bringing the smell of fresh night air with him, to find Morgan ironing cheese sandwiches at an ironing board set up in the kitchen. Patrick was next to her, poking at a flat, smoking black sandwich. "I haven't met your son," Bill said to me.

"Bill, this is my son Patrick," I said.

"Glad to meet you, Patrick. Hey, man, I'm sorry about your newt."

"Hi, Bill," Patrick said dully, shaking hands.

Bill strolled into the other room, and then we heard him calling in great excitement. "Patrick! Patrick! Come and see! He woke up!"

We all rushed in. There on the paper towel was the newt, standing on all four feet and looking as alert as it is in the nature of a newt to look.

"That's not the–" Morgan started to say. I reached out and grabbed her around the neck, then put my finger to my lips.

Patrick's eyes were glued to the newt. "I thought he was dead," he said wonderingly. He reached out a finger to stroke the newt's back, then carefully lifted the edges of the paper towel. "I better get him back into the tank."

Morgan, Bill, and I filed back into the kitchen and sat down at my tiny kitchen table.

"Amazing what recuperative powers these amphibians have," he said.

Morgan had sat down and was tipping back in her chair, her blond hair flipped over. "Pretty smooth," she said to Bill. "How did you know where to find a newt?"

"Everybody who reads your mom's column knows about the creepy crawly store on Clement Street," he said. "I have two more in the car, just in case. By the way, I heard it's almost your birthday. I brought you something." He handed her a paper bag. Morgan took the bag eagerly. "What is it?"

"You'll see."

Morgan drew out a filmy scarf, the kind the women who work in Financial District banks use to dress up their plain work blouses. "Oh, I love it, Bill, thanks a lot," she said in her patented sincere-sounding voice.

"Oh, great!" he said. "I'm so relieved. It's hard to know someone's taste when you've never met her." He didn't see when the scarf, pushed aside and forgotten, slipped to the floor under the table.

The four of us sat down to dinner. "We are lucky guys, Patrick, to get to have dinner with two of the prettiest girls in San Francisco," Bill said. Morgan rolled her eyes at me.

When I turned back from the stove with some warmed-up peas, though, Morgan and Patrick and Bill were all wearing napkins on their heads as a joke and grinning at me. Bill had hung his jacket over the back of his chair and stuffed his tie in his pocket.

After dinner, with Bill's hand warming my back through my blouse, I told them to go do their homework. Morgan stayed at the table with us. "I don't have any homework," she said, and then added, automatically, "I did have some vocabulary words to do. But somebody stole my assignment sheet."

"I've been reading that this is a favorite turf for the vocabulary-word gangs," Bill observed. "Your spelling words are probably on an unmarked truck right now, speeding toward the border."

"That's funny, Bill," Morgan said.

Patrick came back out of his room to hug me goodnight. "Night, Mom."

"Say goodnight to Bill," I said, and then watched, surprised, as Patrick reached up to put one arm around Bill, who had half-stood to receive it. Shy Patrick, who was still working up to hugging his own grandma.

"Night, Bill."

"Night, Patrick."

"Call me the Hawk."

"Night, Hawk."

Now it was several years later, and Bill and I were married. Once, coming down the mountain with Patrick on a hike, Bill ran into an acquaintance who said of Patrick: "Who's this guy?" Bill said, "This is my boy, Patrick." Bill remembers—will always remember—how

Patrick leaned backward into him then, and Bill reached his arm around him. They claimed each other then.

But Bill never did figure out how to get on with Morgan. She was loud, exuberant, and messy, happiest when the music was turned up and everybody was talking at once; he was quiet, neat, happiest on a bike ride, or when the two of us read our books together at the kitchen table.

IT was clear to me that my marrying Bill had been good for Patrick but not good for Morgan. How then could I reconcile staying with him, when I would have told you, as any mom would, that I'd do anything for her happiness?

It was so hard, sometimes, separating their lives from mine. In an Irish play, *The Mai*, by Marina Carr, the grandma tells her children:

> There's two types of people in this world, from what I can make out: them what puts their children first, and them what puts their lover first. And for what it is worth, the nine-fingered fisherman and myself belongs to the latter of these. I would gladly have hurled all seven of you down the slopes of hell for one more night with the nine-fingered fisherman and may I rot eternally for such unmotherly feeling.

I wanted to be a good mom, wanted it desperately, even, but their childhood coincided with the prime of my life, my career, my romances, all the pleasures and distractions of an urban life. I would not hurl them down the slopes of hell for a night with a nine-fingered fisherman, or even a ten-fingered fisherman. I was their mom, and this was their childhood. But at the same time, I was a woman who had just found the man she wanted to spend the rest of her life with.

I was already in love. Bill cried at TV 49ers games. He was funny and smart and even working-class Irish-American, as I was. I liked the way he murmured, "I love this. I *love* this," when we made love.

When we parted I felt neither relief at being alone nor panic at being abandoned: being apart from him was just like being with him, except that sometimes I missed him. He was a light presence, the kind you could live with forever.

I was midspan in my own life, and this was it–my chance at lasting love.

WHEN Bill and I had been seeing each other about a month, he took Morgan out on a date to dinner and to see A Christmas Carol, just the two of them. By then he and I knew we were serious. He arrived wearing a suit and tie and carrying roses. Morgan was waiting on the couch wearing the blue dress with wide round collar that her dad had given her.

"It was awful," Bill confessed later, as we were sitting on the couch after Morgan had gone to bed. "It was awkward making conversation, and I was so nervous I couldn't remember after the theater where I'd parked the car. Morgan had to lead me to it."

"Bill's a nice guy, but he's a dork," Morgan said when I went in to say goodnight. "He couldn't even remember where he'd parked his car."

BILL told me he had, a few years before we met, gone through a period of mourning for the children he would never have. He hadn't met anyone he wanted to take that step with.

A couple of weeks after our weekend in Inverness, he read in the paper that it takes a while for fertility to return after Norplant and suggested I make an appointment right away. I was, after all, already forty-two, he added–unnecessarily, I thought. Dr. Jones, the tall, thin, sandy-haired chatterbox who'd been my doctor there for years, gave me his blessing and his private phone line so I could reach him without going through the switchboard. I started taking folate to prevent fetal spinal deformities.

Sometimes, though, as I moved around the house, putting roses in a vase or freshening the dog's water bowl, I felt a blank fear. Oh, God, did I really want to do this?

I talked to my friend Sally on the phone. "If having a baby is the answer," she said, "then you have to ask yourself, 'What's the question?'"

I bristled, as if she had accused me, a mom, of having the wrong motives. I wasn't just being softheaded: anyone who considers a new baby while her oldest is practically living in the dean's office can't be accused of idealizing motherhood.

I had the Norplant removed. A week later I sat in the examining room, where there was nothing to read but *Baby Talk* magazine and *Diapering Digest*. I thought, I must get a laptop. There was still a bandage around my right arm where the six Norplant capsules had been taken out. Dr. Jones examined me, then said, "Ten percent of women lose their ability to become pregnant by age forty, but women of proven fertility are outside this statistic."

After he left, I snapped my bra on briskly, stepped into my pants. A woman of proven fertility.

chapter 8

I T was Christmas of Morgan's sophomore year, and the four of us were driving through Marin County to my family's. Patrick leaned over the seat, his breath warm in my ear. "Would you eat a bowl of live crickets for forty thousand dollars?" he asked. He was reading from the *Answer Book*, a tattered paperback we kept on the backseat.

"I'd do it for a lot less than forty thousand dollars," Morgan said.

"I wouldn't do it for fifty thousand," Bill said promptly, keeping his eyes on the road.

We were still deliberating that one when we were lurching over the speed bumps in my mother's mobile home park in San Rafael. "We think they were put there in honor of Mickey," I told the kids.

"We know, Mom," the kids said together. My older sister used to barrel down drowsing Yosemite Drive in her Pontiac Firebird, her kids grabbing onto the backs of the front seats, little old ladies blowing off the side of the road like dandelions.

The park is called Contempo-Marin, but my kids called it GrandmaLand, as it didn't allow children. My mother had lived here fifteen years, since shortly before Morgan was born, in a black-and-white mobile home, the smallest one in the park.

When we arrived, her blue Geo Metro was parked in the drive-way, yellow plastic flowers stuck in its antenna, library books and videotapes in plain brown boxes spread across the backseat. Robin's black Mustang sat under the aluminum roof of the carport, with the rest of the cars behind it and along the two streets: Shannon's re-stored orange Corvette and Adrian's Bronco.

Missing as usual were the cars of the three Big Kids, as we had al-ways called my brother Sean and my two older sisters, Mickey and Connie. They lived in Washington state, Idaho, and Utah respec-tively, and so were never around for Christmas. They always sent the same presents: the table inside would hold a block of aromatic goat cheese from Sean's goat cheese farm in the Bitterroot mountains of eastern Washington, secondhand Patagonia vests from Garp's, Connie's sprawling secondhand store in Salt Lake City, and intricate handmade Christmas stockings from Mickey, who worked as a wait-ress in Post Falls, Idaho.

Morgan was right behind me as I entered the trailer, the screen door banging behind us. I paused to let my eyes adjust to the gloom. Rows of Christmas cards hung on a string across one mirror, flutter-ing in the breeze from the wall heater below. A spindly tree stood in the front of the TV, with presents stacked nearly halfway up it. We added ours to the pile, dumping them out of shopping bags and turning the messed-up wrapping jobs (mine) to the tree. My mother was at the counter, ladling instant coffee into cups, her head nearly grazing the swinging light fixture. She was five feet ten, three inches taller than I was, and still beautiful, with huge round brown eyes and the small nose we had all inherited. For a brief summer long ago, she was a dancer for Sally Rand in Las Vegas, earning sixty-five dol-lars a week. "I couldn't dance a step," she told us.

My twin, Adrian, slim and cool in a red sweater and white pants, sprawled on a stool next to the counter. We are fraternal twins, not identical, but share the strong family resemblance all the kids do. Above her head were two rows of our black-and-white high school senior pictures, which we accuse mother of hanging there to embarrass us in front of the people we bring over. In mine the gaps in the pearls lent me by the photographer have worked around to the front, and I have the frosted hair and whitish lipstick popular in 1970.

"Hey, you old bat," Adrian said.

"Old bat yourself," I said, looking at her with the usual twinly mixture of envy and admiration. Adrian has always been as lithe and graceful as a cat, though like me she has never outgrown jeans and sweatshirts. She got married in a dress but carried pants rolled up in her purse.

My brother Shannon looked up from his armchair. Two years younger than Adrian and me, he was tall and handsome, with thick gray hair under black eyebrows. He wore a green Rafael Lumber sweatshirt. "Hey, Dare, Bill," he rumbled in his deep voice.

Bill greeted everybody and got himself a beer. Then the screen door banged again, and in came my little sister Robin, all blond hair and outthrust jaw, a "total fox," as Bill calls her. I could hear her two kids, Tony, nine, and Katie, ten, talking to Patrick, then the thunk of the freezer lid as they got Popsicles from the porch freezer. I caught a glimpse of green—Tony had taken to wearing his grandma's bright green cardigan sweater everywhere, so he was easy to spot.

"Where have you been? I thought you'd be here at twelve," Mother said to Robin.

"Stopped off to shoot pool and have some belts of Scotch," Robin deadpanned, tossing her purse on a chair.

"I hear Dad got an apartment in Fairfax," Adrian said.

And that was when I remembered, with a tightening in my stomach, that Morgan had called him up a few weeks before on a whim and invited him here today. "He'll never come," I'd told her, and forgotten all about it.

"How can he afford that?" Mother was saying.

"It's SSI. He only pays a hundred fifty dollars. State pays the rest."

"Oh, that's fair," Mother said. "Walks out on his family, and ends up on Easy Street."

"I took Rory over there," Shannon said. Rory is Shannon's son by his third wife. "We took Dad out for pizza."

"I don't know why you would want to do that," Mother said. "You don't owe him anything. Seven kids, and he never changed a diaper, not one. Closest he got to a diaper was the day he paraded around the yard in one, for a joke."

"He worked hard, didn't he?" I asked. "You told me once he was the best carpenter in the valley." I remembered Dad, grinning, bare-chested, shouldering his way through the other men at the fair to drive ten nails straight into a two-by-four with ten blows of the hammer.

"He did, when his lordship was in the mood. He wasn't always."

"He had trouble finding work sometimes," I offered.

Mother laughed without humor. "Trouble looking for it, you mean. You kids are the only thing he ever did worth doing, and it wasn't an hour's work for him, altogether. Now can we talk about something else?"

Morgan was listening, the corners of her lips raised, her mouth open slightly. She loved being at my family's. They never saw the sulky hellchild I described to them.

"Morgan, let's walk over to the duck pond," Katie said, coming to stand near her adored older cousin.

"That's a good idea, Morgan, why don't all you kids go out and run around for a while?" Mother said.

"Okay, Grandma," Morgan said.

"I'll go, too," Bill said, surprising everybody except me. He'd been listening quietly from his chair, but he hated the small smoky trailer and usually seized any excuse to get back outside. I squeezed his hand as he went by.

"How is she these days?" Adrian asked when Bill and the four kids were gone.

"Not great," I said, not wanting to spoil the day by going into it. "Her grades came up a little. She had a B in computer math, a C in World Literature, a D in Modern World, and an F+ in biology."

"What does that F+ mean?" Shannon rumbled. "She flunked, but they liked her hair?"

"She seems to be losing the hang of things–of school, and even of friends. It's as if she's slowly drifting out to sea," I said.

"I'm at sea, too," Robin said, pouring herself a glass of white wine from a bottle of Kenwood Chardonnay we'd brought. "What are we talking about?"

"Morgan. Dare's worried about her."

"I don't get this," Mother said. "I never had any trouble with you kids when you were in your teens. You all raised each other."

"Yeah," Adrian said dryly. "The babies Mickey and Connie had as teenagers were no trouble."

"Or my getting married as a senior in high school," I chimed in.

"Or Robin and me dropping out," drawled Shannon.

"This scar on my forehead is cosmetic, not from crashing in a car with my drunken live-in boyfriend when I was a teenager," Robin said.

Mother had picked up a present with her name on it and was shaking it, ignoring us. "Mickey said to tell you that if you ever needed to, you could send Morgan to her in Idaho," she called over her shoulder.

"I would never send her away," I said, startled. "That's nice of Mick, though."

"Jessica's joined something called the Bitches of Power," Shannon said. "She got sent to a halfway house, and told us she likes it better there than home." Jessica was Shannon's thirteen-year-old daughter by his second wife, Suzanne. They had since divorced and Shannon lived alone.

"You must be out of your mind with worry," I said to him.

Shannon shrugged and looked away.

"Morgan's a good kid," Adrian said to me. "She's just rebelling right on schedule. You're the one I worry about."

"Me?" I said. By now everybody had lit up cigarettes. I leaned away from the smoke, trying not to let them see me do it. "She's the one who never does anything she doesn't want to do."

"Well, who does that sound like?"

"Who?"

"Everybody in this room," Robin put in.

"Morgan seems happy today," Adrian observed.

"She's always happy with you guys. She likes being a Daly."

"And you don't want her to be one, anymore than you want to be one yourself," Adrian said.

I was jolted. "I'm never happier than when I'm with the family. I dream about all of you guys at night. Never of my city life." I did, too. My sisters and brothers populated my dreams, flopping on couches, throwing strange parties, showing up everywhere.

"Yes, but you got out. You went to college, you married your English teacher, you got a job and got famous."

"I'm not famous."

"You are."

"What does this have to do with Morgan?"

"She's everything you've gone away from," Adrian persisted. "It's all back—*in the flesh*."

Just then Morgan banged back in through the screen door, and in the light from the porch door we all seemed to see it at once, the way the fabric of her blue cotton top caught on the generous swell of her breasts.

Mother turned her glance away, thumbed at a Bic lighter until the flame snapped on, and lit her Merit Ultra Light.

"I got cold," Morgan said, although she'd never been cold in her life. She wanted to be with the family. Still sitting on the counter stool, I pulled her onto my lap and sat with my arms around her. She relaxed backward against me, and I held her tight.

Two hours later I was sitting on the wooden steps outside. We'd eaten lunch and opened the presents. To all appearances I was just keeping Adrian company while she smoked a cigarette, but actually I wanted to keep my eyes on the entrance of the park.

"Why are you so jumpy?" Adrian asked.

"I'm not," I said.

I let my gaze stray down the street. All the mobile homes had red or green gravel in front, as if colored for the holiday. They had that blank, expectant feeling, like a TV set turned off, that streets get on Christmas, just before they explode with overexcited kids pushing shiny new bicycles.

We could hear in the trailer behind us Robin and Mother singing "House of the Rising Sun" as Shannon played the guitar, his rough baritone the only voice on key.

I heard an engine backfire. I stiffened. "What's *with* you?" Adrian said.

I pointed. There, lumbering across the small concrete bridge that marked the entrance to the park, was Dad in his 1949 green panel truck. Fred was in his lap, with his nose out the window.

I yelled, "Dad!" and he lifted a hand and pulled over.

"Oh, man," Adrian said. "Who invited *him* here?"

"Morgan did," I said. "He's her idea of a good role model."

Dad stepped down from the truck gingerly, as if the pavement were land after a long sea voyage. He wore the rumpled jeans and slightly too small Saint Vincent de Paul thrift-store shirt he always did, being as indifferent to clothes as a baby. He snapped his fingers at Fred, who leaped to the sidewalk and came over to me, wagging his tail. "Hello, Fred boy," I said, scratching his head. He licked my face. "How's life on the ranch?"

"Hi, Dad," Adrian said.

"Adrian!" Dad said, his glance taking in both of us. "How are my little twin babies?"

"Not bad," I said.

"I'll warn the troops," Adrian said, stubbing her cigarette out in the glass ashtray. She disappeared inside.

"Hi, Pop," I said, crossing the sidewalk to him. "I thought you weren't supposed to be driving anymore."

"Hi," he said, with a crooked grin. "I'm not. State of California had its way, I'd walk everywhere." He swayed ever so slightly. "And as you see, that's not a great idea."

Dad's chin was covered with white stubble, and he reeked of beer and cigarettes. On his feet he wore fuzzy bedroom slippers. I surveyed him unhappily. "Nice outfit."

He glanced down at himself. "I had to gird myself for this homecoming. Say, you wouldn't have a beer on you anywhere, would you?"

"You don't need a beer, Pop."

Dad didn't seem to hear me. He was staring out the window at the mobile homes, some with plastic roofs rigged over the driveway for shade. "Funny to think your mom and I both ended up alone, living in vehicles, fifteen miles apart," he said.

"You live in a studio apartment now, Dad," I reminded him.

Morgan came banging out the screen door, a string of Christmas ribbon trailing from around her neck. Two more sticky bows from packages clung to her hair.

"Whoa, it's beginning to look a lot like Christmas," Dad said.

"Hi, Grandpa! Adrian said you were out here."

"Yep, out in the cold," Dad said. He sank down on the red painted steps and patted the place next to him. "Take a load off," he said to Morgan. "We rebels have to stick together."

I went inside. Robin was slicing a pie in a kitchen so thick with cigarette smoke that she looked for a second like an Impressionist painting. "Hey, Dare! Is it true that Gene's here?" Robin called him Gene because he'd been long gone by the time she was born. She wasn't even sure he was her father.

"I'm afraid so," I said. Everybody watched me as I got a beer from the fridge and walked back out.

I handed Dad the beer. "We're going to need another for the kid," he said, taking it.

"She doesn't need any beer," I said. "She's only fifteen."

"You worry too much about people drinking, Mom," Morgan said. "Everybody in the family thinks so. You should just let people have fun. I won't really drink it, anyway. I'll just hold it and keep Grandpa company."

"No."

Dad drank his beer in one long pull, and then rose to his feet. "I'm ready," he said.

Dad followed me in. Robin was still slicing pie, Adrian was gathering discarded wrapping into empty Macy's bags, and Shannon sat with the guitar he'd been playing stilled on his lap. All around, half buried in wrapping, were opened presents. Mother had got everything she asked for: a book tape of *I Claudius*, bookstore gift certificates, art brushes, and a subscription to *New York* magazine. Mother read even more than Dad or I did.

She sat very still in her armchair, wearing her new yellow duck slippers, the tiny Christmas trees in her ears flashing off and on. "What are you doing here, Gene?"

"How're tricks, Lee?" Dad asked, standing in the middle of the room. No one knew when they had last seen each other. Years ago. He smiled and opened his hands palms up to her, as if to show he had no weapons. "I brought you something," Dad said. We could hear the hum of the heater in the sudden stillness. He reached in his pocket and brought out a small wrapped package. Mom took it from him and put it down next to her drink. She didn't glance at it.

"Thanks," she said.

"It's a watch," he said.

"I said thanks."

They spoke in the manner of people who are convinced they see right through each other.

"I was hoping to talk to you," he told her.

"I want you to leave, right now," she said. "If you don't, then I will."

"I wondered if you wanted to go for a drive sometime," he said. I looked at him in surprise.

Mom looked at him contemptuously. "A drive?" she repeated.

She was still staring at him. He might have been a specimen in an apothecary jar. "Not today," Dad trailed off. "Sometime. Think about it."

"You're seventy-two now, Gene," she said at last, "so it's possible you simply don't remember this, but a number of years back, you ran off and left me to raise seven kids on my own."

Dad sighed. He had backed up more, and was standing near a small upright piano Mom was learning to play. I took a stool by the counter. "You were in no danger of starving."

"Yes. We were in no danger of starving," Mom said. "Your kids went to a present giveaway down at the community center. They came hollering home with bags of groceries and games, thinking they'd got away with something. They didn't know–yet–they were the poor children the presents were for."

Dad lifted his chin. "I'd sure like to be an innocent bystander just once in my life," he said. "Other folks seem to enjoy it so much. Like you, as innocent as the driven snow."

Mom got up and walked out of the room. The screen door banged behind her as she went outside.

"Hi, Shannon," Dad said, after we had all watched Mom leave.

"Hey, Dad," Shannon growled.

"You still running that lumber company?"

"Yeah."

"How's it going?"

"Good."

"You're the manager now, I hear?" Dad said. Their voices were almost identical.

"Yeah."

"How many people you have working for you now?"

"About forty." Shannon leaned forward, his drink sloshing in the glass.

Dad's mouth squinched sideways. "Guess you're a big man now," he said. "Peddling merchandise for others, for their glory and profit."

"Something like that."

Dad was swaying as he stood, like a fighter offering to take on all comers. "I hated lumberyards," he said. "Used to bolt before I could complete my list of materials. All those forklifts trying to run over me, managers trying to straighten me out on what I needed."

Shannon pressed his lips together, but said nothing. Robin, licking pie from her fingers, had come to sit on the arm of his chair. She'd been regarding Dad steadily since he came in. "You once passed me in the aisle at Lucky Market," she said to him. "You had a bag of Butterfingers in one hand and a six-pack of beer in the other. You looked straight at me, and didn't even recognize me. Your own daughter."

"You evidently recognized me," Dad said to her. "You might have said hello to me. Your own father."

"Are you?"

"Am I what?"

"My father."

"Why don't you ask your mother!"

"I'm asking you."

"I guess I don't understand the question."

Robin crossed her arms. "I don't look like anybody else. I'm taller, I'm blonder, I'm different. You left before I was born. Are you my father?"

"You are the image of my mother," Dad said. "You walk like her, you gesture like her."

"You didn't answer my question."

Dad drank his beer and looked at her. "Oh, I thought I did. I am your father," he said.

There was a silence. Nobody spoke. Then Robin said, "No, you're not. You're nothing to me but a pair of carpenter's overalls left behind in a closet." In the hush that followed, I heard a skateboard go by on the street, and a dog barking at it.

"You're going to have to learn to eat shit now, Dad," Adrian said from behind me. She said it quietly, matter-of-factly.

Morgan was sitting on the rug by the tree, following the scene. The bows still askew on her hair, she stared at Dad like everybody else, but her mouth was gentle. I had seen her look at the cat that way when his ear was torn in a fight. Part of me felt sorry for Dad, too, but part of me wanted Morgan to see him like this.

Mom came back into the room. "It's time for you to leave now, Gene," she said. "Nobody is buying what you're selling today."

"I just got here," he said. "The kids and I are talking."

"Then I'll leave," Mom declared. She had her car keys in her hand.

"Don't go," he said. His hand jerked at his side, as if he had been about to stretch it out to her.

Mom paused. She filled the doorway, a shadow with the light in back of her, only the flashing Christmas tree earrings clearly visible. "What is it you want, Gene?"

"I want a corner by the fire. Slippers and a pipe. I want back in."

"You should have thought of that before you walked out," she said.

Dad had turned to face her. He looked small, shrunken in his clothes. He didn't look big enough to have ruined anybody's life. "Don't get your panties in a twist," he muttered. "I'm leaving."

He turned and walked to the doorway. I followed him out, putting off the time when I had to explain why I had arranged to have Dad over to ruin Christmas.

He was snapping his fingers at Fred, who leaped through the open window into the cab of the truck. Dad no longer seemed drunk at all, but the bitter odor of beer washed backward from him. He crumpled the empty can he held and handed it to me.

"Thomas Wolfe was right," he said. He got in the truck. It grumbled to life after several misfires, startling an elderly woman passing by with her poodle. "You can't go home again." Then he was gone.

Morgan was standing on the steps, watching. "You're pretty hard on Grandpa, Mom," she said. "I think he's really smart. And he's funny."

I went up the steps and put my arm around her. "Don't admire him, sweetie. He has nothing to do with you. You're not a Daly."

"I am too a Daly," she said, shrugging slightly to free herself from my arm. "You just don't want me to be."

chapter 9

I DIDN'T hear from Dad again for months. He reminded me of the bird that once flew into my summer school classroom. It came flying straight past the teacher, whapped into the windows, and beat its feathers frantically for a minute trying to get out. Then it found an open window, and was gone. That was Dad in my life. Whap! Then gone again, with a flutter of wings.

When I tried to call him after Christmas, his phone just rang and rang. I called a friend of his who told me he had gone back to the desert.

That worried me. He was too old for that now.

School started up again and went on with its round of Morgan crises. I was called in by the dean in April. I cried most of the way home from Lowell this time, huge wrenching sobs that made it hard to steer the car, and that I could hear myself over the lyrics of "American Pie" on the radio. I felt humiliated, embarrassed, frightened, and furious, all at once.

The dean told me she'd got drunk at a school dance—or arrived drunk at it—then pushed a girl who kissed her date, Julio.

At a stop sign, I stared at the red Honda in front of me, the light glaring off the metal. What fifteen-year-old arrives at school drunk? I winced at the scene I saw in my mind: my daughter staggering around a softly lit gym floor, talking loudly, drunkenly, while other kids and their dates stared. Then she rushes up to another girl, says something to her, and shoves her–roughly, so the girl loses her balance on her high heels and falls.

Morgan was suspended for two days and had to spend them at a detention center on Golden Gate Avenue, doing homework under the eye of a supervisor. It's where the tough kids are sent.

I dropped her off there the next day and rushed home to clean her room. I wasn't supposed to be in there, invading her privacy, but I didn't know what else to do. I felt as if I was losing her, and it had always soothed me to handle her things.

I took my time, savoring it, playing her tapes. For two hours, I sorted happily through her stuff, finding the tops for pens, mating shoes, hanging up sweaters, taking back my own bras and T-shirts, putting the CDs in the right cases and the loose change in my pocket.

I sat on the bed and read the poetry in her journal, scanning for clues. Her poetry was bleak, and her spelling was worse. All life is a sharade? I felt guilty, reading it, but I was desperate.

I tried not to read the balled-up notes from and to friends. Then I yielded to temptation and unfolded one note on binder paper. It was from her friend Alexis. In large childish writing she had scrawled, "What's up? The reason I'm in such a bad mood is because my Mom wants 2 send me 2 this camp 4 'uncooperative kids.' I said I didn't want 2 go, & that got my Mom really P.Oed. Now neither of my parents is talking to me, and when I asked them why, they said all they're going to do is clothe me and feed me. They don't give a fuck what I do or where I go. Doesn't exactly make me feel good. I don't know if I should be happy, or not care at all."

Before I had a teenager myself, I would have been smug. At least I'm a better parent than those poor schmucks, I'd reflect. I could remember thinking about Morgan's friend Steve, a likable boy with a lock of brown hair over his forehead who was always in trouble. His mom worked a lot, and I used to think smugly that some parents just couldn't establish the right kind of rapport with their kids.

That was before Morgan turned thirteen.

Now I stood reading the note and ached for those parents. I saw them sitting in a cold light at their kitchen table, hearing their daughter's music overhead, and not even feeling they could speak to the child they had loved all her life. I began to see that it could happen to me, too.

As I went on cleaning, I heard the clink of glass in a lower drawer. Inside was an empty bottle of Bacardi rum in a green file folder. I let the dusting cloth fall, and slumped into a chair. The rung of the chair hurt my back, but I didn't bother to shift my position. I put the bottle on the desk, near a pile of binder paper and paper clips and hair ties I'd also cleared out of the file drawer.

Chilled, I remembered half a bottle of California pale dry sherry, wrapped in a pink shirt, that we'd found in her closet at her dad's house two years before.

"Where did you get the wine?" I had asked.

"I probably got it from Dad's shelves, but I don't remember," Morgan had said. Nor could she remember what she had been planning to do with the sherry.

I hadn't been upset by the sherry as much, even, as I had been when she left for school the next day without saying good-bye. I puzzled over that one for days, and then realized: it didn't happen at my house. She hadn't done it to *me*.

This set me back. I had been telling myself—and others—that everything I was doing was out of fear for her safety. Yet hidden bottles of sherry were more dangerous than not saying good-bye to your mom.

Hidden bottles ran in the family. Grandma kept vodka in the freezer and couldn't be called after two in the afternoon; Granddad drank Brown Derby beer while reading Wild West magazines; my uncle, a San Francisco motorcycle cop, died at age forty-eight, surrounded by closetfuls of empty bottles. He'd stopped going out and just stayed in his living room, monitoring the radio as if he were out on the motorcycle. My brother Sean landed in a hospital with a huge blood clot in his heart and another in his lung from neglecting a leg wound while he was drinking. Later he flipped out on booze and destroyed a car, had three guns pulled on him in two days by outraged neighbors, and woke up two months later in the mental ward without knowing how he got there. And there was my dad, who'd been sent to Napa State Hospital a dozen times to dry out, like a sleeping bag that had fallen in a stream.

"Morgan, I want to talk to you about something I found in your room," I said when she came home from detention at one o'clock and flipped on the TV. They were supposed to spend the rest of the day "under parental supervision." What was that? I felt as if I didn't know anymore.

"Whatever it is, I don't want to talk about it," she said. "You aren't even supposed to be in my room."

I showed her the bottle. "What's this?"

"A bottle?"

"Morgan, this worries me a lot."

"I'm not an alcoholic, Mom, if that's what you're thinking." Morgan's eyes were fastened to the *Ren and Stimpy Show* on TV. "Everybody in the family knows you are worried about that stuff too much, because of your dad."

I shut the TV off. "I just want to know how much you're drinking."

"I have been drunk a few times, like on the Fourth of July. But it's not like every day or anything."

Fear tightened my throat. "You've been drunk a *few times*? Morgan, you're only fifteen years old. I want you to go see somebody."

"What do you mean, see somebody?"

"Someone to talk to."

"You mean a shrink."

"Yes."

"All right."

"All right?" I was surprised.

"Yes, all right."

"Okay, then. I'll make you an appointment. I'll go with you."

I left her room, still trying to get over my surprise at how cooperative she was being. She must be scared herself.

Next morning Patrick came in to say good-bye before leaving for school, and I was shocked to glimpse a purplish bruise on his jaw. "Oh, sweetie, what's that?" I said.

Patrick put his hand to his face. "It's nothing," he said. "I have to go to school, Mom, I'm late."

"Wait." I sat him down, and peered at the bruise, alarm rising in me. Had he been in a fight? "Someone hit you. Tell me who."

"Morgan." He raised his head, his anger rising as he spoke. "She and her friends were having a beer party in Dad's attic late last night. Sam and I went in to use the phone. I told her not to do that stuff, that Dad was going to come home and get mad. She started yelling at me, and I got mad and called her a fat ass. 'I'll kill you!' she said. Then she hit me."

I flinched. I had been home, downstairs, oblivious to what was happening. "Then what happened?"

"I was mad. And embarrassed. She did it in front of her friends and in front of Sam. I ran to my room. I was crying."

"Oh, Patrick," I said, kissing the top of his head. I had to pull his head down to do that now. "I'm so sorry she did that." Fury at her surged up in me.

"I hate Morgan," he said, shouldering his backpack, his face averted. "I don't want her for a sister anymore."

"God, don't hate her, sweetie," I said. "She didn't know what she was doing. She loves you. She's always telling everybody how proud she is of her good-looking little brother."

He shut the door softly as he left, but I heard it as a slam.

I was a long time before I could move. The usual feelings raged through me, immobilizing me. The front door had swung open again after Patrick left, and a cold breeze was blowing papers around on my rug, but I just sat there. I would bar the door to anybody--anybody!--who hurt Patrick.

Except his sister.

"I just struck out at him," Morgan said when I confronted her. I was standing in the kitchen, trembling with anger, watching her take orange juice from the fridge and pour it in a glass. "I was drunk. I didn't mean to hurt him." She said she was jealous because her friends had switched their attention to him.

"I've made you an appointment with a teen counselor that everybody recommends," I said. "The earliest appointment I could get for you is in June, after school lets out. In the meantime, sweetie, please, be smart. Take care of yourself. And don't ever, ever, hit your brother again."

We had been trying therapy all along, without much result. One was Kim Gold, a family therapist with an office down on Gough Street, a few minutes drive from our house. She was small, friendly, and businesslike. Jim, Patrick, Morgan, and I had filed into her small office, Morgan taking a chair by me. We liked her. She was able to cut Morgan off with a wave of her hand. Patrick made jokes. We talked for the first time about the divorce. When Kim asked us who was the most unhappy, everybody said Jim was the most unhappy, Morgan next, then me, then Patrick. At the end of the first hour Kim complimented Morgan for having found a way to bring her dad and me together on the phone every day. She said, "For now, just keep right on doing it!" She said that Morgan was acting up to give Jim a focus, because he was alone and Morgan was unconsciously worried about him. I told her that Jim and I had talked every day for the past twenty years.

Jim and I also went to Jody Eisen at Kaiser, our HMO hospital. Jody said Morgan and we were arguing over the solution to a problem--set homework hours to help her keep her grades up--while she didn't agree there was a problem. "She may be hyperactive, and not actually able to sit still at a desk for two and a half hours," Judy added.

"She's out of control," said a counselor in a teen clinic. "What happened with limits when she was younger?" She recommended "containment" at home–minimum standards for behavior, strict supervision, therapy. She didn't tell how we were supposed to enforce all this with hardheaded Morgan.

Nothing I was hearing answered my questions. Why Morgan and not Patrick? What could we have done differently to head this off? Would she have been all right, spared these five years, if I had not divorced her dad when she was five? If I had not married Bill when she was twelve?

DAD had begun writing to me again. Every few weeks a thick, tightly rolled sheaf of yellow sheets would arrive, and I would grab an apple or a cup of coffee and sink into a chair to read it, the pages curling against my hand. I got letters from places all over California, and I read them as if there was something I desperately needed to know.

The first letter was a single yellow sheet in his cramped hand. "And a man's foes shall be those of his own household," he said, quoting from the Bible. It was a book I hadn't known he was familiar with, but it didn't surprise me. Though he never finished high school, Dad had been addicted to books since he learned how to read. "It was a long bleak period from birth to my first book," he told me once, then added, "Pisses me off to think about that period of deprivation."

People told Dad how lucky he was to have reading as a mainstay, but that's not how he looked at it. "It's just another of the shells a hermit can crawl into–though I do try to limit my addiction somewhat. My letters to you are meant to be a counterirritant, no doubt–keep print flushed out of my system."

He said he had turned tail and worked his way back south again, his life flipping past him like a torturous movie reel behind his eye-balls. "Better keep a sharp eye on your own kids," he wrote in that aching hand, "it might be your father back to haunt you. Better not look in the mirror. Better break all the mirrors in your house."

Other letters arrived, and I learned that images from the past kept him twitching: children left in a car while he went off to play the slot machines, kitchens lined with packing boxes. "There's no way I can sneak back to the past, tidy things up a bit," he wrote in despair. "I've been an absolute asshole–God knows we need no further proof. The episodes speak for themselves."

He remembered my brother Sean at fourteen, when Sean had gone with him on a building job to Lake Tahoe. "I bought a startling ski jacket and a puffy hat with ear flaps for myself–and nothing for him. Remembering his delight in my bizarre appearance has dogged me down through the years. That moment of cold shoulder from his father could have been the moment he began to expect nothing from life."

He remembered, too, the night that none of us kids has forgotten, when he came home drunk and was hitting Mom in their bed.

In a letter from Bishop, which according to the map was in the Sierra Nevada below Yosemite, Dad said, "As you know, I barged around in a separate world. You were part of your mother's en-tourage–I might say that you came fully into my awareness that fa-mous midsummer at the foot of your mother's bed."

My stomach tightened as I read. I knew what night he was talking about. I read on:

"Last night, lying in my sleeping bag, a picture floated before my eyes, a tiny bedroom, me slapping your mother and hoarse, ele-mental cries of distress coming from the foot of the bed. I remember it as clearly as if it had happened last night."

It was the worst of all the bad nights. I was eight years old. I stood at the foot of Mother's bed, the floorboards cold under my bare feet. I stood in the shadow, outside the light cast by the lamp, and said, over and over, "Don't, Daddy. Don't. Don't hurt Mommy."

"I'm all right, Dare, go to bed," Mother called to me, but her voice was muffled, strange.

Dad looked over at me and froze with his fists in the air. He let his arms fall. "You heard your mother," he said. "Go to bed."

When I went back to the bunk beds in the room across the hall, I lay with my cheek on the iron railing. I knew from her breathing that Adrian, who slept in the same bed with her head at the other end, was awake, too. Above us was Mickey, crying softly into her pillow. The cries and thumps continued from across the hall. "You Irish frump," I heard him say.

I was sure she would not get up to light the kindling in the morning, would not be there next time I got off the bus after school. He was beating the life from her the way you beat dust out of a mattress, and there was nothing we could do about it. Adrian was right there in the bed with me, I could feel her terror as her feet jerked against my leg, but I might as well have been alone. I hugged the cold iron railing of the bed and listened.

In the morning we woke to find Mother stuffing kindling and newspapers into the stove as usual. She was pale, and later she went to the doctor and came home with her arm in a sling. Dad was gone for four days, and came home with a new Airedale puppy. Life went on as usual.

I was amazed that Dad remembered that--and to learn that the memory of it plagued him. When he acknowledged that childhood terror, some of it seemed to recede.

His mood seemed to lighten when he at last turned his wheels toward the desert. In the few letters I'd received, he had begun writing to me about this new apparition he was seeing in the rearview mirror of the truck he lived in, "this geezer with blue-veined legs, the new weakness in his shoulders, dimming eyesight." Looking at that reflection, he said he felt "the first honest affection for myself, from myself, I've ever known: the more ghastly I become, the more I overflow, wanting to throw my arms around that haggard creep in the mirror–somehow forgetting for a fleeting instant that that haggard creep is me. Wanting to slip to the floor, hugging each other, choking with laughter at what has happened to us."

IN May of her sophomore year Morgan came home at six o'clock on a Friday with two black kids. "You remember Tommie," she said, nodding her head at the taller of the two boys, "and Ricardo." Ricardo was lighter-skinned than Tommie, wearing a green knit hat, both hands thrust into the front pockets of baggy jeans. I remembered him. I had found a bottle of beer in his jacket pocket at Morgan's twelfth birthday party. It had been hot in the room but he kept his jacket on for a long time, and when he took it off I saw the tip of the bottle, opened, leaning out of it. It was the first time I had seen anything like that at one of my kids' parties. Jim told him to leave, and he did.

The last time these two came by to see Morgan they had stayed out on the sidewalk–I peeped at them through the blinds–and afterward I found an empty bottle of St. Ives malt liquor stuck between the railings in the front garden. Morgan hooted at me when I showed it to her and asked if those boys had been drinking beer. "That was probably some homeless guy who left that there," she said.

Now they sat at the table, and Morgan laughed and talked too loudly about some girl who had "busted out" another one down at "the Pit."

"What are you up to tonight?" I asked casually.

"We're going over to Robbie's house. Tommie forgot his backpack over there," Morgan said. The two boys sat huddled, elbows on the table, eager to leave.

"You are?" I said lamely. I didn't know what to say. It was only six o'clock, and for a change she wasn't grounded: I had no pretext for not letting her go. I didn't like these older boys. It didn't make sense for Morgan to be hanging out with them.

I sat down. "What school do you guys go to?" I asked, and an awkward conversation followed. My only weapon was talking to them, trying to get them to see me, to bring me into focus. To them I was only a vague outline, a middle-aged woman in bear slippers, a pair of lips talking to them until they could politely get out of the house.

Morgan, in an oversize hooded blue sweatshirt, handed them two orange Simply Sodas from the fridge and they popped them open. Her hazel eyes shone.

They were just kids, just someone's sons, but I could not leave the kitchen, could not go back to the white letters waiting on my blue computer screen. Morgan did not belong with them. They would draw her into the twilight city, into the night screaming with dangers. And then they were going. Morgan grabbed her jacket, "Bye, Mom."

"Morgan," I said. She turned, impatient, her hand on the knob. The boys were already thundering down the porch steps.

"Yes, Mom?"

"Please don't go with them."

"I'll be fine, Mom, I'll be back in a couple of hours," she said. "You have to trust me, Mom. I'm fifteen and a half now."

I watched from inside the door as she got into a gray Ford Mustang that pulled out fast. She was a blur of pale skin through the glass.

Two hours later, the phone rang.

"Hello?"

"Could I speak to Morgan's mother, please?" A deep, male voice. "This is Sergeant Haley. We have your daughter here at the Balboa Police Station."

"Your daughter . . . police station." I had finally heard all those words in the same sentence.

I raced to the police station, trying to see through the dark, and the fog, and my tears.

While I waited for Morgan to be brought out, I sat in the shadowy anteroom, more like the small lobby of an unfriendly hotel than a police station. A cop came out, and I rose to meet him, still huddled in my jacket as if for protection from whatever he might say. He told me about the stolen Mustang going out of control on the O'Shaughnessy hill and hitting an embankment with the three kids in it. "She wasn't hurt," he said. "She was wearing her seatbelt." I silently thanked Bill, who had drilled seatbelt-wearing into all our heads.

The vending machine in the lobby flashed HAVE A NICE DAY in red digital letters as he spoke. I kept seeing the car hit the wall, and then bounce, and the heads inside bounce, too.

"She's not being charged with anything," the policeman was saying, handing me her blue backpack, politely not noticing my streaming eyes. The light from the overhead fixture glinted off his badge. "You can take her home."

Then Morgan came out, pale, her hair in her face. She was teary, but also hard, in her black jacket. She shook a Marlboro from a pack she took from her pocket and bent over to light it with her Bic.

"What happened?" I said in the car, the headlights shining on the trunk of a tree in the parking lot. I had not yet started the engine.

"We were going over Portola when the brakes gave out," Morgan said. "Tommie was trying to get to his house in Glen Park by using the emergency brake." Glen Park lies at the bottom of O'Shaughnessy.

"You could have got out, right?" I said.

"No, Mom."

I stared ahead. There are lots of stop signs and a stoplight on Portola before you get to O'Shaughnessy. She could have jumped out at any one of them. She could have said, "Let me out here. This car isn't safe."

But she didn't. Kids like to be cool. She stayed in a car, even after she knew it had no brakes.

"Then what?"

"Tommie lost control of the car as we were coming down O'Shaughnessy. It was dark, and we could hardly see in the fog.

Then the emergency brake gave out, and we hit something, and the car spun around. Nobody was hurt, except Ricardo. He was sitting in the back, and hit his head hard on the back of Tommie's seat."

"The police said it was a stolen car."

"Tommie didn't know the car was stolen. He borrowed it from his cousin." She said it with a sidelong glance. It was the same tone she used when she told me the absences marked on her report card were computer errors.

"You could have been killed," I said, choking out the words. I kept thinking, it's still early evening. What if this had happened at midnight, after they'd all had a lot to drink or smoke? "That boy could have killed you."

All I could think about during the rest of that drive home was that it was Morgan herself who had no brakes. I could not trust her to keep herself out of danger.

I had to get her out of the city.

chapter 10

"CAN she come up there?" I asked my sister Mickey on the phone the next day. "You said if I ever needed to, I could send her to you."

"Sure. Send her up," Mickey said promptly. "I'll put her in summer school."

"I won't forget this, Mick. I'll put her on a plane when school lets out in two weeks."

I got off the phone and went to stand on the front porch in the sunshine. I felt as if I had been holding my breath underwater and had just exploded to the surface for a gulp of fresh air. I imagined Mickey in cutoffs, cup of coffee in her hand, on her deck overlooking the small reedy lake in front of her house. Mickey lived in Idaho, not far from Coeur d'Alene. She loves to think of herself as a can-do person. When she comes down to visit Mom she starts right in weeding, taking stuff to the dump, getting the sagging mailbox fixed. Her hands are always busy, like Morgan's.

When I walked into Morgan's bedroom, she was lying on the bed, talking on the phone. I waited until she hung up.

"You're going to spend the summer with Aunt Mickey," I said. "And maybe stay longer, if it works out."

Morgan paled. "You've gone too far, Mom," she said. "I won't go to Idaho. I'll run away instead."

An hour later she was gone. I found a crumpled note on binder paper on her bed, saying she was at a friend's house. I sat on the bed, switching on the lamp so I could make it out better in the dim room.

"It hurts me so much to know you don't want me living with you anymore. I am sorry for the way I have acted and treated you. But I think that by the time I want to talk to you and work things out I will be in another state."

I cried on her bed for a long time, mopping my eyes with one of her T-shirts. I lay curled in a ball. I was Morgan–Morgan feeling unwelcome in the one place on earth where, according to my own profoundest beliefs, you should always be welcome.

At the same time, I was myself, hurt and scared and angry. I didn't even try to call around and find out where she was this time. I felt as if I didn't want to talk to her, or think about her. I was angry at her refusal to just be a kid, one who lived with her parents and by their rules, like other kids.

After that, as the days passed, I was just holding on, waiting for Idaho. Idaho was the Promised Land, the shimmering landscape where Morgan would be safe and happy. I saw her riding a bicycle down a country lane between green hills. Mickey had promised only a summer visit, but I saw Morgan laughing in a school corridor, surrounded by other safe, normal high school kids.

THAT night she never came home at all. I didn't know where she was, and didn't call anybody to find out.

Then on Sunday night she called downstairs from her dad's: "Hi, Mom," she said. "Will you help me with my English project?"

"You must be out of your mind," I said, and slammed down the phone. I was shaking. I didn't even trust myself to be around her. I was afraid of what I might say.

Yet I sat there at my desk, surrounded by all my own books and papers. All I had ever wanted was to work quietly with her on her English. Back when I first felt her stirring in my womb, I had daydreamed about showing her the uses of the dash.

I stared at my computer. "Writing is fun!" I had scrawled on the beige metal of my computer in black marker, to remind myself. The manila work folder under my coffee cup held exactly two columns, both lame. I usually had six or seven in there, a thick sheaf of paper between me and deadline panic. I sat dusting off the keyboard with my bottle of Dust-Off compressed gas, with its loud hissing noise that made the dog bark.

Losing confidence in myself as a mother had spread to my work. When I had started at the paper six years before, hired away from a magazine to write a column, I had felt like a rising star. That feeling had leveled off, but for a long time I felt as if I was at least holding steady in my little part of the firmament. Now I felt like a star drifting down toward the horizon. I actually felt different going into the building, trying to greet people cheerfully though I didn't know their names, to just keep doing my work, taking that old advice to "never explain, never complain," but feeling a little like a ghost.

Though I prided myself on being a professional, able to write through anything, I was not writing through this. One day instead of working I watched three movies in a row: *The Accompanist, Tombstone,* and *Four Weddings and a Funeral.*

After eight days of strain, I drove Morgan to the airport. "I am going to miss you so much when I'm in Idaho, being bored out of my mind because you don't want me here," she said when her flight was called in the departure lounge. She picked her bulging backpack up by one strap and took the ticket I handed her. All around us travelers were heading for the jetway, tickets in their hands.

We were both crying. "Morgan, you are in my heart every minute," I said. "I love you." I hugged her, and she headed down the skyway, the pack of red licorice I had given her sticking up from the outside pocket of her backpack.

Then she was gone. I went to the window and watched her plane roll away from the gate. The relief I felt was wonderful, and terrible.

When I got home, Patrick was standing sleepy-eyed in front of the fridge. He had arranged the tiny magnetic words we leave there in a sentence: "Who cooks diamonds in the forest?"

"Can you give me something to eat, Mom?" he said, turning to put his arms around me from behind. He was taller than I was now.

"What do I look like? Your mother?" I said as always, as I scrounged in the fridge for tuna salad to make him a sandwich.

My sister Adrian said Patrick was starting to look like a young Marlon Brando. "He would never have looked at us, back in high school," she said. Morgan probably wouldn't have hung around with us either. I had to wait until I was forty, and had given birth to them, to hang out with the cool kids in school.

I asked Patrick to make his bed before going out to play basketball. He responded by pulling his comforter over everything, including his textbooks and a skateboard. "Try it again," I suggested.

"Why do I have to keep my room clean when Morgan doesn't?" he said.

"Patrick . . ."

"I hate this room." He was suddenly raging. "It isn't even a room, it's a back porch. Why do I have to have this room?"

He left, and I stood there almost dazed, staring at his still unmade bed. Patrick never talked like that.

I caught sight of Morgan's green BP gas station jacket hanging from a peg, and it hit me. Freed of his need to be the opposite of his sister, Patrick got to turn into a normal grumbling teenager. I had read that a parent with two kids will tend to describe them in terms of opposites: Amy is shy, Johnny is outgoing. But kids polarize, too. Morgan was keeping Patrick from expressing his natural badness. Patrick was hogging the role of good child.

"You always favor him," Morgan had said to me once. "You don't even notice what a little brat he is. You only notice the good stuff he does, and you only notice the bad stuff I do. Do you remember that time he got in a fight at school?"

"Patrick never got in a fight at school," I said. "What are you talking about?"

"See?" Morgan said. "He got in a fight two months ago and was sent home from school. You don't even remember." I realized, guiltily, that she was right. I had edited Patrick's fight out of my memory, because it didn't fit the way I thought of Patrick.

How many good things had I edited out of my memory of Morgan, because they didn't fit?

Whenever I couldn't find something, my black bra, or my shoes, or the money I thought I'd had in my wallet, my thoughts would go to Morgan, even though she'd never stolen from me. If Bill couldn't find his umbrella, or saw dirty dishes on the coffee table, or a broken pane of glass in the porch, he would blame Morgan.

It was natural. She *was* trouble.

In the Old Testament ritual of Yom Kippur, a goat was symbolically burdened with the sins of the Jewish people. It was chosen by lot, and then sent into the wilderness, taking those sins with it. The Greeks had scapegoats, too—one married couple would be chosen to be paraded around Athens, beaten with green twigs, then stoned, all to protect the town from calamity.

And we had our house scapegoat. We stood now with our bundles of green twigs, beating each other for a change.

A FEW days after Morgan left my brother Shannon called. He shared a rented house in San Rafael, across the freeway from Mother's mobile home park, with his (now) platonic friend, Betty.

"Heard you sent Morgan up to Mickey," he said.

"Yes," I said. "We're hoping she won't get into as much trouble up there."

He snorted. "That's what Suzanne thought." Suzanne was

Shannon's second wife, by whom he had two daughters, Jessica and Tara. When Jessica had joined the Bitches of Power, Suzanne had responded by moving her whole family to a horse farm in Idaho.

"How's Jessica doing?" I asked. His daughter Jessica, fourteen, was a tall, pretty girl with shiny blond hair and her father's black brows.

"I hear she's part of the Mexican underground," he said. "She skips school, she runs away. Suzanne says she threatened her with a knife."

"With a *knife*?"

"Yes. Guess moving the kid doesn't work."

"At least not when the family moves, too," I said.

"We're talking about making her a ward of the state."

"You can't do that, Shannon. She's your *daughter*."

"Those Mexicans she hangs out with could come and kill the whole family. Especially since Suzanne has been calling the police on them."

"Oh, God, I'm so sorry."

"Shit happens," my brother rumbled. "Some kids go bad, and she's one of them."

I walked around my office with the cordless phone, agitated. "Don't you think that's an extreme statement?" I said.

"No, I don't," he said. "When I talk to Jessica, she seems very far away. She's not the child she was."

I paused. "Aren't you afraid for her?" I asked.

"What can I do?" he answered. "I told Suzanne I wanted Jessie to move back here with me. But Suzanne won't let her."

I remembered when Shannon had come late to the family Thanksgiving, bustling in with his jacket on and a big grin on his face, to announce he was the father of a baby girl. He looked so happy, standing in the doorway, his guitar in his hand, clutching a Polaroid of the baby.

"Send her to me," I blurted impulsively.

Shannon barked out a laugh. "That'd be sending her from the frying pan into the fire."

I put the phone down. Running away. That was the deepest of my fears: Morgan living on the streets, in San Francisco or Seattle or New York, cadging change on the sidewalk, sleeping in the park. It was the unseen horror behind that haunted me, stayed my tongue when I was furious and shaking: she might run away.

When I told Morgan over the phone what Shannon had said about Jessica, Morgan gave a motherly sigh. She wanted Jessica's number so she could call her up and counsel her. "I made all those mistakes when I was younger," she said, from the lofty perspective of fifteen looking back at fourteen.

"WE can do that thing we do," said Bill, standing in front of me wiping the frying pan with a paper towel and tilting his eyebrows toward the bedroom. He had started whistling around the house again. He'd even offered to take me dancing.

I looked at him and had an inspiration. "Let's join the Mile-High Club, and do it in Tahoe."

Patrick had gone to South Dakota on vacation with his dad. Morgan was canoeing around a lake with my sister in Idaho. We asked a neighbor kid to look after the dog and the cat, threw books and bathing suits in the car, and five hours later had arrived at the mountain lake we went to every summer.

"Hey, lady, cute butt!" Bill yelled. We were on the cement bike trail that hugs the lake for eleven miles on Highway 89, a path that gives you a fresh blast of blue lake and snow-capped mountain peaks every time you come around a corner. Bill waited for me at the top of a rise. He smiled from under his white Giants hat. "You sure are slow," he said. "If you weren't so cute I'd have to shit-can you."

"I'm just staying with you until somebody better comes along anyway," I answered. Huge mounds of snow covered with dirt sent rivulets running across the concrete path, mud up our back tires and the backs of our T-shirts. Pine needles crunched noisily under our tires.

I hadn't felt so happy in a long time. Mickey had confirmed my deepest feeling about family: that when you were desperate, they would help. That family came first.

It's what my mother taught me. A couple of us and a couple of neighbor kids had lugged a pitcher of cherry Kool-Aid down the road to sell at our stand, a sheet of plywood over two sawhorses. Shannon knocked it over, staining the ground and our shoes red with Kool-Aid, and we all started cuffing him.

All of a sudden there was Mother rushing down the path in her jean skirt, her curly black hair flying out behind her. "He's your brother!" she cried, pulling us off Shannon.

We stepped back, shamefaced. Shannon stood as if he were hanging from a peg, his shoulders hunched, already starting to grin at his release. "He's your *brother*," Mother said again, more softly.

At the end of the ride, Bill and I had a margarita at the Tahoe Lakeview, arguing over whether the lake with its forty shades of blue was prettier in the open or framed through trees. Then we wobbled home on the dark path to the Tahoe Cedars Lodge, the lakeside cottage we always stayed at, to make love under the thin orange blankets.

The Norplant had been out of my system for three months, so I could get pregnant any time. "I've been dreaming of a little boy with soft brown hair, a tiny Patrick," Bill confided sleepily as we lay still plastered to each other in the darkened room. "I keep having this daydream where I whip out my wallet and show pictures of my son."

On the morning of our third day we woke to find a note shoved under the curved iron handle of our room door. It was from Dorothy, the owner of the resort: "Your sister says to please call her."

I had four sisters, but I knew it was Mickey. I'd left her our number, in case of emergency.

I called her back from the phone booth across the road.

"I'm sending Morgan back to you," Mickey said without preamble.

"She's only been up there a week," I said, stunned. I was looking at Bill as I spoke. He was staring away from me, at the road, but I could tell from the stiff set of his head that he had heard. "Why?"

"I don't like to leave her home with Larry when I go to work." Larry was Mickey's husband, a handsome blue-eyed Indian who stayed home on disability because of a nerve disease. "She's careless about the way she dresses and undresses in front of people." Mickey's mind was made up. I was too furious to argue.

I hung up the phone, missing the cradle on the first try. The harsh sun glinted off the metal of the phone booth.

"I don't know if I can do it." Bill spoke into the silence. A couple passed us, their blond little boy wobbling on his bike ahead of them.

"Do what?"

"Live with the noise, and the upset. I don't know if I can stand to come into the bedroom and see you crying on your pillow anymore."

"She's getting older," I said miserably, staring at a blur of trees. "She'll grow out of it." We didn't look at each other.

"Fifteen. She's still only fifteen."

We packed up and drove home, not even turning on our book tape to hear the second half of *Emma*.

BILL was edgy all the rest of the week. He threw away the envelope Morgan's Driver Education slip was in, tossed the newspaper clippings I wanted to save in with the recycled papers, warned me about ink stains when I sat on the couch to read the newspaper. "Don't make holes in the wall," he grumbled at his stepson when Patrick wanted to hang his freshman picture on the wall of the kitchen. He went for long, punishing bike rides and arrived home dripping with sweat.

Morgan came back at the end of June. She seemed glad to be home. "There's nothing to do in Idaho," she said. She had a new

burn on her leg from riding on the back of Mickey's Harley motorcycle. I found ointment for it, my anger at my sister growing with
each careful swab. "Why didn't Mickey take you to the doctor when
this happened?" I said. "You're going to have a scar."

I felt wrung out, used up. It had been three years so far: three years
of waking early in the morning, wrestling with my fears, my dis-
couragement, and my disappointment.

Three years of mistakes–mine and hers. How I had sent her upstairs for talking on the phone all night when she was supposed to
be studying for a Spanish test–and how, stung, she had run off to a
friend's instead.

How, one Mother's Day, she had spelled out "I love you Mom" in
flowers in the grass across the street. I gazed on them blearily, trying
to manage a smile, though I was still wiped out from a sleepless
night–she had not come home the night before.

Even when I thought I was picking my battles, I was doing no
such thing. I'd explode over something as minor as on what surface
she did her homework, and buried in the back of my mind far more
worrying incidents–empty bottles found in drawers, her sleeping in
the afternoon. I had started out as a buddy mom and evolved
painfully into a more parental one, but I had never found my balance. I had flipped out, as Morgan herself would say, over every little thing. Now, when real trouble had arrived, when we were way
beyond homework hours and cheating on tests, I had nothing left.

My reactions now felt, even to myself, strangely muted, as if I was
underwater. Morgan had planned to be in Idaho, so she had no summer job and had not signed up for summer school. She was seldom
home. Kids I didn't know left angry messages, and one painted "fuck
Morgan" on the side of our house. Jim went right out with a can of
paint and stood there painting it out, his mouth set in a line. He and
Morgan hardly spoke anymore.

For two days she had refused to leave the house. "People are trying
to get me," she said. She talked about going to live with someone

named Victor in South San Francisco, and dropping out to go to cosmetology school.

She had begun to see the teen shrink I had found for her, and liked him, but she wouldn't say what went on there, and nothing changed.

Bill had a standing joke. When a friend mentioned teenagers, he would say, "I have two words for you: boarding school." I never thought it was that funny.

I was dismayed by the English habit of sending kids away to school. Why have them, then? A child is someone you have to touch, to smell their hair, to lean over as they struggle with homework. Not someone whose handwriting you recognize as you flip through your mail.

Yet this was the scene three weeks later: Morgan, in ragged jean shorts and black tank top, was close behind me as I followed a woman in skirts down a forest path. It was July. We were dogging the footsteps of the principal of the John Woolman School, a Quaker boarding school in Nevada City.

A kid with purple hair who was etching a design in a wet clay pot nodded at us in one of the low redwood buildings scattered around the leafy hill. It was more like a campground than a school. "It's a working farm," said the principal over her shoulder. "The kids have jobs here, everybody pitches in." A little later, we looked over the fence at the cows the kids help milk. Morgan glanced at them politely. As she stood at the fence, I could see the livid red scar from Mickey's motorcycle.

"We stress personal honesty, integrity, working with others, and academic achievement," said the principal. "Ninety-five percent of our graduates go on to college."

Before they did that, though, they came to live here.

. . .

AFTER the tour, we got back in the car and headed home down the freeway. Morgan's face was rosy with the heat. Neither of us likes air-conditioning, so the windows were open to the torrid breeze.

"What did you think of the school?" I asked.

"It was pretty cool, I guess," she said. "The kids seemed kind of dorky." She reached forward to fiddle with the radio buttons.

"I want you to go there," I said. I caught sight of my flushed face in the rearview mirror.

"I don't want to talk about it."

"Morgan, take a couple of days, think about it."

"I don't want to talk about it! I know I can go there, and I know I can not go there. I'll think about it, but I do not want you talking to me about it. At all. It just makes me mad."

"I'm going to send your application in on Monday." I said it as firmly as I knew how.

Morgan's face was in her arms. All I could see was a bare brown shoulder. It was shaking. "Mom!" she said in a strangled voice. "Why are you saying that! I don't want to live away from you!"

An exit to Marysville came up, and I left the freeway. I pulled into the first gas station I saw, and parked by the water hoses.

"I thought that when you said you'd come look at the school, it meant you would consider going," I faltered. A man in a tank top pumping gas looked over at us, two women just sitting in a car. Her sobs wracked me, confused me. I put my hand on her back, but she quivered under my touch, and I took it away.

"I just wanted to spend the day with you!" Morgan cried. "I didn't care where we were going!"

Silence. Then her voice. "Do you really want me to go there?"

I pulled onto the road. I was supposed to harden my heart, say, "Well, you're going, and that's final."

"Of course you don't have to go if you don't want to," I said. "God, I would miss you so much if you went away."

• • •

THAT'S what she heard me say, but I had also driven her to the airport to catch the plane to Idaho, and to a boarding school in the hills. In early August she arranged to go live with my sister Robin and her two kids across the Golden Gate Bridge in Marin County. She'd enroll at Redwood High, a suburban school out on the marshy land between Robin's house and the 101 freeway. You could enroll in the district if you were staying with a close relative. Robin's husband, Rick, had moved out of their apartment overlooking a canal in Larkspur. Her daughter Katie, ten, would give up her room for Morgan and bunk with her brother Tony, nine.

I had not arranged it myself, but I was so relieved that Morgan would be safe in Marin. I would not give her new number to any of the city kids who called.

On her last night at home in early August, Morgan was slamming her laundry around. When she let the plastic basket fall to the floor with a loud whack, I looked over from her closet, where I was pulling clothes off the floor and folding them into a box. "I don't want you to go," I said. "We're just trying this."

"I'm still mad at you about the boarding school," she said. "It feels as if you just don't want me here."

Her words stabbed at me. As the Robert Frost poem has it, home is where when you go there, they have to take you in. How must it feel, to walk around in your own house, and see yourself reflected in your own parents' eyes as a kid no one wanted? No wonder she was scrambling to find shelter elsewhere.

WHEN Bill and Patrick and I arrived at Robin's on our first visit, we found Morgan out on the deck overlooking the canal, painting little clay pots to line the window of her room, which used to be Katie's room. She proudly showed me the room, with her lingerie neatly arranged in a laundry basket looted from my house. She showed me a flowered print dress she'd found in a secondhand shop down the street. "I'm worried Dad will like it," she said seriously as she modeled it for me. Her dad's taste in dresses came from his childhood in South Dakota in the thirties.

"Are you happy here?" I asked. The room was about half the size of her room at home, the one we'd turned over to Patrick.

"Yes, Mom, Robin's great."

"She even cleaned the house for me a couple of times," Robin shouted. She was in the little bathroom, painting the walls bright red. "She's a wonderful kid. It's fun having her here."

I watched Robin slap red paint on the pipe behind the toilet with such force that paint splattered on the linoleum floor. "What's the matter?" I said, watching her slap at the pipe.

"It's Rick. We're getting a divorce."

"Oh, Robbie," I said.

"And he doesn't want me to work at the bar anymore."

"I'm so sorry to hear that," I told her.

Robin and Rick had been having trouble for some time, but it was especially a shame about the bar. The year before, Rick had bought the Silver Peso—a sixty-year-old Marin County biker dive, with two pool tables, a scuffed old shuffleboard, and, over by one wall, the piano that Janis Joplin used to play. I went in once and there Robin was behind the bar, bartender's apron over her black jeans, her blond hair whipping around, yelling at Rick that somebody's Harley was blocked in. Her kids knocked at the back door, and a big old tattooed guy said, "Robin, your kids want you."

She was thirty. She'd been a deli manager, a salesman for the electronics store called Good Guys, a daytime bartender, a dog groomer, a waitress at Denny's, you name it, without knowing where any of it was leading. And then she was a manager, in charge and in love with the job.

"Can't you go on being the manager?" I asked now. I felt a purely selfish alarm—I wanted to ask, But things here won't change, will they? She can still stay?

"No, he wants me out," Rob said, wiping the floor with a cloth. She was silent a minute, painting, then said, "One thing about Morgan."

"What?"

"She's great. Don't get me wrong. She's great. But we were sitting on that little boat out on the canal, and she had that bathing suit on, and sat in Tim's lap, writhing all over him."

"Who's Tim?" I was confused.

"This guy I've been seeing. He's a butcher at Safeway."

Morgan came into the bathroom. "What are you guys talking about?"

"About you," Robin said. "We have to have a talk about those breasts of yours."

"What do you mean?" Morgan said.

"I was telling your mom what happened out in the boat yesterday. This provocative behavior is going to get you raped someday, and it's pissing me off, and you don't want to do that," Robin said, putting her paintbrush down on the newspaper and looking up at Morgan.

Morgan turned abruptly and went into her room. I followed her and patted her back as she sobbed on her bed. "Robin doesn't mean it," I said. "Robin loves you. You know that."

"I can't help it if I have big breasts," she sobbed. "How can I help that, Mom?"

BY September Morgan had settled in at her new school. "I want to start a girls' football team," Morgan informed the principal, though she'd never played the game or shown any interest in it. She even got a job at an employment office, working in its Jobs for Youths program. She made $5.25 an hour, thirty hours a week. She was counting her hours, saying, okay, that's $5.25 times thirty they owe me, okay, $157.50. I remarked that of course she wouldn't *get* all of that. While she listened in utter disbelief, I explained about taxes.

• • •

Robin said Morgan was doing fine, she was a doll. Then I started to get calls from her. "We all think that Bill must have given you some sort of ultimatum, him or her, and that's why she can't come home," she said one day.

I slammed the phone down. My chest hurt. I called Adrian in Ukiah. A day later, she called back. "I talked to Robin," she said. "She didn't mean that. She's having a tough time with the divorce."

Next day my mother called.

"Well, Robin and the gang are all going to Marine World today," Mother said. "That should keep her out of trouble at least for the day," she added lightly.

I was silent.

"Dare?"

I had control of myself again. "If anybody makes a joke, or makes even one comment about this, I'll break off relations with the whole family."

"I'm sorry, Adair," my mother said, a trifle crisply. "But you kids carry on as if no one had a teenager before. I had seven at one time, and I did fine. Is it true, by the way, that Morgan was in a stolen car? Why would you let her do such a thing?"

"I didn't 'let her,'" I said fiercely. "I just didn't know how to stop her."

"Well," mother said, backing away from the edge in my voice, "I don't know what's going on. But you must realize you spoiled that girl."

"I did not!" I raged. "And if I did, so what! What does that have to do with anything?"

"Well," Mother said, "calm down. Try not to worry so much. Most kids are all right in the end."

Instead of taking offense, she was soothing me. I seemed to get on better with the family when I was like this, my defenses down, not an idea in the world of what to do next.

Next day Shannon called. "I heard all about it from Robin," he said from his office at the Rafael Lumber Company. "She's not mad anymore, Dare."

Robin was not mad anymore, but I was. It had occurred to me that Robin had never really thanked me for the outgrown clothes of Morgan's and Patrick's that I'd heaped on her since her kids were born. As I put the phone down, I felt tired of my whole family. I felt myself closing down to them, as I would on anyone who accused me of choosing my husband over my child.

Yet even as I told myself this, I noticed that the family I was backing off from had joined hands around me. The phone was ringing in every house, from San Francisco to Ukiah, as everyone joined in, determined to heal the breach. It was as if an organism was growing new skin over an injured part, protecting it.

It was peaceful at home. Patrick moved into Morgan's room. We could go to bed without taking the phone off the hook. I could lie in bed without starting at every sound, wondering where Morgan was, thinking up ways to trick her into letting us know what time she got in.

In September Morgan called me, crying, from a phone booth, saying she'd come home after her midnight curfew and Robin had locked her out. I drove over and brought her home for the night. That weekend she and I went to look at a funky apartment behind College of Marin. A spacey young woman named Paula was looking for a roommate.

Then I came to my senses. An *apartment*? She was only fifteen.

Two weeks later, Robin accused Morgan of sipping secretly at her liquor bottles. "The level in each bottle is down at least an inch," she said. "Who else can it be?"

"It wasn't me!" Morgan cried when I asked her about it.

"It wasn't Morgan," I told Robin angrily. I refused to believe that it was until someone could prove it to me. Much later, we learned it had been Tim, Robin's butcher friend. He was fired for drinking on the job.

In October, three months after Morgan had moved in, Robin called me up. "I can't do this, Adair," she said. "I can't raise your teenager for you. It's not my time to do this yet."

"She was a teenager when she moved in," I pointed out stiffly. "What's changed?"

"She just can't stay here. Morgan's very large, you know. She takes up the whole room. I'm large, too, so I thought I could do this. But I can't."

I went home and started searching my files of student writers, looking for Marin addresses, and start calling them all. Morgan said she wanted to stay in Marin and keep going to Redwood.

I had heard that you should gauge your teenager's future self not by how he behaves at home but by how he behaves away from home. Without Mom in the room to rebel against, his grown-up self emerges, like a flower that blooms only in certain light.

Was this Morgan's grown-up self, this child no one could stand to have around for long?

chapter 11

T HAT'S a red light ahead, take your foot off the pedal and slow down!" I screamed when we took the Corte Madera exit off 101. Morgan was at the wheel.

My insurance company had sent me a Parent-Teen Training Aid. It said, "Avoid using the word 'stop' because it often panics a beginning driver. Say instead, 'Bring your car to a stop.' "

"Bring your car to a stop," I said as the red light loomed in front of us. I was jittery, but I was also happy: this was ordinary mom stuff, teaching my child to drive. And she had to listen.

"What?"

"*Stop!*"

We were driving Bill's old 1985 Dodge Colt. It was a good little car for a teenager--automatic, a quiet mauve color, drew no attention to itself.

After years of making do without a car, Bill had bought the Colt so he'd have a way to get up to his parents' house, fifty miles north in Santa Rosa. The route from our door to his parents' door was almost the only one he drove flawlessly, piloting the little car through a series of exits and cutovers until he arrived at the neat adult community in the valley of the moon, and his smiling parents hurried out to meet him.

"I've decided I'm going to be a safe teen driver," Morgan said.

"You are?"

"Yes. Because nobody expects me to. It's annoying."

I glanced over at her. "I miss you, baby," I said. "I don't know where you are half the time."

"Call Susan. She always knows where I am." Susan was one of my writing students. She and her husband, Harvey, had agreed to rent their backyard studio in Corte Madera to Morgan. Morgan would earn extra money for herself by baby-sitting for their two little girls.

"I know she does," I said. But I didn't want to call another woman to find out where my child was. I didn't even want the other woman to *know* that I don't know where my child was. It was logical for Susan to know—Morgan was staying with her, not with me. But that didn't help.

The car swerved, and I grabbed the dashboard. "You have to persuade us that Bill giving you this car is a good idea, by being responsible."

"I'm taking the car down to Santa Cruz next weekend," she answered.

"No, you aren't. In fact I'm marking down the mileage on the odometer," I said, jerking sideways as we scraped by a Pathfinder.

Morgan was chattering, feeling around her seat for a dropped cassette. She changed lanes to avoid a Jeep Cherokee and landed right behind a red Honda Civic. We might as well have been in its backseat. I could have reached out and fiddled with its radio.

"Mom, you have to stop this," Morgan said, tapping the brakes.

"Stop what?"

"Stop sucking in your breath like that."

A car veered near us, and I held my breath. Morgan stabbed at the radio, in a vain effort to drown out my panicky sounds.

"I'm going to install one of those toy baby steering wheels with a horn for you on that side of the car," Morgan said.

"I'm going to need some toy brakes, too," I said.

When we arrived and ran in the rain across the sodden lawn that separated Morgan's little studio from the main house, the room smelled of burned candles. Morgan's futon lay against one wall, covered with clothes and jackets and schoolbooks.

Our plan was to work on the paper for her Shakespeare class. I couldn't read her scrawled draft, so she read it to me while I typed. She wore a wrinkled white Gap shirt and blue Gap pants and was walking in a circle, kicking at the clothes in her path as if she were walking through piles of autumn leaves.

"Titania and Oberon restored their passions," she read aloud to me.

"They rediscovered their love for each other," I typed.

"Hey!" she said, coming over to read over my shoulder. "You changed it."

"It's better this way," I said. "Restored doesn't work with passions."

"Okay, fine," she said, and continued her dictation. After a while she quit dictating, but I kept on writing. I had spent the week reading the play and was eager to set down my impressions. The phone rang, and Morgan answered it. "Oh, hi, Margo," I heard her say. Margo was her new friend. They bombed around Marin in Margo's station wagon, often ending up at Denny's. "My mom's here. She won't let me write my own paper."

"I'll let you take over when I finish the paragraph I'm on," I shouted, and kept typing. Morgan dictated another paragraph. Then she said, "Do you mind if I pick up my room while we work?"

"Yes," I said, my eyes on the screen.

I was typing on the seven-hundred-dollar Mac computer her dad had bought for the express purpose of getting these papers for Shakespeare class done.

"I have to run to the bathroom," she said. "Be right back."

While she was gone, I just sat there, thinking. Though I'd had several months now to get used to it, it was weird having her gone from the house. I couldn't drive or comb my hair or read the new *New Yorker* without being aware of the strangeness of it, my daughter living somewhere else. I couldn't leave my eye shadow on the bathroom sink without worrying about her making off with it–and then remembering.

Yet so much had improved. Redwood was easier than Lowell, and both her attendance and her grades were better. I myself had become a sort of favorite visiting aunt.

I had talked to Robin on the phone again that morning, and her words reverberated through my head. "She should be home with you!" she'd urged. "Think of how much you're missing!"

Remembering, I felt my stomach clench. Of course she should be home with me.

But when she came home, even for a night, she'd start making calls frantically to her friends. "Hi, Sarah? What are you doing tonight? Oh, okay . . . Do you have Kiley's number . . . Kiley! Hey, do you want to . . ." She'd still be calling at nine, or nine-thirty.

"Stay home with us," I'd plead from the couch where Patrick and I were watching TV.

"I can't," she said. "I hate this house." The doorbell would ring, strange kids would appear in the hall, and she'd be moving past the red couch in the TV room, blue hood drawn over her hair. And though she promised to be back at ten, I'd lie awake until all hours, waiting for the series of clunks–boots hitting floor, followed by backpack–that told me she was back in the house.

The cottage was so cold that I was typing with my jacket on. I could see my breath. The space heater I had insisted Susan bring in the last time I was here was back locked in her office, a room off the cottage. The case of lemon-lime soda I had brought lay against the wall. It doesn't need refrigeration, I thought sourly. You could hang meat in this room.

I glanced around. Morgan's junk was strewn everywhere, though her work clothes for her new weekend job at the Gap were folded neatly on a special shelf. Several melted candles stood in the middle

of the floor. Harvey had been grouching at her about leaving cigarette butts in the room ("He sounds just like Dad, Mom!"). She said
he sometimes went in during the day to open her windows and air
out the already cold room.

"How can we get her to keep her room clean?" Susan had called
me to ask. "Harvey is going nuts about it."

Susan called me often. Once she reported with distress that her
little girls no longer wanted to stay with Morgan: she had at least
twice left them in the house while she went to the cottage, giving
them her number but telling them not to call unless it was important. "I don't feel as if I can trust her with anything. It's like, do I
have to tell her that if the kids are bleeding, call the doctor?"

Once she said she'd caught Morgan and her friends smoking in
the cottage. "You know what this feels like?" Susan said to me. "It
feels like, screw you."

Later she gathered up all of Morgan's incense and candles and
hid them. Morgan was now forbidden to light a match anywhere on
the property.

Sometimes Morgan was scheduled to work at the Gap the same
day she had promised to baby-sit for Susan and Harvey. At least once
Susan had locked her out of the house, and Morgan had called me,
crying because she couldn't change her clothes for her shift at the
Gap.

Harvey had got on the phone once, though Susan tried to stop
him, and began sputtering at me about the smoking. "There should
be consequences!" he said. At my suggestion they'd given her a curfew of midnight. Morgan had called them at midnight the night before, with a story about sleeping over at Jasmine's, and then had not
shown up at home until eleven the next morning.

I listened to him, and made soothing noises. Harvey had a solution ready, as Jim always did, and it was usually about our putting
our foot down, as Jim's tended to be. I remembered that stage, when
you still thought grounding them would help. I asked to talk to
Susan again. I was remembering it as though from a comfortable

distance, looking back to those long-ago days when I, too, had been a difficult teenager.

"I admire you," I told Susan. "At least you *know* you don't know how to do it." I meant, deal with a teenager. I was sincere. I admired her for asking for help with "her" teenager. I was happy to offer advice. "She wants rides to school with you," I pointed out. Susan lived four miles from Redwood High School. "Make her a deal. A clean room gets her a ride."

"Do you get lonesome?" I said to Morgan when she came back from the bathroom. I stretched. The unfamiliar computer was giving me a kink in my neck.

"Yes, kind of," she answered. She had fallen back into her bed amid the disordered blankets. "Susan and Harvey turn out the lights and go to bed at, like, eight o'clock. I stay out here. I pee in the yard rather than go in the house to do it."

"How about food?" I asked. I was paying for room and board.

"I've been asked not to eat the leftovers. Susan says she plans meals with them."

I felt so sad--and so furious at Susan--that I had to hurry briskly along, try not to think about it, my child peeing in the dark behind the darkened house.

"What do you eat, then?" I made myself ask.

"I cook something for myself, or Margo and I go over to Denny's," she said. "And Daddy brings me lasagna when he comes."

A 4 Non Blondes song came on her boom box, one she used to play every morning at home while getting ready for school, Linda Perry singing "What's Up." "Twenty-five years of my life and still . . ." Morgan and I both jumped up, and we did one of our slow dances to it, swaying in the middle of the floor. I held her tight as I could, as if I was drawing strength from the feel of her against me. She held tight, too, and we danced to the end of the song. We were exactly the same height.

I remembered when she was a baby and had started crying miser-ably for hours at night. One of my childcare books said it was mostly nervous first-time moms who had colicky babies. Reassured, I put the "Beer Barrel Polka" on the stereo and waltzed her gently around the attic room, in and out of the shadows thrown by the recessed light-ing. I was holding her tight under my chin, but still relaxing my arms.

"This is you, not me," I had crooned to her. "I'm not upset about this at all, myself. We're just dancing." Then off we'd whirl again, be-hind the desk, past the bookshelves, along the hallway. Her colic dis-appeared that night and never came back.

Now I felt my whole body relax as we danced, the song we both loved connecting us. I relaxed my arms and buried my head in her shoulder. The room fell away, and there I was, dancing with my baby.

I WAS hanging a red ball on the tree, trying to get it to hang right. Morgan had to work at the Gap, and so was missing the tree deco-rating for the first time. I was wearing a present she had made me open early, a pair of earrings that were tiny pictures of Shetland sheepdogs.

The blue flames of a three-hour Presto log flickered in our tiny marble fireplace. Patrick had just moved his old school-made orna-ment—a red Santa made from an empty toilet paper roll—from the back to the front of the tree. Bill was in the middle of what I thought of as the Annual Cursing of the Christmas Lights, and had stomped down to the corner drugstore to get some that worked. The phone rang, and Patrick found it under the collapsing cardboard box of or-naments. "It's Susan," Patrick said, handing me the white cordless phone. "Her voice sounds funny."

"Adair, this is not working for me," Susan said, her voice pitched high.

I walked into another room, my hand over my ear to shut out "I Saw Mommy Kissing Santa Claus" coming from Bill's old 70s stereo.

"What do you mean?" I asked. Her tone scared me.

"Morgan is not the person she represented herself to be."

"What did she do?" I didn't add, "now."

"A girl spent the night, and she didn't clear it with me. She wasn't straight with me about the smoke in her cottage last week, and there are half-open soda cans all over the place. And she doesn't even know her schedule at the Gap. I can't depend on her as a baby-sitter."

"I'm sorry, Susan," I said. I felt guilty, as I nearly always did talking to Susan. I had shifted the burden of raising my rambunctious teenager onto an innocent near-stranger. "I'll talk to her," I said.

"I want her to move out. By January first."

Before I could answer, a voice broke in. "This is the operator. Will you take an emergency call from Morgan?"

"I'm sorry, Susan," I said. "I'll call you back."

"I hate Susan," Morgan sobbed into my ear. "She's mean to me all the time now."

"I'm sorry, sweetie. It doesn't sound as if the two of you are getting along very well." I was apologizing to everybody tonight. "She said something about ending this arrangement pretty soon."

"I don't want to stay here anyway, Mom," Morgan said. "I want to live with someone who loves me."

My heart contracted in my chest. "I love you, sweetie," I said. I felt my arms lift so I could put them around her, but she was twenty miles away. "Come home."

"I don't want to live in the city," she said. "I wasn't happy there. Besides, I like my school here."

We were silent a moment. "Well, we'll figure out something," I said.

The next day Shannon, who lived in San Rafael, said he had an extra bedroom she could use. He lived in a different school district, but she could drive there in the Dodge Colt. I was grateful to him, and prayed it would work out: sooner or later, even I would run out of siblings.

When we moved Morgan's stacks of clothes on hangers, her

portable fridge and futon and half-melted candles out of the cottage, putting them into the station wagon for the ride over to Shannon's house, Susan hugged me good-bye. "You have my sympathy," she whispered. I froze, and stepped back from her. I had allowed her to criticize Morgan while Morgan was under her roof, but with the last box we carried out of that cottage, her Morgan-bashing privileges ended.

"WHAT did you get on your *Midsummer Night's Dream* paper?" I asked her one day as we were taking the tree down.

"I couldn't get it to print out," she said.

"What's the matter with the printer Dad gave you?"

"It's still in the box. I haven't had time to hook it up."

I felt like a chump. "Your dad bought you a computer and I practically wrote the paper for you," I said. "All you had to do was get it to school."

"I'm sorry, Mom. I'm doing the best I can."

As I went on taking off ornaments, I kept thinking of a children's book I had seen called *Mama Will You Love Me?* In it, an Eskimo child asks her mama if she will love her always. "Even if I drop the ptarmigan eggs?" says the child. "Even if you drop the ptarmigan eggs," promises her mother. Even if she puts salmon in her parka, or runs away and sings with the wolves in a cave. "What if I turned into a polar bear and I was the meanest bear you ever saw?"

"I will love you."

Morgan seemed to be asking me the same questions. Mama, will you love me if I dye my hair purple/eat too many curly fries/sneak out/start smoking/lie to you/get arrested/wear out my welcome in every new place you send me?

The answer, of course, is yes, I will love you.

But I won't always *like* you.

• • •

Iт had rained all through Christmas vacation, and we'd all been cooped up for days. When Patrick begged to be taken snowboarding, I showed him a newspaper photo of a car stuck up to its windows in snow. "It says *blizzard*," I said again. "The Highway Patrol says to stay away from Tahoe unless you want to get stuck." I'd already had to buy a new iron after Patrick melted the wax off his snowboard with the old one (and I ironed my new blouse with it before noticing).

"The roads are closed, and winds are gusting up to one hundred miles an hour," Morgan shouted from the TV room, her eyes on the newscast where a man was pointing soberly to the Pacific Ocean and drawing circles.

"Let's just go up and see," Patrick pleaded. He had hounded me into letting him open his big present of snowboarding boots a week early, but this would be his first chance to try them out.

I looked at Patrick's face, closed and still, braced against disappointment.

"We're going," I said, clicking off the TV. "Bed, bed, bed! We're leaving at five in the morning."

"And you're coming with us," I said to Morgan. She'd always managed to get out of coming with Patrick and me on our trips to the snow. "I want you to come, and so does Patrick." I looked at Patrick, but he said nothing. He was wary around Morgan now, as a child is around a dog that has been known to bite.

"All right, Mom," Morgan said.

"Want to come, Billy?" I asked Bill, though I knew he didn't like to ski and had so far resisted every entreaty to come to the snow with Patrick and me.

"No, you three go. I'll stay here and finish taking down the tree, then go see my parents."

By six-thirty we were on the empty freeway in a car crammed with mismatched skiwear, headed across the sleeping state to the Kirkwood ski resort, which is an hour south of Lake Tahoe. At first it was dark and the kids were quiet. Stars appeared as we headed into the country, and then the growing light of dawn. Miraculously, the weather had cleared.

Half of the backseat of my little Toyota folded down, so we had been able to bring both Patrick's snowboard and my dingy pair of cast-off rental skis. As the sun began to rise we were passing apple and peach orchards, and the light slanted through the fruit trees in the morning mist. It cast a red glow on Patrick's face where he sat squashed in next to the equipment, *Snowboarding* magazine open on his lap. He had a subscription, and read it even in the summer.

"I'm starving," Morgan said from her place in the seat next to me. "Can't we stop for breakfast? Look, there's a Denny's!"

"We just got on the road," I said. "Why didn't you have a bowl of cereal, like Patrick?"

"I hate cereal," she grumbled. She slipped a tape in the cassette player, and rap music filled the car. Patrick's head snapped up from his magazine. "Morgan!" he yelled. "Turn it off!"

"It's Snoop Doggy Dogg," she said. "I want to listen to it."

"I'm reading!"

I turned my blinker on, pulled over, and switched off the engine. "Hey! Why are we stopping?" the kids asked.

I didn't answer. We sat there in silence a minute. Cars swooshed by on the freeway. The sky to the east cast a reddish glow.

"Okay, Mom, let's go," Morgan said. "We won't fight."

I started the engine. "And if you do, we agree that it means you want to hear my English poetry tape all the rest of the way to the snow?"

"We know, Mom."

I gave them each a 7UP and a bagel, and pulled onto the freeway. I switched off my headlights.

"I had a dream that I had become a psychiatrist," Patrick said.

"You'd be a good one," I observed over my shoulder. "You've always been empathetic."

"I'm empathetic!" Morgan protested next to me. "All my friends agree I'm the most empathetic person they know." She was wearing her blue pajamas with clouds floating on them but had promised to change in the car.

"You're good with your hands," I told her.

Patrick said to me, "I'm making you a cup in ceramics," adding, "only it's a little messed up."

"I hope you're making me a small engine in your small engine maintenance class," I joked to Morgan.

The miles sped by. I told them stories of when they were babies. Patrick liked to hear how he refused to eat a cookie if it was broken, and how he had said firmly, at age two, "I have a boy's round hand, and a boy's round face."

"You were fearless," I said to Morgan. "You always went right to the top of the jungle gym. I loved it, but it scared me." She smiled, pleased.

"I might be getting a D in math," Patrick said.

"I wish you would go for help at the Math Center," I said mildly. "That's what it's for."

"The Math Center's for nerds," he grumbled.

"Don't tell them you're my brother," Morgan said.

"I've been thinking a lot about Joe Foley," Patrick said. Joe was a boy in his ceramics class who had died suddenly of a heart attack. He'd had a congenital heart defect. "He was a good friend of mine, Mom," he said. I was glad to hear him talk about it. I had found a red ceramic jug hidden in Patrick's drawer. Letters scratched in the bottom said, "This project is dedicated to Joe. I will see you in Ireland/Heaven."

Morgan listened quietly as the first snow-covered mountains loomed in the windshield. "I've decided I can get my GED early and take classes at College of Marin, Mom," she said when Patrick had finished talking about Joe.

"Out of the question," I said. "You're going through high school, not around it." Somehow being in the car made this a friendly exchange, though my arms had tightened on the wheel.

For years the three of us had driven to my mother's pool on

Sundays. The rule was that, on Sundays, none of the three of us was allowed to bring a friend. If the kids brought friends they all sat in the back and talked to each other, and all I heard was the occasional remark floating over the seat: What's your mother's name? Is that her real hair color? Doesn't she have a boyfriend or anything?

When it was just the three of us, we talked about important stuff, like whether we'd rather be eaten by a shark or stabbed to death, and whether you could lick a whole car in a day. Patrick would confide his plan to have a stuffed-bear factory when he grew up, so he never ran out of toys, and Morgan would say she wanted to be a writer and an actress and in retail sales. Practically everything important I know about my kids is something they told me in the car.

I remember driving with my own mother. I was thrilled to be up front with her, sitting beside her, instead of squashed in the back with my six brothers and sisters, watching the back of her head. She always asked for two dollars worth of regular. Coke cans rolled at our feet, and the upholstery smelled of the sun coming through the windows. I was usually being driven to the dentist, but she'd tell me of her dreams to have a house on a hillside, with a south-facing kitchen, and I'd tell her my dreams of being a writer.

At Kirkwood, Patrick took off by himself to snowboard on a higher hill. "I'll teach you myself," I told Morgan. I rented a pair of skis for her and showed her how to snowplow with me over to the nearest chairlift, trying to remember what I had learned in my intermediate lesson the year before. "Stand into the turn, weight on the downhill ski."

The chairlift led, we found out at the top, to an intermediate slope. "Just follow me," I said, and for a while she did exactly that, following me in wide turns down the hill. She fell twice, getting right back up and taking off again.

Then the blob of purple that was her knit hat was shooting past me. "Wait!" I cried. "I haven't shown you yet how to stand up in the turns . . ." She was skiing straight downhill, holding her poles awkwardly, then more confidently and began making wide turns as if she'd been doing it all her life.

After a while Morgan and I skied and snowplowed to another slope to find Patrick, who was Joe Cool on the snowboard in a flannel shirt. I watched him sway down a slope, as graceful as a sea lion slipping into the water. His pants were big enough for two. Next to him I looked loaded down, with my Gore-Tex jacket and poles and the two long sticks on my feet.

Patrick swooshed up to where we were standing, his board kicking up spray.

"How're the new boots?" I asked.

"Perfect, Mom," he said in his new, deeper voice. "This is the most fun I've ever had in my life."

"I want to do that, too," Morgan said, watching enviously as he unstrapped one foot and dragged his board behind him back over to the lift line.

After only two hours on skis, Morgan no longer fell at all. "You're what they call a natural," I told her.

"I am?" she said. "Really?" She grinned.

As the day went on she grew more reckless, and I grew more cautious. I'd freeze at the tops of hills. I was watching a stretcher go by, pulled by a snowmobile, only the tips of the boots of the fallen skier visible, when Morgan yelled, "Just follow me!" and then headed straight down the slope.

The kids fastened each other's boots, and offered each other gum while waiting for a scared mom to complete her wide turns and come down the hill. "Come *on*, Mom!" Patrick would shout.

Finally I started skiing fast over little snow clumps, going several inches in the air before landing. I believe the kids call this "getting air." They kept speeding ahead of me. "No one can see how good I'm getting," I complained to Morgan when I caught up to her, puffing.

"Tell me about it, Mom," Morgan said soothingly. "You were really good, weren't you? *How* steep was the slope, did you say?"

"Well, on my second run I . . . ," I said happily.

On the way home, we rode in content, tired silence.

As we came down Highway 80 in the slow Sunday traffic, the Bay Bridge was lit up and the downtown buildings were still outlined like Christmas packages, so you saw thousands of colored lights in the darkness. "I wish I could look at it longer," Patrick blurted as we cruised slowly by. "Me, too," Morgan said.

Surprised, I took the Emeryville exit and drove down to the mud-flats along the bay and parked. We got out and I stood between them as we gazed across the water at the lights. The city lights looked all the more brilliant for the cold. We dove back into the warm car and drove home.

Days like that, I thought, were like a string of colored lights on a porch, keeping back the darkness, keeping us safe. If I could string together enough such moments, Morgan would always know where home was, where I was. And then she wouldn't get lost.

chapter 12

W HEN she told me the oil light was on, I told her to take
it to the gas station right away," Jim told me as he lifted a twisted
mass of beach clothes from behind the backseat and dropped it into
a hefty bag that already held wadded school papers, empty Sprite
cans, and jackets. Sand rained down on the cement floor of the
garage we'd had the corpse of Morgan's Dodge Colt towed to.

"So did I," I said, extracting one of my own sweaters from the mess
and putting it aside.

Morgan had asked her friend Mike about it instead. Mike was in
her small-engines maintenance class at Redwood. He lifted the
hood, checked, and said, "She's full of oil."

"What do I do when the oil warning light comes on and there's
plenty of oil in the car?" Morgan then asked the teacher.

"Ignore it," he'd said. "Problem's probably in the wiring."

Late one night several days later, as she was driving the 101 freeway back to Shannon's after a school play, a grinding noise, loud
enough for her to hear even over the blasting of the radio, filled the
car. She pulled over. The bone-dry car had thrown a rod.

Thank God, I thought when I learned about it. It happened late at night, and not in the middle of the day, when the freeway was crowded.

The car was towed to the gas station where we were now, so Morgan had had no chance to clean it out. She'd asked Jim and me not to look in the backseat when we emptied it—we were giving the hulk to charity—and I'd said, fine. I was exhausted. If there was something she didn't want us to find in the car, then I didn't want to find it either. So many awful experiences had begun with my finding things that sticking my head in the sand now had a strong appeal.

But the mechanic had made us do it.

"Look at this," Jim said quietly. He had pulled a half-empty quart-size bottle of Budweiser and an empty bottle of rum out of the mess.

I stared at that bottle. How much drinking was she doing? Was she drinking and driving?

I again experienced a sense of just holding on, like a driver with a runaway team of horses. Trying to keep her safe while she got older. With every birthday, I would think, okay, fourteen. Fifteen! Sixteen!

"We know about your saloon on wheels," I told her when I picked her up at her friend Rachel's, where she had spent the night. Rachel lived near the school with her parents and her two brothers. We hadn't yet figured out what system of buses would get her from Shannon's house to school, and Morgan often found it easier to just stay with Rachel.

She'd brought Rachel's older brother to the car to meet me. Zack was a skinny kid with frizzy bleached-blond hair and big blue eyes. His worn steel-toed boots were untied. Morgan was wearing his jacket.

"Hi, Zack," I said. Cute kid, I thought. I turned back to Morgan.

"I don't know how that bottle got there, Mom," she said. "I wouldn't drink and drive. I'm not that stupid. Besides, you told me not to."

"Did the bottles hop into the back on their own?" I asked, wearily. "You wouldn't let anybody drink in your car, would you?"

"Of course not, Mom."

I didn't believe her. All I could think of, for a minute, was something that happened when I was sixteen. I had heard that Stevie Garchik had been killed in a car. His older brother had been injured.

Stevie was in my class in grammar school, a boy with spiky sand-colored hair and a sharp nose. He once grabbed my hand, looked at my fingernails, and said, "Clean them or cut them," but I didn't hold it against him. For one thing, he was so thin that the class joke was "*Gone with the Wind,* by Stevie Garchik." He told me once that when he grew up he was going to be the water-skiing champion of the world. He and his family spent a lot of the weekends up at Lake Berryessa, in Napa, with their boat.

None of the kids in the car had been wearing their seatbelts. Nobody did, back then. They were on their way to a party, and the paper said the driver of the car, a Dodge Dart, had been drinking Annie Green Springs apple wine. He swung too wide on the curve coming down into Fairfax, and the car hit an oncoming Rambler. Three of the four kids in the car were killed instantly, including Stevie, who was sitting in the back.

I still remember where I was when I heard about Stevie. I was walking down a road in San Anselmo, when I ran into a friend who told me the news. The trees blocked most of the summer light overhead. Cars went by, and Stevie was dead, just like that.

WHAT a great idea it had been of mine to give Morgan a car, I thought the next weekend. I was driving my own car south down Highway 5, past cows and farmland and wrappers blown up against the chain-link fence on the side of the freeway. I was too full of my whirling thoughts even to switch on the radio. I felt now as if I was making not just stupid mistakes with her but dangerous ones.

On the seat beside me, sliding around every time I changed lanes, was a shoe box full of my dad's letters. I had brought them all, hoping they would give me clues to help find him. Impulsively, I had taken a week off to drive to the Mojave Desert. I didn't know whether I was escaping from Morgan or searching for Dad, and it didn't seem to make much difference. I just threw everything I thought I'd need for three days into a laundry basket, tossed the basket on the backseat, and got the hell out of Dodge.

It had been fifteen months since he'd left. Six months before, his letters had stopped. This worried me. For Dad, writing was like breathing. He was probably just mad, and going through one of his phases where he refused to send his writing to me. But he was seventy-three now, and I remembered how he sometimes tottered as he walked.

His last letter had been postmarked Barstow. I checked in at a motel, then went out to find where in town a person would go in search of books. I knew Dad came in once a week on a food and book run. I walked into a drugstore and found myself twirling a rack of paperbacks with garish covers. "Have you seen an old guy in here looking at the books?" I asked the woman behind the counter who'd been watching me.

"Had a dog?" she said.

"Yes. Little black-and-white one."

"He doesn't much care for the books we stock."

I felt ridiculous asking it. "Did he say where he was, uh, parked?"

"Parked?"

"He lives in his truck, out in the desert."

"Oh. No."

I went back to the motel. The switch for the TV came off in my hand, and I found myself lying on the bed, trying not to smell the fusty bedspread. People walked by outside, shouting to each other. I studied Dad's letters until I had at least the semblance of a plan for finding him. I reached for the phone to call Bill, and then dropped my hand. What if there had been some new development at home?

I should never have turned that car over to her. She was too young for it, no matter what the state said about the driving age. When I finally got up to break the paper seal on the bathroom glass and brush my teeth, I could hardly stand to look at the weak, vacillating mother in the mirror—the one whose child was reckless and troubled and needed her.

I woke at five. The stars were still out, so bright I could almost read my map by them. I left the plastic motel key on the table, threw the laundry basket back in the car, and drove east.

I had already realized this was stupid, looking for a single van in a desert. I should have asked the cops to look out for him, but Dad didn't have a driver's license. They would take his van away from him.

I took a northeast road out of Barstow, looking for a dry lake called Coyote Lake, which Dad had mentioned in a letter. The sky lightened. Pale mountains stretched away to the north in jagged procession. I rolled the window down, but it was cold, and I rolled it back up. Two teenagers went by on motorbikes. Later I passed them spinning in circles off the road, shooting their pistols.

I was thinking about my dad. He had been remembering so much of the past. I wondered if he remembered the day at the dam.

HE had come to the dam one hot day, showing up bare-chested in a pair of jeans and work boots. We kids were all in the water, shouting and splashing. Mother sat on the rocks in a pink shirt tied at the waist, chatting with the other mothers. Dad sat on the rocks above us for a while with a beer in his hand, watching. I was paddling near the shore in an inner tube. We got no swimming lessons. You just waded into the water and got in deeper as you got older, until you found yourself one day falling forward in a kind of drowning, kicking motion that might resolve itself into an awkward dog paddle, if you lived.

All of a sudden he dived in the water in his jeans and came up alongside me. "Come on, Dare," he said. "Let's swim across the dam."

"I can't swim that far, Daddy," I said. I was six.

"You just think you can't," he said, water streaming off the tattooed blue eagle on his right bicep. "Your mother is teaching all you kids to be sissies. Now come on. Give me that thing." He lifted the inner tube over my head and heaved it over on the rocks.

He swam out, and I followed, the green water around my chin. "All you have to do is swim to me," he said, and I kept paddling. I could hear the shouts of the other people in my ears, see the blur of pink out of the corner of my eye that was my mother, receding, but my world had shrunk to the two feet of green water between my dad and me.

"Wait up, Dad," I said, each motion of my arms pulling me forward only a few inches. I kept trying to use my feet, but only churned the water and made myself more tired. "I need to rest." I was trying to reach him so that I could grab his shoulder.

"Oh, you can do it. Don't be a baby. You're halfway there. I'm not going to let you quit now." Dad was swimming lazily backward, always just out of reach.

"No, Dad, wait!" I called, crying now, gulping water. "Please!"

I was churning the surface of the lake, a tiny waterspout. When my foot slipped down, I could feel the subterranean cold down there under the warm surface water. I saw myself sinking down into the darkness with my suit billowing grotesquely, my lungs bursting. If I could just reach that shoulder, that streaming tattoo, I would be safe.

Dad kept swimming. "I want you to find out that you can swim all the way across the dam," he called. Each time I got close, I was sure he would let me rest, wait for me, relent, but he never did.

"We're almost there," Dad said, swimming ahead of me, his blond hair sleek and dark against his head, so that he looked like a seal. As he got closer to the shore, he swam faster, further out of reach.

Yet for me he *was* the shore, the shore that retreated every time I got close.

"What are you blubbering about?" Dad called, impatiently. "Look, you made it."

And I had. I could feel slippery cold moss under my feet. I stood up, then pulled myself out of the water and onto a rock. Dad was already standing on a higher one, looking at a soaked pack of Lucky Strikes he had taken from his back pocket. "So now you know," he said. "You can swim all the way across the dam."

I ignored him. I sat on a rock, hugging my knees. I couldn't stop trembling.

The sound of a splash told me that Dad had plunged back into the water.

I stayed where I was for about a half hour, until I saw my dad loping back up the trail to the fire road. When I heard the roar of his truck starting up–he always drove in, although you weren't supposed to–I eased myself back into the water and paddled back across the dam. He was right. I now knew that I could swim across the dam, or any distance I needed. I was no longer afraid of drowning.

I was afraid of my father.

AFTER an hour of driving, I spotted a single column of smoke hanging in the blue sky, and to my astonishment there was the old bakery van, parked among some mesquite bushes. A sawhorse stood outside.

When I parked and walked over, my sandals sinking in the soft dirt, there was my father in a short-sleeved shirt, writing at his picture window, the glow of the sun on his face. I smiled. A burden I only half knew I'd been carrying slipped away, and I knocked on the window.

"Dare! I'll be goddamned!" He opened the door and I climbed in. The truck smelled of dog, ripe bananas, cigarette smoke, and gas. I sat on the bunk. Dad was still gaping at me. "What brings you all the way down here?" he said. "Somebody die?"

"I was worried about you."

"You were? Why?"

"Look," I said, raising my voice in sudden frustration. "You can't just disappear, Pop."

"Disappear?"

"Nobody knew where you were."

"I disappeared for years and nobody cared."

"You're an old man now, Dad. Something could happen to you. Don't you want at least one person on the planet to know where you are?"

"One always does. Me. How the hell did you find me, anyway?"

"You dropped clues in your letters. I just followed the trail of bread crumbs."

"Ah."

"You stopped writing."

"No, I didn't." Dad pointed to a stack of closely written yellow pages. "I just stopped sending it to you."

"Why?"

"We had a deal. We were going to trade scribbling for scribbling. What did I get from you? The equivalent of postcards."

"Sorry, Pop. I try–"

"I suspect my letters were better than you hoped for," Dad interrupted. "A scribbling dad is one thing. A dad who scribbles better than you do is quite a different kettle of fish." He said this slyly, watching my face.

"I don't think that's it, Dad." I looked out the window at the desert stretching to the horizon, only a few mesquite bushes scattered here and there.

He followed my gaze, watching my face as proudly as if he had thought up the desert himself. "The light this morning would have Van Gogh pissing his pants. Look at it! How many jaundiced old bastards get a freshly painted world to wake up to every morning?"

I looked. Emptiness in all directions, stretching to the purple mountains. In the distance a flock of sheep, leaning up against each other.

"Aren't you lonesome out here, Dad?"

"I have the wildflowers, the squirrels, the occasional blue jay. They're good people, the blue jays, despite their reputation."

Dad made me coffee. He spilled the first cup, and had to make a second one. "I got a doctor in some little two-bit town to give me some baby tranquilizers to help me sleep," he said.

"Have you been drinking?"

"Drinking out here would be like using a cane in paradise," he said. "I haven't had a drop since that delightful Christmas reunion with the family."

"Why did you start drinking anyway, Dad?" I asked, after we'd moved outside and were perched side by side on the sawhorse, our faces to the sun now well risen over the eastern mountains. Dad was tossing raisins to a chipmunk that watched us from a distance. "That's Reggie," Dad said. "He comes closer every day." I thought he hadn't heard my question, but then he said, "I was forty." He threw another few raisins and looked at me sideways. "Couple of years younger than you are now. I had already failed at school, and in the army, and I realized I was going to fail as a father," he said.

"But you had seven kids," I said.

"Yes, I did," he said. "Can you imagine how that felt, to get up every morning, and look at the crowd of you little kiddies, facing another day of not knowing how to go about being your father?"

"I can," I said. "I know how it feels to fail as a parent." I set my coffee on the ground and gripped the sawhorse with both hands. Sorrow had suddenly gathered in me. Dad was waiting, but for a few moments I couldn't speak.

I suddenly knew what my dad had felt, all those years ago, as he sat in his workshop under the house, working on his projects, hearing the footsteps of the family over his house: that acute consciousness of what a good father, a good man, would do and say, and the anguish of knowing that you are falling short. Dad couldn't stand living with what his family reflected back to him every single day: a man standing apart. That daily erosion of self. It must have been so lonely.

Dad gazed at me. "Oh, it's not really me you're upset about, is it?"

I shook my head.

"What's my favorite hell-raiser done now?"

"She wrecked that nice little car we gave her to get to school in. Ignored the oil warning light and it threw a rod on the freeway."

"Well, well, Dare. Every kid totals his first car. You just have to expect it. I went overboard. Totaled, what, my first five or six."

"Kids die in cars, Dad. And there were bottles in the car."

"Take away her driver's license. Bring her home. Do what you have to do."

"What she'll let me do, you mean."

"What she'll let you do," he agreed. He drew on his cigarette. "I know it's been rough on you, and on Jim and Bill. I have no sense you could do much better than you have, though. Trying to maneuver such an explosive element as Morgan through the pitfalls is not easy."

I watched the chipmunk seize a raisin in his little front paws and eat it. "Everybody thinks we should be tougher."

"I'm not sure I'd agree with that. She's too much like me. If you and Jim with your combined fly weight put your foot down, you would probably have to forward Morgan's mail to some crib in Winnemucca. A girl's equivalent of my string of guardhouses and a federal lockup."

I was confused. "What does that mean?"

Dad paused to fumble out his cigarette makings. "I could never submit to the army's authority over me. She'll never submit to your authority over her. You've been saved by a combination of timidity and incompetence."

"Thanks, I guess," I said.

"Hang in there," he said. "You got a tough kid there, with a lot of horsepower. She's willing to risk her life, but you can never take in that it's come to that. With your nature and upbringing, how could you? Morgan's got you so far outclassed, there's no hope—unless you can prove you're smarter than she is."

"How?"

"Stay with her, even if it gets hard. Get that energy aimed in a positive direction. I always thought I could have been deflected from my path of destruction if some half-bright person had thought it worth their while to take me in hand. Before my habit of rebelling got so ingrained that I couldn't be appealed to."

The sun shone on my face, relaxing all my limbs. I felt as if someone had just thrown open the door to my dark cellar, and invited me to climb on up out of there. Dad was the only one who told me that I was doing what I should be doing. I felt as if I didn't dare move, for fear of breaking the spell. "So you don't think I blew it?"

"Fuck no. You may have flubbed a bit here and there, but who hasn't?"

I let out a breath.

Dad chuckled. "You've really been Monday morning quarterbacking yourself, haven't you? Hell, everybody makes mistakes. Only way to avoid that is to do what I did. Race out the nearest door."

"I did make a lot of mistakes."

He threw more raisins. "You're not in my class."

We watched the chipmunks a while. I could hear cars whizzing by on the road. "What did you think your life would be like after you left?"

"I thought it would be easy," he said, rolling a cigarette on the worn cloth of his knee. He licked the cigarette closed and looked off into the distance. "People disappear every day. They're disappointed with the life they fell into, move off the grid, begin a new life, with a new wife, and a different set of kids."

"But that's not what you did."

"Didn't even come close. Nietzsche said that almost anyone has enough enterprise to commit a crime, but few are able to prevent the memory of that crime from stunting or ransacking what becomes of their lives from that point on. We are all saddled with our own funk. You are deluded into thinking it's okay if no one is looking. But the severest critic of all is missing nothing, forgetting nothing."

Dad stood up. "I set up my tape recorder a day or two ago. Inadvertently chose one of Shannon playing his guitar and singing. Tripped me down a mineshaft. A sickening plunge into a darkness. Wistfulness, longing, might-have-beens–and instantaneously an overpowering urge for a nice highball–prepared in a bucket."

As we headed for the van, I reached over and put my arm around him. He gave me a humorous look, and I took it away.

"What are you going to do, Dad?"

"Oh, I know I can't stay out here any longer. Hell, I knew it before I left. Pat says she has arranged for me to get that HUD apartment again. Apparently she's even taken it upon herself to put my few poor sticks of furniture back in it." Pat was the friend who had helped Dad get the studio apartment in the first place.

"Come back with me. You don't need this old van anymore. Just leave it here." I patted the van, and then jerked my hand back. It had grown hot as we talked.

"No, you go along, get back to that kid of yours. I'll nurse this musty old elephant-shooting platform home. I have to say good-bye to the desert. Might be a while before I can get back here again."

"I DON'T want you to drive anymore for a while," I told Morgan when I got home. She was visiting, playing solitaire on my computer. "I'm worried about you."

"I know you are, Mom," she said. She got up to give me my chair.

"I'm giving your license back to the DMV."

"Okay, Mom. I'll take the bus."

"And you'll see the counselor, the one I found for you before you went up to Idaho."

"Yes, Mom," she said. I felt more in control than I had in months.

USAA, our car insurance, refused to remove Morgan from our

policy when I called up to give them the happy news that she wasn't going to drive anymore. "She might drive anyway, now she knows how," they said. I hung up on them. I was on a crusade, trying to rewind the clock back to before Morgan was a driver, and they weren't cooperating.

I walked over to the DMV with her license and handed it to a woman at the window. "This is a provisional license, right?" I said. "I can give it back to you and cancel her right to drive?"

"Yes," said the woman. And took back the shiny little square.

I walked out, and into the Metro Hotel on Divisadero for lunch, feeling hungrier than I had in a long time. It was first time in months that I really felt like a mom.

A mom saying no.

HAD also had Morgan start seeing Dr. Koffman, a substance abuse counselor at Kaiser Hospital. When Jim and I went to meet him, I thought Koffman looked more like a football coach than a shrink. He sat on the edge of his chair, leaning forward with his hands linked tightly over his belly and peered at us from below tangled brows. We took two of the leather chairs facing him. "I'm very worried about your daughter," he said. "While I listened to her, red flags were going up all over the place."

"What do you mean?" I said. What I meant was, whatever it is, please, please handle it for me.

"She has oppositional defiant disorder."

He handed me a card that said you had to have four of eight identifying features.

1. Loses temper often
2. Often argues with adults
3. Actively defies adult rules
4. Deliberately annoys people

5. Blames others for own mistakes
6. Touchy or easily annoyed by others
7. Often angry or resentful
8. Often spiteful or vindictive

I handed the card back, trying to hold his gaze and keep my re-action from showing on my face. Morgan was never vindictive. As for the other seven, what teenager wasn't?

"She has minimal good points," he said. My arms tightened. It was possible that he had forgotten that he was speaking to us about our daughter. "I believe she has a narcissistic personality disorder. That's a disorder where you think everything revolves around you. It gets people in a lot of trouble."

Then, perhaps seeing my expression, he added hurriedly, "But she's a great kid. She told me you were her best friend, Adair, that she loves you more than anything."

I smiled thinly. Morgan *had* been talking in a wild new way, say-ing how smart she was, how she got A's on all her tests, how high school, while okay for other kids, was wrong for her. She'd been talk-ing like that for a month, and when she did she sounded a little nuts. But I didn't like hearing it from Koffman, or the way he said it.

"I can't tell you my major concerns, because of confidentiality," Koffman went on. "You couldn't do anything about it, anyway."

Rage at them both coursed through me as I shut his heavy door and followed Jim out of the building. Let her tell her awful secrets to Koffman. Let him deal with them.

ONE Saturday Morgan and I were lying head to toe on her small bed at my brother's house in San Rafael, giving each other foot mas-sages while talking and listening to her Blondie CD. Somewhere someone was using a leaf blower. Under my legs was a pile of CDs in splintered jewel boxes. "Pull my toes," I begged, and she pulled each toe in turn. Shannon's roommate, a waitress named Betty, was singing to the radio in the room across the hall as she got dressed for work. Betty had welcomed Morgan's coming to use the little spare room because she got half of the five hundred dollars we paid for rent. Otherwise she didn't seem to know there was a teenager in the house.

"So what's going to happen?" Morgan said. "Am I just going to live at Shannon's forever?"

"No," I said, seizing my chance. "Come home. You can take the bus to Redwood High School as easily from our house in the city as you can from here." Our house was ten miles south of the school, and Shannon's was ten miles north.

"I don't want to live with Bill," she said. "Come and live with me in Marin."

"I want to," I answered, "but I can't. Bill can't live in Marin. He'd have to commute to work by bus." I stared at the blue ceiling. I was filled with longing for a moment, seeing the two of us in a sun-filled house below looming Mount Tamalpais, blasting Madonna on the stereo, Morgan bringing her friends home, no one there to worry about the jackets and backpacks they dropped on the floor or the dirty dishes they left on the coffee table.

"What if you were separated?" she said.

"But we aren't," I said. "Bill and I like being married to each other."

"I know you do, Mom," she said. "It just feels sometimes as if you had to choose him or me, and you chose him." Morgan had stopped massaging my feet and was looking at me.

I flinched. I wondered if she could hear my heart beating faster. "That's not true," I said. "I would never do that."

But I knew that to her it looked as if I had.

I used my thumbs to gently rub the soles of her feet, as she had taught me. "What about Patrick?" I said. "He can't go to Lowell from Marin County." He could have, I realized as I said it, but he wouldn't want to. He'd stay with his dad, and I'd see him only on weekends, as I did Morgan. I'd get one child back only to lose the other one.

"Come home," I urged. "I'll buy you rice milk. I'll remind Patrick I told you that you could have your room back. I'll hook cable up in there."

"That sounds good, Mom," she said. "Only . . ."

"Only what?"

"Can Zack sleep over sometimes?"

"You mean with you, in your room?"

"Yes."

I said nothing. I kept rubbing her feet. Morgan had been seeing a lot of Zack since she had started spending so much time at his sister Rachel's house. I wished I could say no, are you out of your mind? What planet are you living on? But I didn't have that luxury. I wanted her home, and I wanted it to be her idea.

"Is Zack really a big part of this for you?" I asked carefully. "You would really come home if I let you do that?"

"Yes, Mom," she said. "It's a big factor. It would mean you really recognize my new maturity."

I didn't recognize her new maturity. I still believed that you could tell who a teenager is by whom they hang out with. Zack always wore a stiff black jean jacket with "6"s all over it and had told me he worshipped the devil. He was going to continuation school after having been expelled from Redwood for smoking pot.

What I recognized was that she was sexually active and would go on being so whether I let a boyfriend share her pillow or whether I threatened to get the cops if he so much as held her hand. It was a battle I had already lost.

And saying no had never been easy, when it came to Morgan. What would happen if I didn't let him stay? Would she say, "All right, Mom, you're right. I'm only sixteen, and it's crazy to think my mom would let my boyfriend stay over"? I couldn't imagine it. My dad's words came back to me. "She'll have her way if she's shot for it."

I was aware that I was now making choices I would never have made before. This was not parenting by the book: this was triage. It was keeping her alive until the right sort of help could be found, or until she got good sense. Ever since she had stayed in that car rushing downhill with no brakes, I had lost my confidence that she would not knowingly put herself in danger. If I didn't let Zack stay, she would just spend all her time at his house, doing God knows what.

"Will you promise to use birth control every single time?"

"Duh, Mom. I'm not an idiot."

"Promise me."

"I promise."

"Okay, then," I said. "It's a deal."

I reached forward and hugged her legs. "You're coming home!" I said. "Oh, sweetie, I'm so glad. We'll come and get your things this weekend."

In our now familiar routine, Jim and Patrick and I went over in the station wagon. "Other people get to take trips," Patrick grumbled, as we turned into my brother's driveway. "We just get in Dad's car and drive Morgan's things around the landscape."

"Thanks for letting her stay," I said to Shannon, as I squeezed into the car and held my arms out for him to hand me Morgan's rust-edged ficus plant.

"Sure," he said.

"How's Jessica, anyway?"

"Haven't heard. She's in Texas, her mom thinks. Ran off with some guy." He lifted one shoulder as if to ward off a blow, then turned and walked back into his house.

THE sight of Morgan's boom box covered with stickers, her cardboard boxes full of boots, and her posters being carried back into the house made me happy in a way I hadn't been in months. I had hung her leopard-print bulletin board on its old nail and put yellow roses from the front yard in her paper-bag vase by the bed. Patrick lugged the tropical-print Z Gallery armchair she had insisted on taking with her through the kitchen. Zack followed with a box of candles. I hadn't known he was coming. He was just there all of a sudden. He had dyed his frizzy blond hair blue and stuck it up with Aqua Net hair spray into a kind of pinecone. Morgan followed him, carrying a box full of textbooks. I reached out and patted her arm as she went by.

After eight months of what we had come to call her "Junior Year Abroad," she was home. I watched Bill, on the sidewalk below, carrying Morgan's Macintosh to the back gate. The printer was balanced on top, its cord dangling between Bill's feet. As he nudged the back gate open with his foot, he had the look on his face I knew so well, the one of determined cheerfulness. He still believed the kids were fooled by it.

That night Morgan asked me to let Zack stay over.

"All right," I said reluctantly. Then I added, "You'll remember your promise, won't you?"

"What promise?"

"About being careful."

"Don't worry, Mom."

We all went to bed, exhausted from the move. Some of us anyway: I kept hearing loud sounds of lovemaking coming from the room next to mine, groaning and bedsprings, and then a bed banging against the wall, and laughter. I found a pair of earplugs in my dresser drawer, stuffed a pillow over my head. Still, the sounds penetrated, and I comforted myself by imagining her hanging out on some street in another city, asking passersby for cash, her unwashed hair stringy on her pale forehead. I imagined her sitting beside a car on a deserted road with her head in her hands, bloody from a car wreck. I thought of my niece Jessica, off in Texas somewhere.

She was not any of those things. She was warm and dry and safe, and, from the sound of it, happy.

"Have you at least asked them what they're doing about birth control?" Bill's voice came muffled from under his own pillow. The dog whined from his mat beside the bed.

"There are condoms all over her room," I pointed out. They were stacked on the bedside table, under the bed, in the dresser drawers. "I have to believe they actually use them."

The sounds in the next room subsided, but Bill was wide-awake now. He switched on the lamp. "I'm terrified about her moving back," he said. "I don't know what I'll do if the screaming and door slamming start up again."

"It won't," I said. "She's much better now, as long as she gets to have that boy."

I didn't sleep well, and the next morning I went into Morgan's room with a glass of water. "Going to school is all you two have to do," I said, holding the glass threateningly over the two huddled forms under the blanket.

After they scrambled out of bed, I drove them to the bus stop. Zack's blue hair was scraping the roof of the Toyota, so he had to ride leaning over. I kept looking in the rearview mirror and grinning. "Cut it out, Mom," Morgan said, smiling herself.

"Want some deodorant?" I heard her ask him. In the mirror, I saw her holding up a tube of Fresh Start. We were almost to the Golden Gate Transit bus stop on Van Ness, where they would get the bus to Marin. "Not right now," he mumbled. I laughed, and Morgan said to me, fondly, "He can't handle deodorant this early in the morning."

"Bye, Mom," she said when I let them out, kissing my cheek. "See you tonight."

I merged back into traffic. I tried to spot her in my rearview mirror, but a bus cut in front, and she was lost from view. That was all right.

I would see her tonight.

SENDING her away had, a few months before, felt like the only way to keep her safe. Now bringing her home, paradoxically, felt the same way. I could not keep her out of cars or stop her from drinking or from riding with those who did. But I would see her every day. That had to count for something.

We settled in. Patrick moved all his things to his room up at his dad's. Morgan took the bus across the bridge to Redwood, often with Zack. There was only a month left of school, and then she'd switch back to a city school for her senior year. The usual yelling and fighting between us had resumed, but she was seeing a therapist, and I'd had a long breather, and felt as if I could get through it.

ONE Sunday I had ducked into the bedroom to change a shirt I had dribbled coffee on, when all of a sudden Bill was there. He leaned toward me, his green-blue eyes filled with light, and then he kissed me, his lips dry and warm, his mouth opening. He smelled of soap and tasted like red wine, and I kissed him back eagerly.

Now all I wanted was him. Oh, sweet man. A car alarm went off somewhere outside, and we kissed some more, harder.

Then he was ripping back the bedspread and we were both racing out of our clothes. The dog lay beside the bed under a shower of my clothes. He looked like a yard sale. Bill jumped under the covers when I was still raking my bra over my head.

"First naked in the bed," he crowed.

I jumped in. I was cold, but he was warm, and I plastered myself against him the way I used to stand on the floor heaters when I was a kid. We kissed, and then I had to take off my watch—the weight of it was too much. I took his ear in my teeth, and he shivered.

A breeze pushed at the curtain we had dropped over the open window, and the last of the afternoon spilled around its edges. The house was hushed, except for our loud breathing.

The doorbell rang. We paused, waiting. It rang again, and again. It didn't stop. It just went on and on, ringing through the house. "Let me in!" Morgan screamed from outside the front door. She must have been leaning on the bell. And then banging. She rattled the door against its chain.

Bill rolled away from me, onto his back, so abruptly that I felt cold again.

"I'll be right back," I said. He nodded, not looking at me.

"Just a minute!" I called, grabbing a robe, undoing the chain.

"Why didn't you let us in, Mom?" Morgan said. "I rang and rang!" I caught a whiff of tobacco as she and Zack rushed past me, back from another weekend at his house.

"Jesus, Morgan, what's wrong with you? Why were you ringing like that?"

"Nothing's wrong with me, Mom."

I followed them to the kitchen. They dropped backpacks and jackets on the floor. "Can I get you a Coke, honey?" Morgan said to Zack, her head already in the fridge. His hair was blond again. He was sitting at the table in a black T-shirt with a death's head on it, his shoulder blades sharp, like tiny shark fins.

"Can I have a beer?" Morgan asked me.

"Of course you can't have a beer." I kept wondering if I could ask them to go upstairs to her dad's. Though it didn't matter anymore– I had just heard Bill's shower turn on.

Her head was still in the fridge. "There's never any food in this house," came her voice. "Honey, do you want a bagel?"

A white china butter dish fell from the side of the open refrigerator door onto the black-and-white linoleum. It broke on the floor, the yellow wedge of butter mixed in with the two broken halves of the dish.

Morgan didn't notice. She sat down. "Mom, Zack and I have to go away for a few days."

"Pick up that . . . *What?*" I said. "What are you talking about?"

"Everything's all messed up. We have to go away to think." She had jumped up again, this time to look in the freezer. She took out a frozen pizza and was ripping the pizza impatiently out of the box.

"What do you mean?"

"I can't stand school. I'm not sure I can be here anymore."

"I'll have him arrested," I said.

"What?" she said.

I looked at Zack until he raised his head to look at me. "You're eighteen, and she's sixteen." I bit the words off one by one. "If you go anywhere with her, I'll have you arrested and thrown in jail."

He looked at Morgan for help. She was trying to jam the whole pizza in the microwave, so that it curled up at the edges.

I found Bill in the bedroom. He was putting his blue blazer in the garment bag now hanging on the back of the door. For a second I was confused. Was he going to New York to meet with cookbook authors again and I had just forgotten?

"What are you doing?" I said.

He straightened out the blazer. I could see only the side of his white face. "This is never going to end. She was like a feral animal, ringing that bell." He examined his ties on their metal rack in the closet and pulled off five, folding them and stowing them in a zippered pocket of the garment bag.

For a moment I couldn't talk. My stomach hurt, and the air in the bedroom seemed suddenly too thick to breathe. My sight narrowed down to his hand as he picked up his wallet and keys and stowed them in his pockets.

"Where are you going?"

"I just called Sharon. She says I can stay over there for a while." Our friend Sharon lived a few blocks away in a huge Victorian with her sister. She edited Bill's cookbooks for him on a freelance basis and took him to the opera when she had an extra ticket.

He picked up his book and put it in his briefcase. Then he came over and took me in his arms. He rested his chin on my shoulder, and spoke softly, despairingly. "Last night I dreamed that the house was full of cats, and that Morgan was tearing it apart. She had taken everything off the walls, torn up the floorboards. I was terribly upset in the dream, because you had told me it would be all right, to just let her do it, that change was good."

I stood stiffly, and then went to sit on the bed. I forced myself to speak. "It'll be all right, sweetie. This is all going to end, one day soon. She'll come out of it. I read somewhere that if they look like normal teenagers, then they will look like normal adults. In the meantime, you're supposed to think of them as on LSD."

"What if she *is* on LSD?" Bill said. "This isn't normal acting out. She isn't getting better, she's getting worse. The truth is I think she's on drugs."

"She's not on drugs. She just wanted us to open the door." I felt everything collapsing. Go, then, I thought, in a rage. Then–stay!

He said nothing. We stood there miserably. "I love you, but I just can't face another day with her. I'll call you from Sharon's."

And then he was gone.

I was in the bathroom, washing my face, hiding from Morgan and Zack. In a way, I had sensed this was coming. Since Morgan had re-turned home, Bill had been edgier than I'd ever seen him. He was mopping the kitchen floor every twenty minutes now, or so it seemed. Patrick had been staying up late on the couch to watch TV, and once Bill dropped the remote next to his ear three times, to show what it's like to be woken in the night by the loud clunk of a falling remote. He went for a hike on Saturday while I was at a work-shop in Marin. "I'm going to go hiking every weekend from now on," he announced when he picked me up at the bookstore. He didn't say "we."

He talked to all his friends about Morgan and asked them about their own teenage years. He invented what he called the "Law of the Worse Teenager." He'd invoke it when we read about a girl who ran off with her gym teacher, and one who allowed her distraught mother to drag Monterey Bay for her body while she was spending the weekend with a boyfriend.

I had been so sure of him. I thought he would keep doing it, keep holding on. I stared at the toilet paper roll I was twisting in my hand. I thought love would conquer all, I guess.

Then I heard Patrick knocking softly on the bathroom door. "What are you doing in there, Mom?" I threw cold water on my face and came out.

"Nothing, sweetie. Just something between Bill and me." I patted his shoulder and went to the kitchen.

"Where's Bill?" Morgan said immediately. Zack slouched in his chair.

"Bill isn't here? Where'd he go?" Patrick said.

"He's gone to stay at his friend Sharon's. We had a fight."

"We can blast the music," Morgan said. But she didn't look as happy about that as I would have expected her to.

At bedtime, I got into Bill's side of the bed. I tried to figure out how to turn his alarm off so that it wouldn't wake me at six A.M. I couldn't sleep until I pulled his pillow against me and pretended it was Bill.

Next morning he called from work. "This is stupid. I miss you. I'm no good on my own."

"I miss you, too. But nothing here has changed."

"I want to come home. We'll get through it."

ONE morning near dawn several days later a yowling woke me, and I got up to let the cat in. I opened Morgan's door, and she and Zack were sitting on the bed, fully clothed, talking. They looked like any two people sitting on the bed talking. "What are you doing?" I say. "Why are you so wide-awake?"

"We drank too much coffee," Morgan said. I closed the door and went back to bed. I lay there sleepless.

I knew it would take more than coffee to make those children so wide-awake at four A.M.

AS we were lying in bed that Saturday night I told Bill I wasn't sure anymore about having a baby. The day before I had thought I felt my period starting. It had turned out to be only the standard drip, but I had felt a stab of fear. That afternoon I swiped a birth control sponge from my friend Donna's bathroom.

Bill's face got very sad. He stared up at the ceiling. "I've been having a sinking spell about it, too. Morgan's so awful to be around these days. I can't imagine bringing another sixteen-year-old into the world."

I absorbed that. He had only seen her as a teenager: he didn't know. He didn't know that even as a hellchild of sixteen, she meant more to me, enriched my life more, than anyone except her brother. But that was my experience, not his.

I rolled over and put my arm around him, spoke into the warm hollow of his neck. "Maybe the real problem is that we're thinking too much again. This is supposed to just happen," I said. "We're supposed to get drunk one night and make a baby."

Two days later I felt definitely premenstrual. The small of my back ached and I was unable to button my jeans. I felt relief. Bill admitted to feeling relieved himself. We talked about my getting a diaphragm. "No," I said. "If I was ever going to have a baby again, this would have been the time. I should just get fixed and be done with it."

In the end I was afraid. I didn't want to tempt the fates by asking for a third healthy child. I didn't want to sort through thirty little jackets at a preschool again. And it was more than that: I felt, obscurely, that having a baby would be a way of turning my back on the baby I had just when she needed me most.

I went back to Dr. Jones and got a tubal ligation, ending both birth control sponges and talk of new babies forever.

SCHOOL had ended in early June. Neither Zack nor Morgan had a job or was going to summer school.

Morgan was finishing her junior year at Redwood High School, taking the bus there every day, but I'd been making her come back to the city every night. Zack's parents, Jeff and Wendy, were nice enough, and they lived in a pleasant house on the edge of a field in Larkspur. But they were seldom home, and when they were they seemed distracted. Once I called there for Morgan, and they had Credence Clearwater turned up so loud in the living room that they didn't hear the phone ringing. They couldn't find her even though it turned out she was there all the time. Zack had a room down in the basement, with its own entrance.

After I told Morgan she had to come home every day, I'd had a steady rain of abuse showered on me, and endless requests to stay at her friend Julie's, or to stay with some guy who was house-sitting in Marin, or even to stay at Grandma's while Grandma herself was in Salt Lake City.

"Suck dick," Morgan said one day when I said Zack could not stay over for the third night in a row.

"What? What did you say to me?" I asked the sullen stranger who looked so much like Morgan.

"Sorry, Mom," she said. "But it makes me so mad that you think you can have it all your way."

I walked out of the room, so shocked that I felt as if the room were tilting. I remember only a few months ago, bragging to somebody about how close she and I had stayed, how she never called me names and never said she hated me.

chapter 14

"DARE? This is your father. I need your help."

"What's wrong?"

"I was sitting on the toilet and reaching for my pants," he said. "Then I woke up on the floor."

"Jesus, Dad," I said.

"I'm scared to sit on the toilet again."

I sighed and switched off the computer. "Okay, Pop," I said. "I'm coming over to take you to the doctor."

My father had returned from the desert a couple of months after my visit with him there and was back in his apartment. I had been to see him once or twice, and had persuaded him to accept a daily hot noontime meal from Meals On Wheels. He complained bitterly about the taste, but I noticed he usually ate some of it. I had found him a cardiologist for his high blood pressure, and called him now to arrange to take Dad in. Dr. Taylor, his regular doctor, had fired him as a patient after Dad called him a quack. Taylor had said, tersely, that it was someone else's turn to be Dad's doctor.

When I walked in his unlocked door he was sitting shirtless and in jeans, at his writing table, looking like a frail Hemingway in a new beard. "I've been thinking about cremation," he said. "There's an outfit in Novato that does it for a thousand dollars."

"You're not dying, Dad," I said. "You just fainted. People do, especially if they just sit in a chair all day long and then suddenly get up to go use the toilet."

"It didn't happen to you," he said sourly.

"Anyway, I thought you wanted to be interred in the same box as Mother, so you could spend a fun-filled eternity making her regret the things she said about you," I said, trying to cheer him up.

"I've changed my mind," he said.

"About being interred with Mom?"

"About going to the doctor's."

"I drove all the way out here, Dad. When I'm already behind in my work."

"I don't want to see the doctor. Goddamned quacks. Money grubbers."

"Dad . . ."

"Say, this'll amuse you," he said. "Shit my pants yesterday on the way home from the bank. Did it so cagily doubt if anyone noticed. What I worried about for years, coming off drunks. Finally happened. Got home, took a shower, which was the end of the worst thing I can imagine. What do you think of that?"

"Depends," I said, grinning at him. Inwardly, I was dismayed and resolved to mention it to the doctor.

"How's your new typewriter?" I asked "Still too noisy?" He had bought himself an old Royal typewriter at a junk shop. He said he needed it to type up a list of his favorite words.

"Yeah, makes a racket. At least it means that for the moment I can't hear the thumping that comes from next door. That goddamned literary Aztec Hindu. He's the editor of the house organ, that newsletter they slide under the door. He lets his respiratory device thump all night against my partition, whereas he has three others where it might be placed. He and his mother–the tote bag knitter–you remember, she left one dangling from my doorknob–are as close to being a nemesis as the building affords."

"Has he complained about the typing?"

"Someone has. Hell, his machine wakes me up. He can enjoy the sound of mine. We know my contribution to the literary world pales in comparison to his linguistic spaghetti, but I refuse to be silenced on that account." Dad stood up. "So you see your poor old father is far more sinned against than sinning, in this pond for old people waiting to be gassed. I'm ready to go, I guess. What time do we have to leave?"

"Not right away," I said. His torrent of words had not stopped me from noticing he was gripping the table. Pity swelled in me. He thought the doctor was going to tell him he was going to die. "How about a bowl of oatmeal?"

"That would be fine," he said, with a trace of his old grandeur.

I cooked the oatmeal for him, dropping in four or five spoonfuls of brown sugar, the way we both like it, and set it in front of him. As he ate his eyes kept flicking around the room.

"I could take you shopping after the doctor's," I offered. I was emptying ashtrays and cleaning off surfaces with a sponge. It made me happy to know what needed doing and be able to do it.

"Not today," he said. "I'm not up to it."

He watched me wash his dishes and sweep tobacco flakes off a table into my cupped hand, then mop the floor. "I don't believe I've seen you with a mop in your hands before," he said as I scrubbed at a dried coffee stain. Mentally, I added "instant coffee" to the list in my head: cane, trash bags, Ensure, new sheets, Saint-John's-wort, multivitamins.

As I cleaned the table I came across a check for $125, a refund for the typewriter I'd returned for him. He didn't know how to deposit a check anymore. I put it in my pocket. I picked up his various bottles of pills and squinted at them to see which needed refilling. I plucked Dad's glasses off his face and cleaned them on my blouse, then put them on so I could read the prescription numbers. Then I dialed the drugstore. You would have thought I was launching the space shuttle, I felt so competent.

When he realized I was ordering prescription renewals, Dad became agitated.

"I just give them this," he said, waving his blue plastic pill case, the ones with pills in it arranged M-T-W-TH-F. "They do the rest."

I kept reading numbers to the pharmacist. "You always have to cross me," I heard him mutter.

When I finished ordering prescriptions, I glanced at my watch. "We gotta go, Dad."

Dad's spoon clinked against his bowl. He slowly lifted the last bite to his mouth. "Have I shown you my new pen?" He waved a blue pen at me. I brought him an ironed shirt I found in his closet, one of the castoffs Bill had sent over a while ago. "It's time, Dad."

I put all his bottles of pills into a white garbage bag to show them to the doctor and sort out what Dad had been taking, found one of his shoes under a chair and the other in the kitchen, and we left. Dad stopped in the lobby downstairs and used the tiny key on his ring to get his mail out of the rack of metal mailboxes. He handed the envelopes to me without glancing at them, and I stuffed them in my purse. I'd go through his mail at home and pay the bills. I took his arm to steady him and we went out the door.

We drove through bright sunshine to Larkspur.

Dad didn't say a word all the way in the car. At the clinic, he refused to bend over so the doctor could assess what had caused the fainting. "I'll pass out again if I do that," he muttered. The doctor shrugged and made a note. "He's fine," he said to me. "He just needed his blood pressure medication adjusted." He said not to worry about the accident Dad had had on the way home from the bank but to let him know if it happened again.

"What does he know?" Dad said as he shuffled after me back to the car. "He's a heart doctor. This is a brain problem."

I suppressed a surge of irritation. "There's nothing wrong with you, Dad."

He whipped his head around. "Are you a doctor?" he said.

I was silent.

"I've decided to take you up on your offer to take me to Safeway for some grocery shopping," he said when we were back in the car. "That is, if your busy schedule permits. Big-city hotshot like you."

I told him I didn't have time to go to Safeway and wanted to go to Lucky's, as it was closer. "You must do exactly as I say," he said when I told him that. "Then everything will go fine."

"Sure, Dad," I said. And drove to Lucky's.

Dad sulked in the car while I shopped for him, throwing in milk, Danish, Reese's peanut butter cups, cheese slices, a pound of chicken chow mein from the deli, sandwich bread, Smart Start. I reached for rice milk, and then caught myself. Morgan was the one who liked rice milk. The two of them were getting mixed up in my head.

The shopping cheered me up as much as the cleaning had. I felt as if I had changed into blue tights and a red cloak. I am Shopping Woman! I can find your food items, buy them, drive you and them home, and stow them in the fridge for you, all in an hour!

Next I drove him to the drugstore so that I could pick up the prescriptions I had renewed for him.

"I need those pills," he grumbled when I returned to the car and told him his Tranzene wasn't ready. It was the baby tranquilizer he had started taking in the desert when his bad dreams kept him from sleeping.

"I told you the drugstore had to call the doctor for the refill, and he hasn't called back," I said.

Back at his place he roared at me again. "All I wanted was the Tranzene," he said. "I thought I made it clear to you that I wanted it today. You couldn't even do that."

"I couldn't get them," I snapped. "Shoot me."

"I'll be glad when I am rid of you for good," he muttered.

I put the groceries away, slamming the cupboard doors as much as possible. "I'm leaving, Dad," I said when I was done.

He said, shortly, "All right, you can go."

I picked up my purse. I said, close to his ear, "Be sure and call me again when I can interrupt my work and help you out, Dad." I slammed out of the apartment, picking up along the way my only victory for the day: a jug of bleach that he had paid for but that was for me. Ha!

IT was a few days later. Bill was clearing the dishes and feeding the leftovers to the dog. The phone rang. I wiped my hands and answered it, knowing it was probably Dad. One day I called for my messages from my office and there were thirteen, all of them from him. He wanted his Tranzene prescription, the same one he had yelled to me about before. "I can't figure out how to get it renewed," he said. I called the drugstore and asked them to call him to say it was ready.

But it wasn't Dad this time. "I have to break confidentiality," said a breathy nasal voice. After a second, I recognized it as belonging to Dr. Koffman, Morgan's counselor at Kaiser. "Morgan is using all kinds of drugs–LSD, methamphetamines, marijuana, alcohol–and legally I have to tell you." I stared at the black diamond pattern on our linoleum. I knew already, of course. But now Koffman was making me face it, forcing my ostrich head up out of the ground: Morgan was doing drugs. She was sitting in basements or in bedrooms, lighting pipes and downing pills. I saw the still childish contours of her face hazy behind a veil of smoke.

"How do you know?"

"She asked for my help in stopping. I asked her what she'd been doing, and she told me. That's when I said I had to tell you."

"Where's she getting the drugs? From Zack?"

"Yes. And his friends."

"What did she say when you said you had to tell me?"

"She said she would deal with it herself. She swore at me and said she was sorry she told me. She even shouted that she would sue me."

I was silent.

"I told her, 'Morgan, I'm in a quandry,' " he went on defensively. 'If I tell your mom, you'll never trust me again. If I don't tell her, I'll have an ethical problem.' "

"What if she continued to see you and submitted to drug testing?" I said. Meaning, please, God, don't throw this back in my lap.

"Our work together is over. She'll never trust me again."

"What now, then?" I said numbly. Bill had come over and put his hand in mine.

"We have to send her down the hill."

"Down the hill?"

"To the chemical dependency program at Kaiser. They'll assess her problem, and she'll probably be required to go to AA. There'll be family therapy. And weekly drug testing."

I put the phone down. I rushed past Patrick and Bill to the bathroom and threw up. "Mom, you're sick!" Patrick said. He and Bill had followed me into the bathroom. "Sweetie?" Bill said. When it was clear I was finished, he handed me a towel and patted my back.

"It's your sister," I said to Patrick, using the towel to wipe my mouth and streaming eyes. "Koffman says she's been taking all kinds of drugs."

"Jesus," Bill said. "I'm so sorry, babe."

"SHE was stoned when I ran into her at the county fair," Robin said on the phone a few minutes later, unsurprised. "Remember, I told you."

Of course she had told me, in the sense that she had said those words. But she had not told me in the sense that I had wanted to listen.

I went upstairs. Jim was making a pie, his big square hands all floury. He kept working as I told him, his mouth twitching downward. The rolling pin crashed down on the table, and rolled so hard he tore a big hole in the dough. He balled it up and started over, whomping the dough down hard and then slamming the roller down on it. "Can you think of any reason why I shouldn't throw Zack down the stairs?" he said.

I enjoyed it for a second, the sight of Zack cartwheeling backward down the stairs, his frizzy hair flying. Then I shook my head. Zack was not the problem.

"I KNOW about the drugs," I said to Morgan when she came home. Unable to work, I was cleaning out my desk drawer. "I thought they weren't supposed to tell," Morgan said angrily, her voice rising. Cody got up and started barking at her.

"He had to," I said over the dog's barking, suddenly so furious that it came out as a hiss. "After what you told him. After what you've been doing."

"I can't believe you're on his side!" Morgan cried. "You're not my mom anymore!" She ran through the house to her room. I followed her.

"You should reconcile yourself to long-term therapy, and to the drug treatment program, whatever it turns out to be," I said.

Morgan burst into tears. "You're so mean!" she cried. "You never used to talk to me this way."

I thought again of the drug smorgasbord she'd been enjoying, and hardened my heart.

"What do you expect?" I said. "After all the shit you've been pulling."

"You did a lot of stuff, too, when you were my age," she sobbed. "You did whatever you wanted to!"

"I did . . ." I stopped. It had never occurred to me before, but she was right. I did do whatever I wanted.

"Yes, but what I wanted to do included going to school and getting good grades, and it didn't include drugs," I said.

"You got married when you were still in high school!" Morgan said. "How did that make your mother feel?"

"We're not talking about me," I said. But I paused. How did it make her feel? I had never even given it a thought. I had wanted to get married, so I did, and that was all. "I don't know," I said. "Please don't cry," I said to Morgan. "You know I can't stand to see you cry."

She sobbed in my arms, and I smoothed her hair. My wild child so full of talk and, it seemed these days, so little else. I held her, but my eyes were open, and I stared at the closet doors.

I went in to make a salad for dinner. I had spun the lettuce dryer too hard, and was picking lettuce off the linoleum floor when Morgan came into the kitchen and stopped a few feet away from me. "Is my room mine?" she asked. "Do I own it? Can I do anything I like to it?"

"Well, not exactly," I said. Pity flooded me, and I pushed it back. We went into her room.

"Is the desk mine?"

"Yes." It was the one she put together herself as a freshman.

"The bookshelf?"

"Yes."

"The CD holder? The lamps? The end tables? The green sheets?"

"Everything is yours but the bed," I said finally. "That's Patrick's."

She seized the end of the mahogany bed and started tugging it toward the door, as if she were going to jerk that double bed right through the doorway.

"Hold on," I said. Together we dismantled the bed and took it up-stairs to Jim's. "What are you going to sleep on?" I asked when we were done. But she didn't answer, and I didn't really care.

Next morning there was a small black wooden box on the kitchen floor in front of her bedroom. A sign taped to the box said: MORGAN'S MAILBOX.

I opened the box to find a crumpled piece of binder paper with "Mom" written on it in black marker. I unfolded it. "I love you, Mom," it said. "But I just want to be left alone for a while. Anything you want to give to me goes in here. Pretend there's no door to my room."

I folded and then refolded the note, smoothing the corners in slow motion. She was running away from home—without leaving the house.

I sat down, still holding the note, and looked at the white plate my mother had stolen from my wedding with Bill and then returned to us with pink roses and congratulations painted on it. I shifted my gaze, and there on the opposite wall was the black-and-white photograph of my mother that I'd found and blown up, of her standing at the sink with a cup of coffee in her hand, wearing a man's shirt with the sleeves rolled up and a denim skirt, exactly the way she always looked.

I remembered a day when I was sixteen, almost exactly Morgan's age now. I had called my mother at work.

She was the catering manager at the Elks Club. Most of us kids worked there on the weekend, too, and as I waited for the busboy to get her, I imagined her coming hurriedly to the phone while three or four people awaited her instructions. "Send somebody out to anchor those tablecloths with ashtrays, or they'll blow away," I heard her say.

"Mother?" I said.

"Adair? What is it? We're really busy here."

I blurted it out. "Johnny and I are going to drive to Reno. Is it all right with you?" I don't know why I said that. The truth was that Johnny and I had just come back from Reno. We'd been out driving, eating cherries out of a paper sack from a roadside stand, and had just sort of kept going, just for the thrill of being able to drive anywhere we liked. We'd gotten to Reno, walked around, eaten some Kentucky Fried Chicken in the car in a parking lot, and then driven home again, all in one day. I sat next to him the whole way, listening to "Red Rubber Ball" on the radio. Nobody even knew I'd been gone.

I can't remember what my mother said. I only remember that it was something careless, something tired and disappointed, like "Do what you want."

"I have to go," I said abruptly, and put the phone down. It missed the cradle, and after a few moments started a high-pitched beeping.

I felt as if someone had shot a cannonball through me, that if I looked down I would be able to see the cartoon edge of the new hole in my middle. Then I heard myself crying, the sound wrenched out of me.

I cried all that summer afternoon. My little black dog, Danny, licked my bare feet, then thrust her muzzle into the circle of my arms, trying to lick the salt tears from my face.

My brothers and sisters came in curiously, looked at me, and left again. They asked what was wrong, and I said, "Nothing."

"She's upset about something," they shrugged to each other. We were by then a house of six teenagers: there was always somebody sobbing on the couch. Adrian pushed a cold can of Tab into my hand, stood there uncertainly, and then I heard the screen door bang as she went off somewhere.

What could I tell them? That I felt for the first time in my life like one of them, just one of her kids? That there was, for her, nothing special about me after all?

When I was little, I had trailed my mother like a lover as she moved from washing machine to sink to clothesline to making beds. I hated to use the word "she" for her. Not "Where is she?" But "Where's Mom?" It made her too separate; it implied that she had a life apart from me.

She was large and freckled and amused and smelled of suntan lotion. She was mysterious, with her own square toilet paper called Kotex behind the toilet. She wore red lipstick and would leave pink stains on her L&M's, on coffee cups, everything. The kitchen was filled with her kisses. She loved Doris Day and sang along to "Que Sera, Sera"--whatever will be, will be.

When I was trying to pull myself out of one of the laughing fits we were all subject to, or just wanting the shock of the experience, I would imagine that she was dead. It was like imagining the world with all the color drained out of it. I did it for the pleasure of knowing it wasn't true, that when I got off the school bus out at the highway and walked up Lagunitas Road, there she'd be, hanging out the wash in the yard, or standing with her bathing suit already on, impatient for everybody to get home so we could get in the last two hours of daylight at the swimming hole.

In my zeal to make myself stand out from the others, my clamoring greedy brothers and sisters, I wooed her with wet, pale blue forget-me-nots gathered on the lot above the road and blackberries with prickly stems still attached where I tore them from the bush in my haste. I brought home glowing notes from my teachers, and I tried to do things to make her laugh, like the time I painted a box blue and filled it with worms and gave it to her for her birthday. I heard her on the phone for days afterward, roaring with laughter as she told her friends about it.

In return, she smiled at me as I sat doing my homework at the picnic bench that served us for a kitchen table. She welcomed me into bed when I came into her room in the night, letting me curl up in the warm hollow of her as she slept on her side. She would say to the other kids, "Why can't you be more like Adair?" This did not endear me to them especially, but I was so inept in most ways, so ridiculous with my glasses and short bangs, that they didn't mind.

The dog was licking my hand. I finally sat up, wiped my eyes, and opened the now warm Tab with a bubbling pop. I was through crying, but I wasn't over it. I never did get over it. Something had been taken from me that day. Even I thought I was just being hysterical, overreacting. But I never got back the feeling that I sat warmly in the middle of my mother's love. I got some of it back, but not all of it.

From then on, there was sometimes the slightest frostiness on her part, as if I had betrayed her by growing up. She started calling me "Adair" sometimes, when she was annoyed, though the family always called me Dare.

I started saying "she," as in "Is she home yet?" It felt good to call her "she." It implied separateness. She, she, she.

When I was seventeen I fell in love with a handsome twenty-one-

year-old lift truck operator named Michael Lara. I ran off to Reno to
marry him the minute I turned eighteen, in the middle of my senior
year of high school. He had wide-set brown eyes, and said he would
love me until the day he died. We drove to Reno in his faded red
Chevy, with the rest of our wedding party–Adrian and her boyfriend
Johnny Malaspina–squashed in the back. I wore an ugly blue dress
with a gold frog pin. I don't even remember if my mother was there
when we drove off. I knew only what I wanted, what I felt.

Mike and I rented a hilltop apartment in Fairfax where birds circled below the living room window, and I listened to morning radio
shows directed at housewives. I wrapped vanilla wafers in waxed paper, and packed them into his black lunch pail along with salami
sandwiches and love notes written with a purple felt pen. I wrote my
own absence excuses for school and went home on Sunday mornings to eat doughnuts with my family. I avoided my mother's room,
with its strong pull of the brushes scattered on the vanity, her
clothes, mother herself reading in bed after working two shifts the
day before, the other kids lounging around the bed. Instead I went
into the living room, switched on the old Fisher stereo, and talked a
lot about how nice it was to have my own apartment.

The marriage–grand word for our puppy arrangement–lasted
seven months. When our soulful looks into each other's brown eyes
and frantic though inept wriggling under the blankets gave way to
heated arguments about whose turn it was to clean up the dog's
messes, I moved back to my mother's house as if nothing had happened.

Now, sitting in my kitchen, remembering what Morgan said, I realized for the first time why I had done that, been in such a rush to
leave my mother's house.

I had done it to punish her for her new coldness. "I'll make you
care," I was saying as I fingered the gold frog pin on the blue dress I
had bought to get married in. "You can't leave me. I'll leave you first."

Was this what Morgan was doing? Punishing me, in a sense, for
leaving her for Bill?

• • •

THE next morning, Saturday, Bill and I took our usual walk over to 24th Street. Cody had to stop to bark at Toto, the terrier who lives on the corner. Two blocks later he paused as always at the greengrocer's on the opposite corner, hoping for a handout. "They don't feed me at home," his brown eyes claimed. "Any help you can give me would be appreciated."

I snapped the leash on him. I reminded myself I had a good career, friends, a good marriage, a sweet son, even a nice little dog and this view of the bay from 14th and Castro, a view like a painting, with long cargo ships passing on the blue water.

But I was battling feelings of dislike toward Morgan. As a writer, I wanted to revise her, cross out some things, give her a different voice.

I thought about how she demanded credit for attending class regularly, even though she did it only because the vice-principal at Redwood had done everything short of hanging a beeper on her. I thought about how she had quit her math class, saying, "That teacher doesn't know how to teach, Mom."

I was not furious because she lied to me about what she was doing. For teenagers lying is like breathing. I was furious at her for having so little regard for herself that she could turn herself into this awful drug-taking kid. I was furious because she wouldn't let me feel proud of her, or hopeful about her. I was furious because it was just so stupid, and because I was so scared.

"Are you brooding?" Bill asked as we walked along. "I'm just facing the facts," I said. "She's not going to come out of this by herself."

He stopped me on the sidewalk and took me in his arms. I clung to him, wanting just to stay there. "What if she won't agree to go into the program?" I asked him. "What will we do then?"

DAD, meanwhile, was still convinced he needed brain surgery. One day he went by cab to the hospital, and then couldn't tell them why he was there. The nurse who called me said, "You should be here. He needs help from his family."

"I'm teaching a class tonight," I said. "I can't leave the city." I had begun to teach an occasional writing class at night.

"I see." I could hear, in her pause, her stoic acceptance of a world filled with nice sick old men and hard-hearted daughters. I was sure that when I said, "I'm teaching a class tonight," she heard, "throwing a party."

Lucy called, too. Tall, always eating potato chips, she worked part-time at Dad's building, serving as social worker for the 140 old people living there.

"We haven't seen you in a while," she said. "When I go in to check on your dad, he's sitting there in his armchair reading your old letters."

I was silent.

"I don't get along with my mother," Lucy went on, conversationally. "She's seventy-two, and half the time I want to smother her with her own pillow."

"You do?"

"Sure. I could never do for her what you're doing for your dad," she said. "I wish I could, because I know it would be better for me. We have to come to some resolution with our parents before they die. If not, all that stuff that is in us will stay in us."

"How is he?"

"Not good. He's begun to pace the halls at night, and we can't let him do that. This house is for people capable of independent living."

"Can't the county help him?"

"What do you mean?"

"When we were young he abandoned us to the system. He said Marin County wouldn't let a family starve. Well, now it's his turn. It's thirty-five years later, but Marin County still won't turn a demented old man into the street."

There was a brief silence. Then Lucy said gently, "I do understand. In my line of work, I see a lot of angry adult children."

"I live forty miles away, in the city," I defended myself. "I'm too far. He has six other kids. Three of them live right there in Marin."

"But they won't help, you said."

I looked down. The paper clip I was clenching in my hand had bitten into my thumb.

"No, they won't. My twin would, but she lives too far."

"Well, who does that leave?" she said.

When I hung up, I sat staring at the wall a while. I knew who it left.

Some days I'd come home and check my voicemail, standing there at the window, impatient, only to hear a series of identical messages, each the sound of my dad's breathing, then a sigh, then "Well, please call me," and a click.

I'd reach my hand toward the phone and then snatch it back, already hearing him demand to know why I hadn't found him an appointment with a brain surgeon, or what I was plotting with Lucy.

Meanwhile, I talked to social workers and doctors and tried to find out what services for seniors were available in Marin County. I knew he would need a board and care home soon. I paid his rent when it came due and otherwise did nothing.

I paid no attention even when his bank called. "Your dad is here trying to close his bank account, and it's the one his social security is deposited into," they said.

"He probably just wants my name off the account," I said. "Just do that for him," and thought no more about it. I had put my name on his account so I could help him pay bills. If he wanted it off, fine. Let him pay his own bills.

Next day he called me. "I'm looking for that check for a hundred twenty-five dollars that was on my table the day you came over here and messed with my things," said the cranky voice in my ear.

Embarrassment flooded me. "I took that to pay myself back for the cases of Ensure I brought you." My fury was powered by guilty feelings. I never thought he'd remember that check, which I had just stuffed in my pocket, thinking Dad would never be able to figure out how to deposit it himself.

"I thought the Ensure was a gift," he said.

"Well, it wasn't," I said curtly, though it had been, in the sense that he never offered to pay me back when I bought food for him. Still, I felt guilty: taking a check from an addled old man. I deliberately conjured up the image of him walking down the steps of our old house, the shadow of the trees dappling his back, keys jingling from his belt. When I remembered him, it seemed to be always from the back, me watching as he walked away.

At the same time, part of me wondered how often I had used these images as an excuse to let him down, do less than I could for him. Bad dads were actually easy to care for: you could take care of him or stay away, according to your mood, and still be considered a saint either way.

"I want my writing back," he said. "And my Polaroid camera."

"Those letters are mine," I said. "You sent them to me."

"Things were different then. When are you going to bring them?"

"When I get around to it." I hung up on him, and went to my bed. Cody was curled up on the bed in a patch of sunlight, and I reached out and buried my face in his hot fur. Dad had never before asked to have back the only thing he'd ever given me: his writing. I knew he was half cracked, but it hurt anyway.

I thought he'd forget about it, but he kept calling, wanting to know when I was bringing his papers. "If you want your writing back, you can come and get it," I said angrily, knowing he couldn't. He could hardly manage the walk to his bank anymore.

One Sunday morning, when Bill and I and the dog returned from our walk for coffee, a voice hailed me from the front garden. "Dare," it said. I looked up and saw my pale, angry father standing in the front garden, wrapped in his old orange parka. He looked like a frail stick, made of anger.

"Hi, Dad," I said as I went up the steps and unsnapped the dog's leash. "How did you get here? Do you want some coffee?"

"None of your tricks," he said. "Just give me what I came for."

He followed me into the house. I couldn't help watching his face, but he never glanced at anything. So I stepped on a chair and got down the cardboard box filled with the yellow sheets I had been collecting from Dad for ten years, all his journals and letters. His life work, and my inheritance. I gave him the Polaroid camera, too.

He couldn't lift the box. "Can't you put a handle on it for me?" he asked.

"How will you get it home?"

"I might buy a car, take the stuff home in it, and then junk the car. What do you think of that?"

"Great plan, Dad," I said. "Wait here, and I'll put your stuff into a bag for you."

I found Patrick's old snowboarding bag in the closet in Morgan's room. She was still asleep under the jumbled comforter.

I brought the bag back to my office, where Dad perched on the edge of my computer chair. I kneeled on the rug and began to switch the yellow sheets into it, handful by handful, as he watched with suspicion. "I'll know if anything's missing."

One sheet fluttered to the side and I began to read it. "Fumbling through my battered old trunk--old dentures, jock straps, notices to appear--trying to find something to amuse you," it said in that painful scrawl.

"Can I keep this page, Dad?" I said.

"Put it in the bag."

The phone rang. As I turned to answer it, I crumpled the page I was holding and shoved it in my pocket.

It was Iris, out at the ranch. "Do you know where your dad is?" she asked. Her voice was high, agitated. "He isn't answering his telephone."

"He's here," I said.

"There? At your house?"

"Yes."

"Well, isn't that nice to hear?" Iris said. "You two must really be getting along."

"Yes, he's my new best friend," I said. "Do you want to talk to him?"

"Well, maybe this would be better coming from you," she said. "Somebody shot his dog."

"Oh, my God," I said. "Oh, Jesus." My sorrow was immediate, and for that first moment all my own. I saw once again the little black-and-white dog with his nose out the window of Dad's truck.

"Who would do that?" I said.

"I don't know," she said in a bewildered voice. "We just found him this morning, still tied up outside his doghouse, shot in the head."

I saw the dog lying in the dirt, his eyes glazed.

My anger had rushed out of me. I looked at my dad where he sat in the orange jacket he'd refused to take off.

"Dad." I touched his arm. "Dad, that was Iris. It's Fred. He's been shot. He's dead."

Dad flinched away from my touch. He glanced at the window, then back at me. "I did it," he said.

"What?"

"I shot him."

"How did you get out there?" I said stupidly.

"Bus."

"Why?" I was still bewildered.

"It's humiliating to have a dog who reads you at a glance–who knows with his deep sense of pack rank that you are a person of low status. I don't need to be reminded of that."

"I don't understand, Dad." Again I was bombarded by images– Fred in the desert, chasing tarantulas. Dad sneaking him in the side door, while the management pretended not to see. "You shot him with a gun?"

"With one of those guns I made. Iris said she wouldn't take care of him anymore."

Dad sat there, glaring, his jacket pulled around his throat. I stuffed the rest of his papers in the bag as fast as I could. I had to get him out of the house.

When I was done, he said, "Can't Michael drive me?"

"He's not old enough to drive. And his name is Patrick, not Michael."

"Call me a cab, then."

I did, and Dad marched out into the rain, hauling himself down my steep steps with both hands on the railing, like a man letting himself down a rope. I carried the bag to the bottom of the steps.

"I would have taken Fred for you," I said.

"Drop dead."

"You first," I said and went back up the steps. He settled down to wait, in the rain, for the cab. He pulled the bag toward him.

And I went back in the house, and told Bill I was fine, I really was.

chapter 15

JIM knocked at the back door and I grabbed my purse. The drug clinic was down the hill, as Koffman had said, and it sometimes felt like that as Jim and I got in the red Volvo and drove there: as if we were going downhill. Jim, who usually couldn't drive down a street without exclaiming over the Victorians we saw along the way, was silent, barely glancing at the houses interspersed with housing projects we were passing.

He had nothing to say about the architecture of the Kaiser drug clinic. It was a brand-new facility down on Webster Street, across the street from the Northern police station, in the part of town called the Western Addition.

Morgan was already there, attending the teens' group–or at least I hoped she was. Though we were only two weeks into the program, she had already begun to miss meetings–and the weekly urine test for drugs.

Jim and I always arrived too early, and had to riffle through magazines as if we were at the dentist. I flipped through a magazine and tried to read an article about garbage bags. I learned that drawstrings aren't as sturdy as flaps and handles. The best bags for lawn and leaf waste was Glad with Quick-Tie Flaps. Jim was reading *The New Yorker*. He thought nothing of swiping a magazine from a waiting room if he was in the middle of an article, and I remembered how I always liked that about him, that tiny unexpected bit of larceny. I looked at him again, and saw that he hadn't bothered to put on his glasses.

He borrowed mine to fill out the pink form in which we recorded our activities for the week. "Number of 12-step meetings attended in the last seven days." Then, "List or circle what you are feeling today: love guilt joy boredom optimism depression enthusiasm fear jealousy revenge anger happiness frustration restlessness anxiety confidence self-pity sadness serenity peacefulness inadequacy irritable tired."

I watched Jim circle "depression" on his sheet. I circled "love" and "anger."

It always felt oddly intimate to me to be there with Jim, united again, watching his large square hand as he wrote our names in the book. We'd already met privately with Dean, the director of the clinic, an athletic-looking man who seemed to be made from all squares and rectangles. Dean had let us know what was in store for us all: "Twice-weekly drug screenings for Morgan, outside Al-Anon meetings for you two and Bill, outside teen AA meetings for Morgan. And Mondays we'll see you all here for the eight P.M. family meetings."

We were instructed to remove all the wine and beer from the refrigerator and not to drink at all ourselves for the duration of the program, an instruction we took to mean don't drink in front of Morgan. I locked our wine and beer in the walnut chest in the living room and stowed the key in a book about General Montgomery. When our friends Joan and Bob came over to go to a party with us, we had to buy a six-pack to take with us, as all our beer was warm and in jail.

"What if she won't go?" I had asked Dean. "She tends to be the one who decides what she's going to do."

"You have to explain to her, firmly, that if she drops out of the program, then she can't continue to live at home."

Jim and I had looked at each other. "People keep acting out until they run into something solid," Dean said, seeing our looks.

We agreed to everything.

At the same time, even on this third visit, I found myself sitting hunched over with my hands in my pockets, counting down the time until I could find myself back on the sidewalk. Morgan wasn't the only one with an oppositional disorder. Life in my family had not prepared me to be part of a program that required me to sit quietly while someone explained the beliefs and rules that would govern my life from now on.

I don't do well in groups. I had never belonged to a group in my life, and as far as I know neither had anyone in my entire family. I suspect that for Dad the army was a group—that's why he walked away.

We're Irish-American, and come from a long line of poets and dreamers and hardheads dedicated to the proposition that every man should be allowed to go to hell in his own way. When one of my relatives was required to go to a psychiatrist as part of an application for job disability, she sent me a memo in which he had suggested his patients' schedule their vacations at the same time as his. "Do you *believe* this?" she wrote me. "Let him schedule his vacation to coincide with mine." Dad had told me proudly of the therapy session at Napa State Hospital at which he had proposed they choose up sides for a circle jerk. "I must have made some twenty trips to mental institutions," he added. "I can't imagine why I did it. I must have been crazy."

No one in my family except me had ever seen a shrink they weren't ordered to. I lasted only two months. "How did that make you feel?" a couples counselor I was seeing with a boyfriend had said when I told her about all the stuffing coming out of my koala bear when I was seven. I didn't see where she got off asking about a private koala bear. I hated the way she poked around in my childhood, taking my funny stories and my rogue father and stripping the color from them, reducing them to bleak lines in a psychology textbook.

Yet the people I respected had almost all, at one time or another, been in therapy. I could tell who they were, because talking to them wasn't like walking through a mine field, trying not to hit all the un-exploded mines. I wanted Jim to get some therapy, and, of course, Morgan. Bill's floor-mopping was clearly a cry for help, and my mother was the poster girl for the unexamined life. I just didn't want, myself, to give more than name, rank, and serial number to the other mommies and daddies in the drug program.

They might have known quite a lot about me already, of course. By now I had been writing my column for six years and was pretty well known. People sometimes stopped me in the street and introduced themselves to me. But in the program we were all just worried parents. If they had heard my name outside this building, they didn't let on.

My restlessness in the group meetings didn't mean I didn't believe in the program. I did. I needed to, to the point of desperation. I would follow a cloaked stranger into a dark alley, if he told me help with Morgan lay at the end of it. What I knew how to do—have fun with her, show her I loved her—hadn't been enough. It was time to turn it over to someone else.

From six to eight P.M. we sat on upholstered metal armchairs and had our parents' education meeting, in which we had chalkboard lessons in active listening and signs of addiction and stages of alco-holism. We learned how to give ourselves a time-out when we were mad at our teens. "Does anyone here know what a time-out is?" asked Monique, our group leader, dressed in black pants and black sweater. I stared at her. Not only did she know the answer to every question she asked—a teaching method I've always found irritating—but so did we. Jim and I often found ourselves answering her questions anyway, like the good students we had been.

Across the room were Olin and Adrienne, Bianca's parents. Bianca was a thin, blond, wan-looking fifteen-year-old who had given her parents a weary look of disgust as she stalked off to the teens' meeting. Her parents regarded it as a triumph that she had deigned to come this evening. As the subject had moved on to anger management, Olin told us in a Swedish accent, "I am very, very calm. I am never angry about anything, and my wife gets upset about everything." He crossed his long legs, and his long arms, and looked around at us. His wife, blond and round, looked ready to burst into tears. When Monique asked how Bianca indicated that she was no longer listening, Adrienne said she didn't know. "She never listens to me."

Afterward, at eight, the five or six teenagers joined us, reeking of the cigarettes they'd smoked on the sidewalk during their break and asking us for change for the vending machine.

Together we all filed into the big room for the family meeting, which Dean ran. We always went around the circle to introduce ourselves. The meeting was run on vaguely AA lines. When it was Dean's turn, he always said, "My name is Dean, and I'm the co-dependent of a cigarette smoker." He meant his wife, who occasionally sneaked a smoke. I knew he was just trying to come up with something to say, but it sounded lame, and I'd roll my eyes at Jim. Jim leaned away, refusing to let me catch his eye. He was listening intently.

When my turn came, I'd make sure my arms weren't crossed. Morgan was watching, and I wanted to model cooperation for her. Still, I couldn't bring myself to say, "My name is Adair, and I'm a codependent." I always said instead, "My name is Adair. I'm Morgan's mother."

A codependent, I had learned in group, helps ("enables" is the word they use) the user go on using by covering for him. A co-dependent parent would drive a kid to school when he got up late, and then drive his homework over to the school when he forgot that. He'd let the kid stay home sick to study for an exam after he partied on the weekend.

A codependent, in other words, was Jim, who still did the kids'

laundry and dropped whatever he was doing to make them a sandwich. Five days after he fell off the backyard fence and broke his leg,
I caught him in his Volvo, trying to work the clutch with his cast so
he could drive Morgan to her meeting at the Unitarian Church. "I
think I can drive all right," he said, and it took three of us to put him
back in the house.

He was a caretaker, which in life is nice but in the program is
codependent and very bad.

He seemed to know it: he always leaned forward eagerly and said,
"My name is Jim, and I'm a codependent." He told the group about
driving Morgan to school. The group scolded him. "All right, I won't
do it anymore," he said meekly.

He'd said as much before. "I'm not driving her anymore," he'd announce to Bill and me. The next morning at seven, Bill and I would
wait in the kitchen over our coffee, our eyes on the clock. "One, two,
three," Bill said, and then we heard it, right on time: the sound of
the garage door rattling upward, Jim calling, "Morgan?" and her
cranky, "I'm coming!"

I told this story, and a short, birdlike woman wearing a long black
top over black jeans admonished me. "You can't control what Jim
does," she said, "any more than you can control whether Morgan
goes to class or not." Her name was Donna. She and her husband,
Kit, were the other couple we saw most often. He was a contractor,
with rosy cheeks and bright blue eyes. They'd been in the program
nine months. Their son was Matt, a square-shouldered seventeen-
year-old who had got so heavily into drugs that Kit, shaking, had finally given him $1,000 in an envelope and told him to get out of the
house.

"It took me two months to see the value of the Al-Anon meetings,"
Donna told me in a deliberately soothing voice. I had told her I had
been to one and was never going back.

Jim, on the other hand, had already been to four Al-Anon meetings and talked to Morgan about "maintaining your sobriety."

I knew what Kit and Donna and their son had been through. "I knew there was a real possibility that one day I'd be asked to identify your body," said Kit one night, looking across the room at his son. His eyes filled with tears, and so did Matt's. "I know, Dad," he said.

"We've done everything," said Kit. "One of us was always with him. We locked up our knives after Matt tried to attack us with a kitchen knife when he was drunk. We locked up our valuables so he wouldn't steal them. We disciplined him when he broke our rules, even though that only made him angrier with us."

"Sometimes I'd go into my bedroom and just yell and scream about how much I hated what was going on in my life," Donna broke in. "I was angry, I was guilty, I was terrified about finding Matt dead of an overdose. I was overwhelmed with a sense of helplessness that nothing we could do would help our family."

She looked around the room. Tears glistened on her cheeks. Across the room, tears were rolling down Adrienne's plump red cheeks. "One of the hardest things we had to deal with is the shame we felt," said Donna. "People blamed us for not controlling our son. 'Why do you let Matt get away with cutting class and using drugs?' they'd ask. They regarded us as failed parents, and we felt like that ourselves."

Dean's smile disappeared. He looked almost angry. "You are *not* failed parents," he said vehemently. "No one in this room is a failed parent. You are *here*, aren't you?"

Then it was the turn of Aurora, an Hispanic woman in her late thirties, who actually worked at Kaiser herself, as a medical secretary. Her shoulders heaved under her pink sweatshirt. "Nobody told me about this part of mothering," she said despondently in a Guatemalan accent. "I don't like it."

The tension broke as everybody laughed. Aurora waited, smiling a little, then went on. "What if my daughter is one of the ones who doesn't mature out of it?"

We all fell silent. We all knew that some kids didn't. I thought of my friend Aleta, a woman whose teenager had been a lot like

Morgan–sleeping all night on Mission Street to buy concert tickets, getting kicked out of school for throwing out a teacher's Rolodex, dabbling in drugs–and who was now a heroin addict, living on the streets in San Francisco.

"WHERE'S Morgan?" Dean asked at the next Monday night meeting. "She wasn't at the kids' meeting."

"She wasn't?" Anger washed over me. She had left the house at the usual time.

Instead of Morgan, we had Bill. "It isn't about me," he said unhappily to the group. He had come because I had asked him to. "She already rules our every waking moment. Besides, she doesn't even care whether I'm around or not." He had brought his *New York Times*, but kept it folded in his hand.

"You can't not participate," Donna told him, "not if the family is to get anywhere."

She turned to me. "At what point in Morgan's life did Bill show up?" she asked.

"She was twelve," I said.

"And you said before she started acting out at twelve."

"Yes, but lots of kids do."

"You must realize that it affects any child when her parent remarries, and starts to pay a lot of attention to someone else," Kit put in mildly.

"I know it does," Bill said, looking uncomfortable. "I'm just not sure what I'm supposed to do about that, especially now." It was a question I'd long been asking myself.

"How do you and Morgan get along?" Donna asked.

"Not that well," Bill said. "We mostly stay out of each other's way."

"Does she resent you being there?"

Bill met her gaze. "I don't know why she should. I've been as nice to her as I know how."

Just then Morgan came in, wearing a green chiffon skirt, knee socks, and black boots. Her hair was combed back, her eyes made up.

"Why are you all dressed up?" I asked.

"I'm leaving for Marin right after this meeting. I have to see Zack."

"You are not," I said. "You're coming home with us."

"I want to go and stay with my baby," she said. "Nobody cares about me except my baby."

"Your baby's not here," Matt told her, leaning forward with the same gesture his dad had used. Bare knees poked out of oversize canvas shorts. "Your parents are here."

"I wasn't talking to you, Matt," Morgan said. She flashed me a look that said, hey, why is their family picking on our family? I refused to let her catch my eye.

"I've been where you are," Matt insisted. "Back then I thought I was thinking clearly, too. I thought it was a great idea to go live in a dump in the Haight and do drugs until my money ran out."

"I don't want to be here," she said to the group. "I'm not a drug addict. Even when I was doing drugs it was never my idea. I would just as soon have gone to a movie." She turned to Dean. "I must have some other options."

"You do," Dean said. "They may not be appealing. There are local teen shelters, such as Huckleberry House. Or if things get worse, you may need to be in a structured, safe environment."

"You mean a hospital," she said flatly.

He looked at her. "Yes, a hospital."

"Zack was in a hospital when he was sixteen. He said rehab makes people into addicts."

"Do you think that's true?" Dean asked her.

Morgan was silent.

"Not all the time," she said.

I felt so grateful to Dean I practically wanted to sleep with him. I had longed for years for this kind of help, this much direction, this much challenging of Morgan's steady stream of rationalizations, excuses, bullshit.

"It's time to explain to Morgan what will happen if she stops the program or is suspended from it," he said to me.

Morgan swung around. "What's he talking about, Mom?"

"Morgan, this program is our last hope," I said. "It's only three meetings a week, plus drug testing. Why can't you do that?"

"We don't need this program, Mom. We don't fit in here. You don't seriously want this program to be the most important and fulfilling thing in your life, do you?"

"I don't have a better plan," I said. "I've tried just hanging on and waiting for you to snap out of it."

"Snap out of it? Snap out of what?"

"Snap out of it. Stop all the bullshitting, and the sneaking out, and taking drugs, and trying to quit school."

"Why are you talking to me this way?" she cried. "You don't even sound like my mom."

"I am, though." I softened my tone. "We can't keep going like this, sweetie. It's too hard for us." Dean had explained to me that when parents change, the teens change in response to the parents changing. "I need you to stay in this program."

"I can't, Mom. I came in here tonight to say this is my last meeting."

"Then you are saying that you don't want to live at home anymore."

The room was silent. Jim stiffened next to me. On my other side, Bill put his hand on my knee.

Morgan gaped. Tears sprang to her eyes. "What are you saying, Mom!"

"You heard me, sweetie," I said. I was crying too. Jim took my hand. I shook him off. He was part of this. I had made him agree that we would do this, but in this moment I hated him for it.

"I want to live at home," she pleaded. "Don't you want me? Dad?"

"We want you to stay in the program, honey." Jim was twisting and untwisting his hands.

I don't think it could have felt worse if those in the program had handed me a belt and asked me to beat her with it. Or to beat myself with it: it was the same. It had always been the same. I was a tuning fork for her distress: I felt it in my backbone. I wanted to hurry her out the door, away from all these people who wanted me to throw my own child into the street. The air was charged and heavy, too heavy to breathe. Everybody in the circle was holding still, watching our family. Even Eric, a thirteen-year-old who sat looking at the floor most of the time, was watching intently.

"You are supposed to love me unconditionally, and this is a condition," she said mournfully. Her shoulders dropped. She looked at me, and I saw the sweet rise of her forehead, her baby forehead, the part of her I particularly loved because it had never changed.

"If you miss another meeting, then you have to find another place to live," I said. It was what I had been told to say.

"What about school? I love my classes, and I'm getting A's." Morgan was now going to a special program at McAteer High School in the city, one tailored for smart kids who had screwed up in other schools.

"Getting to school will be your problem."

I could see that rocked her. That was new. Everything had changed: instead of walking on eggs, trying to keep her from exercising the unspoken threat—running away—I had seized power. Living at home had become not a sentence, but a privilege. Something you earned. Even the right to go to school had become a privilege.

Morgan stared around the room. Then she picked up her backpack, and came over and hugged me. "I'm leaving now," she said. "Bye, Mom."

She ignored her father. She walked out, shutting the door softly behind her.

• • •

"YOU did the right thing," Dean said in a kindly tone to me as we all stared at the door. "It doesn't feel like it, but you did. This is good parenting."

I was looking at her empty chair. I knew he was right. It had become like a rule: good parenting felt like hell. If I felt like hell, I was probably doing my job.

WHEN I got home from the meeting, Morgan had staged a mock trashing of the kitchen–all the cabinet doors open, chairs up on the table, books scattered around, and my side of the bed messed up. Alarmed, I looked in her room, and to my surprise and relief, she was there. She was sitting up in bed, fully dressed, with her arms wrapped around her knees.

"Are you really going to throw me out if I stop the program?"

I felt chilled. "I don't feel as if I have any other options," I said.

She cried in her room for a long time after I left her room. When I tried to go back in, she asked me to please leave.

THE next day, she packed her suitcase and went off to stay with her friend Holly down the street.

TWO days later I drew up to Holly's house and honked: Morgan had an appointment at Kaiser, one I had scheduled months before. I wanted to make sure she kept this particular appointment, so I was driving her.

"How's it going at Holly's?" I asked when she got in the car.

"Okay." She was flipping through a copy of *Seventeen* magazine. She had not looked at me once.

I just drove. When I glanced in the rearview mirror, I saw a tired-looking woman with puffy eyes, wearing a shirt she'd worn the day before, and possibly the day before that.

In the Kaiser waiting room we sat tensely side by side, waiting for the doctor to call her in. A heavily pregnant girl came in and eased herself into a seat. She had rings on all her fingers, and wore a long black T-shirt that strained against her belly. She glanced over at us blankly, and then her eyes went to the clock on the wall.

Today five Norplant capsules would be implanted in Morgan's upper arm. They would release a low-level hormone, one that would keep pregnancy at bay for five years. By then Morgan would be twenty-one and safely in her senior year of college--we hoped.

There were condoms all over her room, and condoms worked, but only if you used them. Birth control is, after all, a form of tidiness, of having fun without making a mess. I had seen Morgan's bedroom. I couldn't really see her reaching for one in the height of passion, any more than I could see her stopping to hang up a crumpled dress as she was rushing off to school.

I knew it was a risky trade-off--girls on Norplant are less likely to use condoms, and condoms were the only known way besides abstinence to ward off AIDS. But I was more afraid of an early pregnancy derailing her life than I was of the more distant threat of AIDS.

Now Morgan was flipping through an issue of *People* magazine. "If I turn up pregnant, I'll definitely have the baby and give it up for adoption," she remarked, pausing to study a portrait of Princess Diana with her two sons.

I gave this only half my attention. "Luckily we don't even have to talk about that on top of everything else, because if you were pregnant the Norplant people would have called," I said. Norplant insertion is always preceded by a pregnancy test.

In my head, I had been ticking off a list of teenage problems: cutting class, failing grades, smoking, drinking, early sex, drugs, running away, stealing, pregnancy. We'd worked our way down the list, until the last three. Morgan had been busted for stealing a stick of butter in a Safeway on a ski trip ("I don't want you to think I'm taking this lightheartedly, Mom. I didn't need the butter. It was my fault"), and had liberated a twig deer from a parking lot in a prank over Christmas, but there had otherwise been no crime sprees. She had never run away, and she had never gotten pregnant.

Morgan's name was called, and she went in. I tried to settle down with my class notes–I had a new University of California Extension class to teach starting at seven o'clock, and it was already past six. But I couldn't concentrate. I kept wondering where Morgan slept at Holly's. On the couch?

"I have bad news and good news," I heard Morgan say when she came out. When I looked up, she was grinning. "The good news is you can get your hundred eighty dollars back for the Norplant kit. The bad news is I'm pregnant."

Alarm fluttered along my nerves, so that I found myself suddenly on my feet. Then my mind shut down. I glanced at the girl in black, who now sat biting her nails. I said to my exuberant daughter: "I have to teach a class in half an hour, and I don't want to discuss this right now." I could still hold this news at bay, if we didn't talk about it. When we started to talk about it, our lives would be forever changed.

Morgan would be a wonderful mother: I knew she would. But not yet. Please God, not yet.

"Still, we might as well return the Norplant kit to the pharmacy," she said, practically bouncing on her heels with excitement.

"I'm going to hang on to it," I said, shortly. I stuffed it in my purse. I was thinking, I'll have the Norplant insertion done at the same time as her abortion.

It was still light outside when we drove home, and a warm breeze came into the car. Indian summer. At a red light I said, "I was ex- actly your age–sixteen going on seventeen–when I got pregnant my- self."

"Wow, Mom, that is so weird."

"I was lucky to be able to get one of the first legal abortions," I said. I remembered a psychiatrist's clasped hands in a shadowy office, the pattern of leaves on the back of them as he urged me to describe how getting pregnant had made me suicidal. I told him I had considered jumping off the Golden Gate Bridge, though I'd done no such thing. I had thought instead of how much fun it would be to greet Johnny at the door when he came home with his brief-case, me with our baby in my arms. Johnny was the box boy at the grocery store around the corner. We spent years glued to each other in my narrow bed upstairs, exchanging hot kisses, but carefully not going all the way. My sister Mickey, eighteen, already had a baby in a crib at the end of her bed, and nobody talked about college for her.

At four or five A.M., Johnny would creep out of the house, and I would later go downstairs to breakfast as if nothing had happened. Once, over the waffles, fourteen-year-old Shannon jeered at me, calling everyone's attention to the fact that my nightgown was on in-side out.

One day late in my junior year, Adrian, Connie, Mickey, and I were talking in the living room, in the house Mother had bought from the Greeks next door, the house without a straight line in it anywhere.

We had dumped our schoolbooks on the floor, and were sitting around drinking Cokes in the light that came slanting down oddly from the misplaced skylight.

Connie was nineteen, and the oldest girl. She was just visiting for the day. She was all dressed up, as usual, wearing red stretch pants and a red top. "I'm pretty sure I'm pregnant," she said. She told us that when she told the news to Jack, the soldier she'd been seeing, he folded his arms across his skinny chest. "Prove it's mine," he said.

Mickey wore cutoff jeans and a cowboy shirt, tied at her slim waist. She sighed over the head of her baby daughter, Samantha, who was sleeping in her arms. She sighed. "I think I'm pregnant again."

I was sixteen. I squirmed on the faded green couch, crossing and uncrossing my legs. "I think I am, too," I said. Even as I said that, I remembered the exact moment when I had stood under the hot shower, idly counting the days and wondering why my period hadn't come yet. And felt as if the water had turned cold, when I realized I might be pregnant. Afterward, when I found out for sure I was, I felt as if I was walking down a road with everything I cared about behind me, receding in the distance.

Adrian sat for a few minutes digesting our news, twirling the can of Tab in her hands. "I'm not pregnant," she said. "In this family, I guess that's news."

I was confused. Connie and Mickey deserved to be pregnant–Mickey and Ken disappeared in his red Ford Fairlane for days on end, and Connie was nineteen and had moved to the city and worked in a bank. But Johnny and I had never actually done *it*.

Well, at least once, unable to stand it any longer, we had decided it would be all right to let him take it out and just sort of rest it near the right place, just for the excitement of it. Which is of course how I got pregnant.

Mickey's pregnancy was a false alarm. Connie moved back home, wore the same mountainous red-and-white muumuu every day, wouldn't let us turn up the heat, sent me to the store for Tab (always remembering to ask for the change), and made herself eggs and bacon "for the baby." Though she was the last one you would expect to become anybody's mother, she had a son, Jamie, a boy who looked exactly like her, with a round face and dark curly hair.

I had to tell my mother. She was asleep early one Saturday morning, her huge black purse gaping open on the floor, filled with tea cake that she'd wrapped in Saran Wrap and brought home for us. I sat on the wobbling stool at her vanity and waited. She opened her eyes.

"I'm pregnant, Mom," I said.

"Not you, too," she said. I had never seen her cry before.

"My legal abortion freed me up to take a baby-sitting job in Paris for a year, then go to San Francisco State," I said to Morgan now as the traffic surged forward. "When I had you at twenty-six, I was out of college, married, and ready. I'll make you an appointment with Dr. Jones."

Morgan's head jerked around. "You know I won't consider an abortion, Mom," she said. "I could never do anything like that to my baby."

She was bouncing around in her seat, staring out the window at the passing cars. Everything else was forgotten. Her excitement was obvious: she could hardly wait to get home and start making phone calls.

I dropped Morgan off at Holly's and went to meet the class I was teaching that evening, talking about tone and revision and query letters to a crowd of thirty strangers as if writing still mattered to me, when all I could think about was: Morgan is pregnant. When I got home from the class, at ten o'clock, I climbed the back stairs and found Jim setting a slice of melon on the floor for Mike. Mike had by now moved upstairs and become Jim's cat.

"She's pregnant," I said.

"Oh, my God," Jim said. "Oh, my God."

Distractedly, he picked the bowl up again and put it in the sink, with the melon still in it. The cat meowed.

"She'll have to have an abortion," I said.

"But will she agree to one?"

"I don't know." I had slumped down at the table and was using his Swiss army knife to carve the stick of butter on a plate. I did a long series of horizontal cuts, and then slashed back the other way. "I don't think so."

"The idea of her having Zack's baby is more than I can bear," Jim said. "We'll be linked to the little loser for life."

"And Morgan's life will be so different than we hoped. How can she go to college with a baby?"

THE next morning I snapped the leash on the dog and walked down to Holly's. Morgan came out on the red-painted step, and sat down with me when I shook my head at coming in.

"How are you feeling?"

"I got sick at school and had to come home early."

"Have you been throwing up in the mornings?"

"No. Did you throw up in the mornings?"

"No, I got headaches. Took Tylenol although I wasn't supposed to."

We sat in silence for a long time. Then I said, "I have some phone numbers for you."

"What numbers?" she said, taking the paper I pushed into her hand. Mascara stained the bottoms of her eyelids, so she looked like a linebacker. She'd been crying.

"People you can talk to. People who will help you if you decide you want an abortion."

"Okay, Mom."

It was warm on the steps, another Indian summer day, and tiny beads of sweat laced Morgan's brow, like a delicate filigree chain. I reached over to wipe it away with my hand.

"How's Zack?" I said. I had something I had to say to her, and I didn't want to say it.

"Last night I was watching Airheads, and I kept calling him during commercials to tell him what an asshole he was."

I put my arm around her. "What had he done?"

"He wouldn't come over. He had spent his bus money on cigarettes."

I took my arm away. It was too hot. "Would you call him for me, Mom, and tell him it doesn't mean anything when your girlfriend calls you during commercials and calls you an asshole?"

I smiled. "Call him yourself, kidlet."

"He's such a dork," she went on. "I'm going to be shackled to him for life. He'd fall apart if I broke up with him."

"What did he say when you told him you were pregnant?" I was hoping that Zack would insist she get an abortion.

"He says he'll support me in whatever I decide to do."

I digested that, and then said, "I bought some vitamins for you."

"Cool, Mom. I'll come over later to get them. I was going to come over and watch *Roseanne* with you tonight anyway."

I was going to have to say it. I watched several cars go by.

"Sweetie, you can't come home," I said. "That's part of the deal."

"Not at all? Not even for a visit?"

"No."

She didn't say anything. "I love you very much, and I want you to come home," I stumbled on. "But not if you won't go to meetings."

"Doesn't the fact that I'm pregnant make any difference to you?" she asked in a quiet voice.

"Yes," I said. It came out a croak. "It makes it a thousand times harder."

"I'm not a bad kid," Morgan said. "If you don't let me come home unconditionally, you can't be in any part of my life."

I said nothing.

"Bill's the one who won't let me come home, isn't he?"

"No," I said. "He has nothing to do with this." And he didn't. This was my doing.

We sat in miserable silence. I stared at a patch of crabgrass in a crack in Holly's sidewalk. A skateboarder clattered by, and Cody ran down to the sidewalk to bark at him. "Cody!" I yelled angrily, and he came back. I heard a noise, and looked over at Morgan. Her head was in her arms, and her back was shaking. I reached over and stroked the back of her neck.

"I feel as if you don't love me anymore," Morgan said. "I feel that you love Bill and the house and softball and walks to Noe Valley and Cody and your job but not me."

"Sweetie."

"I know it's not true, but that's how I feel," she went on in a torrent. "I never knew how I felt about Bill until now. Bill is a great guy, but I feel he replaced me. I never said to you, "Either he goes or I go, because I wouldn't do that to you. But he came, and I went."

I put my arms around her and kept my head down, so all I could see was the scratched red wood of the porch step through the tangle of our arms.

"When he came, I told myself that you loved us more, and it wouldn't interfere with our life. I always told myself that Mommy's allowed to have boyfriends in her life. Then everything changed, and nobody noticed it but me, or maybe nobody loved it the way it was but me, the way we used to dance in the kitchen, and go places in the car, just the three of us."

I tightened my grip on her. We were both crying, and she talked through her sobs. "The boyfriends you had before had always gone, and I had always stayed. But this time I got it that you and Bill were going to be together and you were just waiting for me to move out so you could be happy and alone."

"Morgan! Morgan, you know that's not—" I cried.

"Just let me talk, Mom, okay? Then I did move out, and you made me come home after a year of neglect, and now I'm miserable and in rehab, where I'm supposed to be fixed somehow so my parents can stand me. They hate the only person who really loves me and that's Zack, and I hardly ever get to see him, and if I can't have my mommy, then I want my baby."

"Sweetie, sweetie, sweetie," I murmured miserably. "Sweetie, I love you so much I am not even safe in the world. You and your brother are my breath, my heart, my everything." My heart thudded against my chest. My skin hurt.

"I know, Mom," she said, and pulled away slightly, so I had to relax my grip on her. "I know you love me. It's just that I can't *feel* it."

"How do you feel about him?" I asked. "About Bill, I mean."

"He's like Cody," she said. "He barks at everyone else and follows you around."

"I should have waited," I said miserably. "If I had known, I would have. I would have kept him as a boyfriend until you grew up."

Even as I said it, I didn't know if it was true.

• • •

AN hour later, when I got home, I realized I had lost track of Cody. Dropping my purse inside the door, I rushed back to the park and found him by the basketball court, a knot of worried strangers kneeling by him and examining the tag on his collar.

Later in the evening, Bill, who looked pale himself, with an uncharacteristic pimple on his chin, handed me back a draft of a column I had given him.

"This is about five different columns," he said gently.

I started to cry.

"It's not that bad!" he said, surprised. "Really, if you just move things around a little . . ."

"It's not the column," I said, standing up to press my wet face into his neck.

"I know," he said, hugging me tight. "I know what it is. Listen, take a mental health day. Rent movies. You like movies."

"I do like movies," I said, piteously.

But instead of going down to Blockbuster I reached for the phone. I needed to talk to other parents about wayward kids, how it felt, what they had tried, how it was going, what it was like for them to go in to watch their child sleep. I knew another mother of a troubled teen: Zack's mom, Wendy.

"Six months ago it would have upset me to have a daughter in a drug program," I told Wendy after we exchanged greetings. "Now I'm upset that she's not in one." As I spoke I watched several women coming back from their aerobics class at the rec center up the street, carrying mats and towels, heading for their cars. "I learned a long time ago that when you let yourself get into a power struggle with a teenager, everybody loses," Wendy said.

"I know that," I answered. But how could you not, when their future is at stake?

"When Zack was younger," Wendy went on, "we were encouraged to use Tough Love. They showed us all these videos," she said, and paused. "In one of them, the kid dies. *Dies.*"

Wendy said she and Jeff had taken Morgan and Zack to church with them, and then afterward to a park, where they handed out tuna sandwiches and sat on the grass in the sunshine, talking. "We tried to get them to see how difficult it would be to manage their lives with a tiny baby. I told them about that assignment they often give in family classes in school, forming the students into couples and having each couple take an egg with them everywhere for weeks, as if it were their baby."

"Did they listen?" I asked.

"They seemed to."

"What else did you say to them?"

"I told them they couldn't come and live with me."

"I told her they can't live with me, either," I put in hastily.

"I'm angry at Zack anyway," she continued. "I went to a lot of trouble to sign him up for computer classes at College of Marin and he quit after two days. Now he's just mooning around here again."

I thought, We've tossed out our pregnant sixteen-year-old daughter–isn't it time for the drug-taking son, the unemployed girl-impregnating boy to get the heave-ho, too?

As if she were reading my thoughts, Wendy said, "Maybe I should tell him that if he doesn't go to school we'll toss his butt out of here."

We were silent a moment. Then I said, "Ever notice how much we complain about our kids? I remember when my girlfriends and I used to get together and brag about the funny things they said."

"I know," Wendy said. "When I'm angry–and he can make me so angry!–I want to spill over with complaints. I feel myself go all hard inside, and that's what comes out when I talk about Zack. And yet sometimes even while I'm ticking off his faults, what I'm really thinking about is what a fine person he is–or will be, when he gets through this stage."

"I don't even take as many pictures of Morgan as I used to," I said. "It's as if she's getting all blurry, going out of focus."

"A friend once advised me to try on the point of view of a mother who has to take her child to chemotherapy," Wendy said. We were silent again, sobered. I could hear faintly, through the phone line, the sound of a door being slammed.

"There he goes," Wendy said. "God knows where."

In the afternoon Morgan called. "You once said you would give me a thousand dollars to quit smoking," she said. "Well, I quit, and I'm calling to ask if that's still the deal."

"That's great, sweetie," I said. "But we'd have to wait to see if you still don't smoke when you're not pregnant anymore."

"That's not fair, Mom," she said, automatically.

"How'd things go at the Daycare Center?" I asked about her easy program of classes at McAteer High.

"Everybody put signs on everybody else's back in media studies. It was fun."

As I listened I noticed that the pile of her clothes that Jim had washed and that I had left stacked on a table was gone. She must have been here while I was out with the dog. With a sick feeling, I wondered if she had watched from the intersection to see me leave.

The next day she called to ask if Zack's parents and we would each pay half the rent if she and Zack moved into the one-bedroom apartment in the basement below us that Jim was renting to a young accountant. She had even found out about getting on General Assistance, the city program that pays indigents $300 a month. "If you emancipate me, I can qualify for it," she said.

"No way, José," I said.

Later when I went to my desk, I found on my computer chair a handmade booklet made of stapled binder paper, complete with table of contents, entitled "My Fair Deal to Mom made by Morgan for Mommy to read."

"I will cooperate fully with the program for a trial period of thirty days. At the end of this period I will evaluate which aspects have been helpful and which have not. I will discontinue the things that did not help. During this period I will remain completely drug and alcohol free, excluding coffee and cigarettes. I will get to and from meetings on my own. I will be punctual. I will attend meetings with an open mind."

There was more. I read it and smiled, holding the stapled note. I had a large collection of such notes, going back years: Morgan trying to convince me to let her stay up and watch *Thirtysomething* with me; Morgan scrawling a note in crayon telling me that she was very sick and that Patrick had a fake cold. Morgan writing: "No Matter how horribley unfair & mean to me latley I still love you even though you haven't noticed the sacrafices I've made to observe your brutal disiplineary actions. I love you, Mom. Merry Christmas eve." Morgan explaining high school to me: "Part of going to the Winter Ball are dressing up, dinner, the dance itself, and the after party. Remove one of those aspects and you rob me of a valuable high school experience."

I loved her notes. I saw them as her desire to reach me, to try to get her reasonable arguments through my thick head.

"What's this about getting a job?" I called her up to ask.

"I'll work until November, and then I'll take the high school equivalency exam. I'll go to College of Marin and work part time, and then apply to Prescott College in Arizona. Zack and I are going to go there when we're both ready."

"And where will you be living?" I asked. "Here? Dad isn't willing to evict his tenant for you and Zack."

"No, a friend of mine is getting an apartment in San Rafael with her boyfriend. It has two bedrooms, and if Zack and I both moved in we would each pay two hundred a month and half of utilities and our groceries."

"All on your own?" I said.

"Yes, Mom. Even though there'll be a poster of Sid Vicious over the mantel instead of a Muir Beach print we'll act like adults. No alcohol or drugs will be allowed on the premises. We can have company, but it won't be a parentless place for people to crash or chill or anything like that."

"Sweetie, you are still only sixteen . . ."

"I'll be seventeen in two months. What I want from you is your recognition that this is a good idea."

"That's all?"

"And two hundred dollars a month for rent until I can pay it myself."

I waited. "I want a chance to earn back your trust," she said. "I want your friendship. And I want you to acknowledge the ways I have matured and the areas where I demonstrate good judgment."

If I agreed to all this, she'd live with me until the move. Otherwise, she warned, "other arrangements must be made."

I felt as if I was looking at myself. I knew what it was like to be in a hurry. I moved out in the middle of my senior year, got married, cooked hamburgers for my young husband before he went off to his lift truck job at the railroad. I was on my own in my senior year, as she wanted to be.

But I made my voice firm anyway. "You have to finish high school," I said. "That's my fair deal."

I was alarmed by all these brisk plans. I was tormented by images of Morgan with flyaway hair, holding a toddler by the hand and a baby at the breast, coming home from her job at Denny's.

I didn't even need the torments of my imagination. I had to look no further than my own family to know what lay in store for Morgan if she had a baby at sixteen. Mickey now had three grown kids, was divorced, and was still punching a clock, at almost fifty. Connie had had a baby before she got old enough to realize that being somebody's mother was never going to come naturally to her.

Morgan was back on the line again in the evening to say that she had called one of the numbers I'd given her, and the people at Kaiser had asked her to ask us what she could expect in the way of support for the baby.

"Nada," I said.

"Nothing?"

"Nothing."

This was not true, of course. Mentally, I'd already redecorated the porch as a nursery and had switched my classes to afternoons so I could baby-sit in the evenings while Morgan went to night school.

She called again at five to ask for the money from her September allowance.

"Your allowance is suspended," I said.

"You can't do that," she replied. "It's against the law."

"So arrest me," I said, and she hung up on me.

LATER when I went to make a phone call, I discovered she'd left a message on the phone. "Ha, ha ha. I'm watching *Roseanne* and you're not."

An hour later the phone rang again. "Aton and his girlfriend had a baby this summer," she said as soon as I picked up. "They don't have jobs and are living with his mother, but his girlfriend says she would have the baby again in a second."

"Please don't decide anything right now," I begged Morgan.

"I already have," she said. "I'm sure I want to keep the baby."

chapter 16

I happened too fast. I wasn't ready. Adrian had dropped by Dad's apartment and was alarmed at what she found. "He's been drinking, and his shirt is on backward. I can't leave him here by himself," she said when she called.

"I'll be right there," I told her. When I arrived, he was sitting on the bed. "Hi, Dad," I said.

"I was waiting for you," he answered. Adrian sat on the bed next to him, pouring tobacco from a red Prince Albert can into a square of white paper. "I'm trying to roll him a cigarette," she said. "He tried to smoke his pen."

I glanced at the countertop. His blood pressure pills lay in a black puddle on the kitchen table–he had spilled them out of the bottle, then splashed coffee on them.

He was wearing only boxer shorts and an old quilted brown jacket. "Nice outfit," I said to him. I took his jacket off, found a shirt in his closet and put it on him, inserting his arms into the sleeves as I used to do with Patrick.

"Where should we take him?" Adrian said.

"The VA hospital in the city, I guess," I said.

I buttoned up the shirt, and held out some pants Adrian had brought over.

He stepped into them and I hauled them up and stuffed his shirt into them.

"I guess I've crossed some sort of line," he said, watching as I slipped his belt through the loops and fastened it. As I stepped backward, he looked around the room, at his couch, his desk, the guitar that lay in a corner. "So this is it," he said. "They're coming to take Dad away, ha, ha."

My throat was tight. "One day my kids will come for me, too, Dad."

"I don't have kids," Adrian said.

"Looks as if my kids will have to come for Adrian, too," I told Dad, and she and I laughed. Then we stood.

"Maybe I could have a cigarette? Everybody gets a last cigarette," Dad said.

"Sure, Dad," Adrian said. She picked up the rollie she had made and it came apart, scattering tobacco to the rug. Tears were rolling down her face. "We should have done more pot in high school," she said. "At least we'd know how to roll a cigarette."

"I'll go to the store," I said.

I walked down the driveway to the Bell Market out on the main street. It was warm, the hills still golden from the summer drought. On the way, I passed a man playing ball with his two sons. When I came back, the man was stooped over the little one, about four, who was crying. He seemed to have run into the telephone pole and knocked his head. "Be strong for me," the man kept saying to the little boy. "Be strong for Daddy."

"Just pick him up," I wanted to yell, wincing at the scene. But the words echoed in my head as I went back up to Dad's floor. Be strong for Daddy.

Adrian had packed a plastic garbage bag with extra jeans and shirts, Dad's jacket, glasses, and pills. I got his keys, wallet, and a dented metal lamp from the table. I knew its base contained about thirteen thousand dollars in twenties and hundreds, all the money he had in the world, and I didn't want to leave it in the empty apartment.

It was his getaway money. He had saved it from his social security, which was five hundred dollars a month. It cost him many economies—he begged me to make arrangements to get cable for him, then canceled when he learned it would cost twenty-five dollars a month, even though he watched TV all day long. "That's less than a dollar a day, Dad," I had argued. "It's nothing."

"Nothing for you, maybe," he had huffed. When I pointed out that he had plenty of cash, he said, "I might need that. Might have to hit the road again."

I lit a Marlboro now, feeling the acrid smoke fill my mouth unpleasantly, and handed it to my father. He took it, and brought it to his face. Adrian grabbed it from him as he was about to put the lit end to his lips. "Whoa, Dad," she said. "Been smoking long?"

We both watched as he smoked the cigarette. I tried not to glance at my watch. I had another class to teach at seven. "When you're ready, Dad," Adrian said. Her eyelids were puffed up and red.

"What if I said I wasn't going?" he said.

I looked at Adrian.

"Dad," she said gently.

We waited. Somewhere in the building a door slammed. What would we do if he refused to go? I couldn't see us dragging him by force down the hallway, Dad grabbing onto lamps and couches as we passed and appealing for help to passing old ladies.

He got to his feet. I caught him as he swayed forward. "Hell, I'm ready," he said.

I looked his door behind us.

I helped him into the front seat of my car. He smiled at me as I fastened the seatbelt around him. "Smartest thing I ever did, having twins," he said.

At the VA hospital, we waited outside, listening, as the psychiatrist asked him questions in a loud voice. "What year is it?" He didn't know. "What month is it?" March, he thought. (It was September.) "What's three from a hundred?" He didn't know. "What were his daughters' names?" Adrian and Adair. "What did he think he was here for?" He wasn't sure.

"I WANT to talk to that girl," my mother said. She wore her purple fleece jacket and a fluorescent pink baseball hat. Bill and I had gone over on the ferry to meet mother for a bike ride, and the three of us were laboring over the hill behind San Quentin, the wind pushing us backward.

"Please don't call her, Mom," I said. "She's already upset."

"I don't care. Look what she's doing to you. Somebody has to straighten her out."

Bill came up behind me. He was trying to pedal slowly. "Adair," he said in a low voice.

I dropped behind Mother for a minute. "What?"

"Why not let her talk to Morgan?"

"No! She'll just make everything worse."

Bill stopped his bike and handed me the water bottle from it. I stopped, too. "Your daughter is on the lam from the drug program, banned from the house, and pregnant. How can your mother make it worse?"

"She'll hurt her feelings. She can be so abrupt." My mother had become fond of saying that when you reached a certain age, you got to say exactly what you thought.

"Somebody has to tell Morgan she can't do this."

"Well, I can't do it. I can't push her into having the abortion, or she'll blame me for it forever."

"She's Morgan's grandmother. She has a right."

I pedaled back up to where Mother had gotten off her bike and was walking it. "I'll give you her number," I said.

"I'm going to call her from the next gas station," Mother said. "I'll make that girl see reason." I threw a dark look at Bill. See what you've done?

We rode on, following the billowing purple of Mother's jacket. To my left I could see the outer perimeter of the prison. Tiny figures in blue jeans walked about. Beyond were the bay and the shining white of San Francisco on its hills. We crested the hill and turned west into the back streets of San Rafael. Mother coasted into a Chevron station. We braked behind her at the small half-shell phone booth at the edge of the station. "Do either of you have any change?" she asked. Bill dug in his shorts pocket and handed her all he had.

"What's the number?"

I stayed on my bike, inhaling the smell of gas and hot tar, while Mother dialed the number I dictated to her.

"Morgan? This is your grandmother. Don't you know you're hurting your mother?"

I jumped on my bike and pedaled out of earshot. Maybe my mother had a right to yell at Morgan, but I didn't have to listen to it. I went off across to the station to the air hose, and unscrewed the tiny black caps on my front and back tire. Might as well give the tires a shot of air.

As I inserted the nozzle, I could still hear bits of the conversation. "What about school?" Mother was saying. "You'll be raising that child all alone without a father. It'll ruin your life if you do this."

"Adair! Watch it!" Bill had ridden over on his bike. "You're going to pop that tire." I released the handle of the pump. My tire was rock hard and bulging.

By the time I got back, the conversation had ended. Mother snapped her helmet back on. "Well, she cried and cried," she said. "But she didn't hang up. Most people do, when they don't like what they're hearing, but she didn't."

"What did you say to her?" I said as evenly as I could.

"I just talked to her. Somebody had to."

The next day, Holly's mother, Judy, called me. I braced myself for yet another painful conversation.

"I have good news for you," she said.

I held my breath.

"Holly told me this morning that Morgan has decided to have an abortion. She's written a letter to the unborn baby. Holly says she's at peace with her decision."

"Thank you, thank you, thank you!" I told Judy over and over before hanging up the phone. I picked up the dog and danced him around the room. I ate a lemon Popsicle from the freezer. Then I called my mother.

"She's decided to have the abortion!" I exulted. "What on earth did you say to her?"

"I just told her you can't do this to yourself. I pointed out she'd be raising that baby all alone, and that she'd ruin her life."

MEANWHILE, I had been going across the bridge every day to visit Dad in the Hillhaven Convalescent Home. The doctors at the Veteran's Hospital had given him a diagnosis of senile dementia and sent him there. Each visit he was weaker and more confused, and my fear would grow as I crossed the bridge.

"Daly" said a hand-printed white slip outside the door of room 32. I looked in, and a Chinese man in a blue-speckled hospital gown stared at me from the cot nearest the door. The index card at the foot of his bed said, "Mr. Chung."

A pair of spindly feet stuck out from behind the orange curtain in the middle bed. I poked my head around, and there was Dad, flattened into the bed. A plastic tube snaked from beneath his hospital gown and over the side of the bed. His head had lolled to the side, and his mouth was open. I caught my breath. I leaned over him to check him for breathing, the way you do with a newborn. I put my hand on his shoulder and then almost drew in back in shock, feeling the sharp bone under the flimsy cloth.

"Dad?"

He opened his eyes and smiled a huge toothless grin, like a child who has spotted his mother. "Hi!" he said.

"How are you, Dad?"

"I'm doomed," he said. I could tell he liked the sound of that word. "Doomed," he said again.

I sat on a white plastic chair. I broke off pieces of a Kit Kat bar I had brought and gave it to him. The backs of his hands shone in the light from the fluorescent light overhead, the skin so loose and transparent it looked as if his hands were wrapped in Saran Wrap. Underneath the shine they were bloody and bruised from the IVs. Strips of white fabric bound his arms to the bed.

I had bought him a beautiful soft French shirt, white, with pockets, that I thought would look great with his jeans, and impress his visitors. It was surely by far the most expensive shirt he'd owned: eighty-four dollars on sale. I decided not to give it to him, though: he would drop ashes on it and burn holes in it.

Dad spoke again. "This job doesn't pay very much," he said, "but it's interesting."

"That's good, Dad," I said. I handed him another piece of the candy bar, putting it right into his hand so he'd know it was there. I ate a piece myself.

Voices came over the curtain from the third bed, where an old woman in a wheelchair was trying to comfort a man who had begun to shout in pain. "I feel as if you are my own son," she said. "I don't want you to die."

"I don't want to die either," the man managed to say. "But if I do, I want to go to heaven." They said the Twenty-third Psalm together, the man gasping out the words through his pain. "Yea, though I walk through the valley of the shadow of death . . ."

A nurse brought him a pain pill and the man gradually grew quieter.

I had brought Dad a portable radio from his apartment, with an opera CD Adrian had made for him already in it, and set it on the table.

As he lay there, I watched his hands twitch on the blanket and remembered that he had talked to me about the decline that comes before the end.

"I want to make a compact with you," he'd said. "Keep your eyes on the first joint of my little finger. If it moves at all, Dare, that will mean I was conscious of what was happening up until the time the doctor listened and shook his head."

I was looking now at the joint of his little finger as his hands twitched above the blanket, unconsciously rolling cigarettes papers. He grabbed my arms and kissed my wrist. I know he was licking the cigarette paper, but I still felt my heart lurch in my chest.

I sat on his bed, still watching.

He looked too comfortable lying there like a rag doll, letting others shift his limbs about for him.

"You're the one who told me that complete adaptation to environment is death, Dad," I wanted to protest. He hadn't said what to do, if I saw that finger moving. I added aloud, "What should I do, Dad? Do your Houdini thing."

Then my mouth fell open. He started trying to get up. He flailed out with his arm, hitting his hand on the stainless steel bar between us.

"Dad!" I said.

"Gotta take a leak," he muttered.

The bathroom in his room had an out of order sign on it, so I found an aide in the hall and waited outside while she attended to Dad.

Old people in wheelchairs lined the hall at irregular intervals. They stared at the floor, or slept, their necks bent. One woman with faded yellow hair sipped from a bottle of juice.

I remembered lying as a kid in my bottom bunk bed between sleep and waking in the dawn stillness of our old house in Lagunitas, then seeing Dad stride past my door on his way to the bathroom. He was naked, and looked like a god as he walked through the bands of light coming in from the windows, the golden light shining on his smooth chest and flat belly. The sight of him reassured me–it was just Dad, going for his early morning pee–and I closed my eyes and went back to sleep.

"All set," the aide said, coming to where I was standing against the wall. I went back in. Dad lay as before, but he smiled at me.

"Smoke, Dad?" I said.

"Sure."

I lit a Marlboro from a pack I had brought and handed it to him. He drew deeply, but as the smoke wafted over the curtain, Mr. Chung protested agitatedly in Chinese.

"There's no smoking in here," said the aide who came in to soothe Mr. Chung.

I got Dad into a wheelchair, an enterprise that involved getting a nurse, untangling the catheter, and finding him a second gown to cover his back. I caught a glimpse of his buttocks, collapsed and flaccid, and his penis, as smooth as a boy's. I was sweating under my blouse by the time we had bumped the wheelchair over the runner for the sliding glass door and were out in the little cement patio next to his room. Over the fence was the parking lot. We sat for a while. I noticed him squinting against the bright light bouncing off the cars, and I put my sunglasses on him. He looked like an old movie star with his cigarette and his shades.

Then I saw him looking around. "Where is this?" he asked.

"We're in Mill Valley."

"Mill Valley?"

"Mill Valley," I repeated. "You remember, where you drove your Buick off Panoramic and had to cable it back up."

"Oh, yeah." He laughed.

I looked around. Several other white plastic tables sat outside other cement patios. An old man in a plaid shirt sat far away from us, smoking.

"Are you his only child?" the woman in the nursing home office had asked, and then, astonished, had written down the names of his six other children. "He had to have that many to make sure that at least one would be talking to him when he grew old," I told her.

"And you're the one?" she said.

"Looks that way."

I had called everybody after Dad went into the nursing home. Aunt Frances, his sister, went to see him, and then called me. "I had no idea he was this bad," she said, sounding shaky. "I thought he was just drunk."

Connie up in Salt Lake City was laughing with a customer in her secondhand clothing shop when she picked up the phone. I told her Dad was in a home. "He probably won't ever get out of here," I said. "He doesn't even know where he is."

"I'm glad you told me," Connie said. "I really do appreciate it. But I feel nothing." She paused. "I can't mourn my dying father. Isn't that sad? Isn't that just pretty fucking sad?"

"I promised myself I'd never see him again after he came at Christmas," Shannon said when I reached him at his lumber company. I understood, but still I felt sad. Dad had said to me that one of the sorrows of his life was that he had let his own father's illness and death pass unheeded. "He didn't have his son to wave him off," he said. His father, Francis, had died alone in a downtown San Francisco hotel room at fifty-three.

"I could do that, could sit with a dying man," Robin said. "I did that with Joe." Joe was Mother's boyfriend when Robin was small, and he became her surrogate father. "But I'm not going to allow myself to be sucked into it."

"He's your father, but he's just another old drunk to me," Mother said. "Who's paying his nursing home bills, anyway?"

"Medicaid," I said. Dad was classed as an indigent.

"He got the kids he deserved," observed Bill, not unsympathetically, when I hung up the phone on the last call.

And he did. No one would come to see this floppy version of the dad who left them in a hot car while he went gambling, now and then bringing back silver dollars to buy himself more time, feeding them to us through the car window as if we were the slot machine.

Tenderhearted Adrian had come to see him several times after he went to the nursing home, but it was hard for her–she lived one hundred miles away.

He had nothing in the Bank of Good Will to make us want to help him anyway. We couldn't say, Sure he's being awful, but remember the time he drove you fifty miles to the dentist?

There was only me, the fifth child. I was not even the one who followed him around–that was my brother Sean. Not the one to whom he pointed out the prize egg hidden in his boot one Easter–that was Adrian.

I knew what I wanted from my family was unreasonable. I wanted them to come see him for my sake, because I needed them. Already the doctors were asking me questions. What did I want them to do if my father should take a turn for the worse? Did I want force-feeding? Would he sign a medical power of attorney, giving me the right to make his decisions for him?

I leaned forward and turned Dad's cigarette around, so he wouldn't smoke the lit end. "We're all alone, Dad," I said. "It's just you and me."

Dad's eyes were blank behind the sunglasses. "Where did you say we are, again?"

"Never mind," I said. "Doesn't matter."

I scraped my chair a little closer to him and brushed ashes off the front of his gown. "Can't take you anywhere," I said.

Then I heard a slapping sound, and there silhouetted against the sun, was Morgan, who had just jumped over the fence to the patio. She had a milkshake in her hand, and handed it to Dad.

"Here you go, Grandpa," she said. "Vanilla. Your favorite."

The tightness in my chest fell away. "Oh, sweetie," I said, getting up to hug her. "How did you get here?"

"I took the bus."

"All the way out here from the city?"

"Sure. I used to do it all the time, remember?"

"How did you hear about Grandpa?"

"Dad told me."

She sat down, straddling the chair. Her Smith snowboarding glasses were pushed back on her head. "I brought him lunch," she said. Retrieving a greasy white bundle from her backpack, she unwrapped a cheeseburger and handed half to Dad, who took it and put it on the table.

"I'm not sure he's up to that," I said.

"What's the matter with him?"

"His doctor says he has the 'dwindles,' " I said, taking the half of cheeseburger and biting into it. "Grandpa would love that word. Dwindling, like an unwatered geranium."

"So what are you saying? He doesn't have all his dogs on one leash?"

I grinned. "Sewing machine's out of thread."

"Skylight leaks a little?"

"A few feathers short of a whole duck."

We laughed, and even Dad smiled. "You hear that, Dad?" I said. "Your antenna's not picking up all the channels."

"Yeah," he said. "I'm fucked."

We laughed again, and then grew serious. For a minute, nobody said anything. I opened a packet of catsup with my teeth and squeezed some onto the cheeseburger, then took a bite.

"Judy told me about your decision," I said in a carefully neutral tone after I had swallowed.

"I don't want to talk about it," she said. "I'm here to see Grandpa."

"Okay." I was willing for her to be angry with me over this. When she was three, and stepped into the street, I'd set her on the sidewalk and yell in her face: "Never go in the street!" I didn't care if she cried: I was willing to have her upset with me, if it would help keep her out of the road.

We had been sitting in silence again, watching Dad smoke, when she suddenly said in a rush: "Grandma was mean to me. She told me that she would disown me if I did this, that no one in the family would ever talk to me again. She said I couldn't have a baby because I'd been on drugs."

"And that's what changed your mind?"

"Yes."

"She called you because she cares about you."

"I know, Mom."

Dad was looking at us through my dark glasses. A breeze fluttered the edge of the paper the hamburger had been wrapped in. "I looked up dementia, and it happens slowly, over years," I told Morgan, deliberately changing the subject. I didn't want to say anything that might change her mind again. "Grandpa must have galloping dementia. A week ago he was living on his own. Today they said he tried to smoke his plastic urinal."

"Let's take him for a wheelchair ride up to that old bar up the street, the Two A.M. Club," Morgan said. "You distract them, and I'll push him."

"I have a better idea," I said. My own words had been echoing in my head, and I suddenly had a hunch. "I'm going to check his chart." Morgan's arrival had filled me with a new crusading energy. I wasn't alone anymore. My family was here.

I left Dad with her while I went to the nurses station. "I need to see my dad's chart," I said. "Gene Daly, room 32."

His chart said, "Senile dementia, uncomplicated type."

Then I looked at his medications. "He's still taking that tranquilizer?" I asked the aide who waited for me to hand back the chart. It was Tranzene, the medicine I had myself urged Dad to keep taking, when it seemed to keep him from panicking and going on drinking binges.

The aide looked at the chart and shrugged. "The doctor wants him to have it. Mr. Daly was taking it before."

"Can I talk to the doctor?"

Another shrug. "He's only here on Friday mornings."

I went back outside, and together Morgan and I wheeled Dad back into his room. Lunch had arrived, and lay steaming on a plastic tray next to his bed. "Maybe you can get him to eat," said the aide who was feeding Mr. Chung. "He's been refusing his food."

"That shows he has a few marbles left," said Morgan, tasting the chicken soup and making a face.

"Put your arms around me, Grandpa," she said, bending over the wheelchair. "Mom and I want to put you back to bed."

We hoisted him in, getting his catheter wrapped around the wheelchair wheel and nearly toppling him into the bed of Mr. Chung.

I gave Dad the Joseph Conrad book he couldn't read and the glasses he couldn't read it with, and some Hershey's Kisses, the only kind we had exchanged so far in this life.

"Buy you lunch at the Book Depot," I said to Morgan.

She hesitated.

"Please, sweetie?"

"And a book?"

"And a book."

As we were leaving, I handed a bag to Morgan. "A shirt I bought for Dad. Thought maybe you could take it back and get something for yourself. Or wear it."

She was young enough to enjoy a soft white shirt.

"I should have known not to come between mother and daughter," Dad said enigmatically when we said good-bye to him.

"You haven't, Dad," I said. I felt like hugging them both. He wasn't coming between us. Morgan had not reckoned up whether her grandpa had been there for her, in deciding that she would be there for him. She was becoming an adult.

ADRIAN looked Tranzene up on the Internet. "It builds up in the bloodstream," she called to tell me, her voice full of outrage. "No one over sixty-five should take it."

It took me four calls to track down the doctor who attended the patients at the nursing home, a Dr. Adams. From the wheezing sound of his voice, I thought he might be one step from a nursing home himself.

"I want you to stop all of my dad's medications," I said. Adrian and I had conferred and decided this was the only way to tell if Dad's condition was being worsened by what he was taking.

"Young lady," he wheezed, "we can't do that."

"My father is dying," I said. "Slowly, day by day, as he lies in that bed. I want the medications stopped, now."

I COULD see for myself that Dad would never be able to return to his apartment. When Morgan had been at Holly's a week, I went over to see her. "Will you come with me after school to clean out Dad's place?" I asked Morgan.

"Grandpa's apartment? Why?"

"He doesn't need it anymore, and there's a list of people waiting for apartments in that building."

"I'm mad at you, Mom."

"I know you are," I said. "But will you help me?"

I let us in with the key I had taken out of Dad's jeans at the nursing home. It was ten o'clock in the morning. For a moment I just stood, looking around the shadowy room. "It smells in here," Morgan said, following me in with the two plastic laundry baskets we'd brought. It didn't of course. It was the absence of smells she was noticing. Like the absence of expression in my brother's face, when he had lived too long by himself in his mountain cabin.

"It's boiling, too," she added, crossing to slide open the aluminum window.

Adrian and I had forgotten to turn off the heat when we'd come to take him out of here, a month before. The little cactus in a plastic pot, the one I'd got him to remind him of the desert, sat on the desk, thriving.

I picked up the nearest thing to me, a blue shirt hanging over the back of his chair. It was dotted with cigarette burns, and I stuffed it into the Hefty bag. Then I put in the red can of Prince Albert tobacco, and a whole row of bottles of pills. I chose a couple of pairs of boxer shorts to take to the nursing home, and threw the rest in the Hefty bag. I threw in the remains of Meals On Wheels dinners on plastic trays, flyers from Bennett House, and a box of birdseed, left over from Dad's days with Luke, the parakeet. I threw in a dog leash, and a bowl that said "Fred" that I'd brought over when I noticed Fred eating out of an empty yellow plastic margarine dish.

When I crossed the room, Morgan was looking at his rows of books. There was the book on Neanderthals that he loved–he was delighted at how they hung their dead in bowers in the trees, garlanded with flowers. "And we call them primitive!" he'd exclaimed to me. Next to it the Ellman biography of James Joyce and the American Heritage dictionary we'd given him last Christmas. "It's now one of my treasures," he had told me.

I opened a drawer of his desk, facing the window, and there was a pistol lying on a stack of Dad's scrawled writings. I picked it up, felt the warm weight of it in my hand. It was handmade. I used to have one just like it at home. On our last visit before he went to the Mojave, Dad gave Adrian and me each one of the guns he had made on his homemade lathe.

I remember that moment in his truck, sitting on the cot next to Adrian. I had picked out my gun–he had made five in all–and was sighting down the barrel when Dad yelled, "Whoa!" He had been pouring hot water from a saucepan into cups of instant coffee, and slammed it down. He reached over and took it from me. "Got to watch you every minute," he had said. He checked the gun to make sure it was empty, and handed it back to me. As he did, he had a new look on his face.

I would have forgotten all about it, but Dad alluded to it often in his letters. He mentioned it so often that I finally got it: in that brief moment, letting him take the gun from me, I had allowed him to feel like a father.

Now even that memory was tinged with sadness. This gun I was holding had to be the one he'd used to shoot his dog. I had thrown my own away years ago, simply because it was a gun.

"Is that a pistol?" Morgan was looking over my shoulder.

"Grandpa gave me one like this," I told her. "But he wouldn't give me any bullets."

"He wanted to protect you," she offered.

"I guess," I said. I looked at her, reached out to flick a dust bunny off her sleeve. "I want to protect you, too," I said.

"We're not going to have a little moment here, are we, Mom?" she asked. She was smiling.

"But that's how you keep love going," I said. "You take care of people. I wish Bill and I had let Grandma help plan our wedding when she wanted to."

"How did Grandma get into this?"

"I should let her feel more like a mom. I should have let my dad, too. Maybe that's all he wanted--a chance now and then to feel like a dad, instead of like a failure."

"Are we talking about you, Mom? Do I not let you feel like a mom?"

"I wish you would come back and live at home. We can work it out somehow." I put the gun into the Hefty bag.

"Not if I have to stay in the drug program. I hate it there."

I went on cleaning. Jammed in one corner of the closet was Dad's guitar. I lifted it out. Dad had told me that when he took the guitar out of its worn case, Fred stood wagging his tail, seeming to want to lick the guitar. "I know he's only a dog," Dad had said, "and his approval shouldn't count, but when you've waited as long as I have, who cares? He's okay in my book."

I wouldn't think about the dog, not now.

I plucked each string in turn. "My-dog-has-fleas-and-how," I sang, each word a higher note. Morgan shook her head. "Keep the day job, Mom.

"Mom?"

"Yes?"

"You're crying." Morgan came over and put her arm around me. I leaned into her, letting my tears spill on her shoulder. Then patted her.

"I didn't know you liked him that much," she said.

"I don't. I do," I said confusedly. "He's my dad. They only come one to a customer."

I had got it all wrong. I had thought it would soothe me somehow to pack his things, the way it had always soothed me to be in Morgan's room when she was gone. But everything in this forlorn room was touched with sadness and loss. I wasn't reclaiming Dad: I was tossing his life into Hefty bags and listening to it rattle on its way down the garbage chute to the basement.

I stuck the guitar in one of the laundry baskets. It was six o'clock and growing dark outside. We had cleaned out about half the small apartment. I had turned off the heat, but I was choking on the to-bacco-scented air and on my own memories.

"We've done enough," I said to Morgan. "I have to go."

And we rushed out, leaving the laundry baskets full of his things.

THE day we had spent trying to empty Dad's apartment seemed to have thawed something between Morgan and me. She was still staying at Holly's, but I saw her often. One day I persuaded her to come with me to see Dean, the drug counselor, with the idea of making her see that she must return to the program. She came willingly enough to the meeting in his small office, which as always was air-conditioned to the freezing point. "Jesus, Dean, a person can get hypothermia in here," she said as we walked in.

Once there, she ticked off her reasons for not coming back: "I like the family therapy, but I feel like an impostor, pretending to be a drug addict like the other kids so we can reap the other benefits of the program."

She hated being labeled, hated the time the meetings took up, hated the jargon. "I have a different plan," she said. It included private therapy, more time at her Unitarian church youth group, "And I suppose I could go to AA meetings."

It made no more sense than some of her other plans to avoid

punishment, but she talked calmly and reasonably. This was a new side of her, and I longed to believe in it.

She was growing away from Zack. One night I had gone over to Holly's to highlight her hair while we watched *My Cousin Vinny* together. Once she paused the movie to call Zack. I heard her on the phone speaking to him sharply, finally saying, "You're so ridiculous. Let me talk to Rachel." I drew strength from this. Bad kids hung out with bad kids. Good kids found their company disturbing, and avoided them.

I could see it on Dean's face now—even he thought she sounded sensible. A drawing taped to the wall above us showed a stick figure of a girl crouched at a window. She had X's for eyes and was about to jump out the window. The scrawled caption said: "My worst day on heroin."

We decided, the three of us, that she would come home. I felt a giddiness rise in me. Yes!

When Morgan had gone out to get a Coke from the machine, Dean and I talked some more.

"Is she going to be all right?" I asked. "I know lots of kids with drug problems think they're not addicts."

"Yes, I think she is going to be all right," he said.

"Why did she do this? Get herself in so deep?"

Dean locked his hands behind his head and leaned back in his chair. "Her intelligence and charm make it more difficult for her. If you're very bright, as she is, you pick up the threads of truth to weave an explanation that's fairly plausible. You don't get as many people saying, Oh, you have a problem."

"How many of your kids stay off drugs after they've been through the program?" I asked, curious.

Dean shifted his feet, played with a pencil. "Very few," he confessed. "Everybody's partying. There's always somebody else to use or drink with, some reason why it's not the alcohol or the drugs that are the problem."

"Then how do you convince yourself that it's worth doing, holding all these meetings, making it your life work to try to help them?"

"We learn to measure our successes in small increments. Sometimes it's enough for a kid to come here to hear that drug counseling is available and he's an okay person."

"And the parents?"

"They learn to listen, and apologize, and express their feelings to their kids. They learn that being the parents of teens requires different skills than parenting a child. Adolescents are supposed to learn to separate, and part of that process is thinking they can take care of themselves when they can't. With a spirited kid like Morgan, they don't get it until they walk into a wall."

"And maybe not even then."

"And maybe not even then," Dean agreed. He reached for his jacket and got ready to walk me out. "The odd thing is, the fact that you're a good mom is part of the reason she's so wild."

"It is?"

"Sure. Morgan has the sense that a well-cared-for kid has—'the world is a safe place and I am loved.' Her bond with you gives her that. He allows her to take risks."

"A lot of people think this is about weak—not to say spineless—parenting."

Dean smiled. "I have a twenty-two-month-old boy at home," he said. "He wants to be held a lot. Everybody tells me, 'That's because you hold him.' I say, 'You try spending a whole day with him and not hold him.' "

THE next day Morgan came walking in the house after school, after two weeks away.

"There shouldn't be conditions to my living at home," she protested as she and Jim and I sat upstairs in his kitchen, talking about the conditions. Above her head was the exuberant poster of

her at age six, wearing a pink knit hat, spreading her arms wide, the
city skyline in back of her.

"We all have to meet certain conditions to live at home, or to hold
down a job, or to get along with other people," I said. "Learning that
is part of growing up." I stood up. "Come on," I said. "Let's go get
your suitcase."

T HE next day, on my usual visit to see Dad, I hopped over the fence
and cut through another patient's room, avoiding the depressing
stroll through the home itself.

There were two men in his room, one of them pushing a stretcher
with a green body bag on it. The back of his jacket said "Coroner."

I looked at Dad's bed. It was freshly made up, the white sheet
folded neatly back over the yellow blanket. I felt as if I was in a
movie, and the sound had suddenly cut out.

In the same instant, I saw that the curtain was drawn back on the
third bed, and it, too, was empty and made up. I realized the young
man who had been shouting and reciting the Twenty-third Psalm
must be the one in the green bag.

Where was Dad?

Mr. Chung was in his bed, following me with his eyes. I looked
out in the hall and saw the woman who was always there, collapsed
in her wheelchair, her pink scalp shining up at me.

"Bring June some lunch! Bring June some lunch!" a woman in
the room next door was calling.

I poked my head in. A woman in a disordered bed, with wild gray
hair, saw me. "Take me to another room!" she said imperiously.

"I can't," I said. "I can get an aide for you."

"Well, that just isn't good enough, is it?" the woman snapped.

When I went back to Dad's room, there he was in his wheelchair,
trying to back it out the bathroom door. I hurried over, grabbed
the chair, and backed him out. "Hi, Dad," I said over his shoulder,

looking forward to his surprise when he saw it was me, and not an aide. I had begun to look forward to seeing Dad smile when he saw me, the way Morgan used to as a baby when I came into the room.

His head whirled around.

"What the fuck am I doing here?" he said.

"Dad!" I said. "You're back!" I wanted to throw my arms around him. The sight of his face stopped me. He was pale and trembled with fury.

"What is this place? Whose clothes am I wearing?" he said, glancing down at a teal long-sleeved knit shirt that had belonged to Bill, and gray sweatpants I had bought him at Mervyn's.

"Who are all these other people here?" he went on without giving me time to answer. "What are they here for? Do you know them?"

"They're all here for different reasons," I said.

"I don't believe you."

"You don't believe me?" After the tender weeks of coming to see him and caring for him, I was stunned by his tone. I was getting angry. This dismayed me. How had I gone so quickly from elation at his recovery to this familiar irritation?

"I need money," he said. "I can't find my wallet."

I took my own wallet out of my purse and gave him what was in it. "There's sixty dollars," I said.

He took it and cast around for a place to put it, finally just leaving it in his lap. "I've been trying to work out why you would leave your father in such a place as this," he said. "I've been trying to puzzle it out all afternoon. Is it because you want to write a novel about this?"

"Dad, you were looney tunes."

He made a gesture as if to brush away my words. "Can you get me out of here? Can you do that, at least?"

"Yes," I said, "of course. Can you walk?"

"Hell, yes, I can walk," Dad said. I unbelted him from the wheelchair, then held out my hand. He took it and rose to his feet. He staggered, and then balanced himself. "Where's your car?"

I led him out down the hall. Several aides looked at us, and one of them took off down the hall. I took Dad out to the blazing parking lot, and helped him into the front seat of my car. "Sit tight," I said. "I'll just go tell them."

I went to the office and found Francine, the social worker at the home, a heavyset woman who hobbled around on a cane. "My dad is better!" I said. "He seems to be all right again. It must have been the Tranzene."

"Tranzene?"

"The baby tranquilizer he was on. We stopped it a week ago, and now he's in his right mind again. Who do I talk to about taking him home?"

"The doctor," the woman said, "but he's not here."

"Can't someone else do it?"

"I'm afraid not."

"But he's terrified. He doesn't want to stay here one more hour."

"If you take him now, he can't come back," Francine said. She blinked at me through glasses so thick her green eyes were wavy.

That rocked me. What if this was a temporary improvement? What would I do with him if he couldn't even go to the bathroom on his own?

I went back to the car. "I'm sorry, Dad," I said. "They said you can't leave yet." I made a move as if to open his door for him, but he didn't move. He just stared ahead. I got in the car and sat there too. Various people in white coats came out to the chain-link fence to squint at us.

"Just take me to the highway," Dad said. "I can hitchhike."

"I can't." I sat miserably.

"You can't?" he repeated.

"I'm sorry. You have to stay here until tomorrow."

I went around and held his door open. Dad stared at the wind-shield.

"Come on, Dad." I touched his shoulder.

He got out of the car, staggering slightly as he hit the pavement. When I took his arm he shook me off. I took him back to his room.

When I said good-bye, he turned his face to the wall. He just sat on the bed, his thin arms crossed over his chest. But his voice stopped me when I reached the threshold. "Please don't leave me here by myself," he said.

"I'm sorry, Dad. I have to."

That night he crossed four lanes of traffic in his hospital gown and holed up in the Kentucky Fried Chicken place. "Call the police," he told the teenager in a paper hat who gaped at him.

But when the police came, they called the nursing home. Dad took off again, and they caught up to him at a service station down the street. They delivered him, shaken and furious and scared, back to his room at the nursing home, and a beeper was attached to his ankle.

"We want permission to give him Haldol," Francine said when she called me.

"Haldol?"

"It's a strong tranquilizer."

"Are you kidding?" I said, enraged. "The last tranquilizer almost killed him!"

"His leaving showed terrible judgment," she said. "He needs to be calmed down."

"What would you do if you woke up after being drugged into insensibility and found you were being held against your will in a nursing home?"

"What else could I do?" Dad said when I arrived to find him barricaded in his room. He had ripped off a piece of his wheelchair and was brandishing it in the air, threatening to use it on anyone who came near him. "I can't just give up. I have to fight this."

I handed him his jacket. "Come on, Dad," I said. "Let's jump this dump."

I drove him to his apartment. I had paid his rent for him. Thin as a rock star, a diaper sticking out of his jeans, he held on to the countertop with one hand and scanned his ransacked apartment with a puzzled look. Two pink plastic laundry baskets lay where I had abandoned them, crammed with his things. The food from his shelves–oatmeal, Wheaties, instant coffee, saltines–was in cardboard boxes on the kitchen floor. "I didn't think you would ever be coming back," I explained weakly.

"I see," he had said shortly, his hair sticking up in furious tufts. "I guess I should be thankful you didn't throw out my chair." He was looking at the huge green chair he always sat in, the one I'd have thrown out in a minute if it had fit into the garbage chute.

I did what I could to restore order and left, feeling embarrassed and guilty. The evidence was right there for us both to see: I had given up on him too quickly.

THAT Friday I drove Morgan and Zack to Kaiser to keep a couple of appointments. She didn't tell me what they were, and I didn't ask. I understood that they wanted to do this hard thing on their own.

When she came home she said, "I need to borrow your car next Wednesday, because I'm going to Kaiser and have to be driven home afterward."

Bill and I were going to New York for a week. I wanted to be there with her, but she had not told me she had scheduled an abortion, not in so many words.

It seemed incredible to me that my daughter would be going through this and I would not be there. I remembered the intense loneliness I felt the morning I woke up in the hospital after my own "D and C." I was trying to read my paperback–a story about the Watts riots–and kept soaking it with my tears. A nurse came in. "Why are you crying?" she said.

"I don't know," I said truthfully. I was just trying to read. I read all morning, waiting for my release, and cried all morning. It was the end of a summer, and even when I was untying my paper gown in the back to admire my tan in the mirror, I was crying. When a bouquet in an ugly duck-shaped vase arrived, sent by Johnny's relieved mother, I cried harder.

Morgan had the abortion while I was in New York. She had arranged the whole thing by herself.

The Wednesday she was scheduled, I went to the Metropolitan Museum of Art. I took the audio tour, but in my distracted state was always looking at the wrong thing, staring at a painting while the recording described a curious stone sculpture. At the huge gift shop, I bought her a black Met baseball cap and a sweater pin shaped like a little chair.

Outside the museum, a clap of thunder made me look up. Black thunderclouds were massing like the storm over the building in *Ghostbusters*. Then the sky went dark, the taxis all snapped on their lights, and New Yorkers in Jill Sanders suits and Nikes smiled at one another in that expectant, hushed moment before the rain clattered down. A slim man went by wearing only red sweatpants and a black garbage bag worn provocatively low on his shoulder blades. I ducked into the doorway of a coffee shop and asked where the phone was.

"It's the stupidest thing I ever did," Morgan said testily, but there was a note of relief in her voice. She was talking about the abortion. She said that Zack had cried and stayed right in the room with her.

When I got back to my hotel, I switched on the TV and watched *Oprah*. A mother who had lost her seventeen-year-old daughter in a car crash walked forward to meet another seventeen-year-old, in whose chest her daughter's heart was beating. I sat on the big double bed and cried as hard as I ever had. It was as if I was the mother whose daughter had died, and at the same time I was the mother whose daughter had been saved.

chapter 18

DAD stayed furious, but a few days later I made up my mind to go see him anyway.

"I was just about to go on a toot," Dad said on the phone when I called him up.

"Oh, that's too bad," I said. "I'll come some other time."

"I didn't say I was going to go on a toot for sure," he said hastily. "There's still time, if you want to come over."

"**H**EY, Pop," I called out when I banged in his door.

"Hey, yourself." The top of his gray head was just visible over the rim of the green chair.

I had two small zebra finches in a cage, plus a book called *Zebra Finches*.

"They're just trying you out," I said. "If they don't like you, I'll take them back."

Dad lifted an eyebrow. "What am I going to do with those fucking birds?" he said. But he didn't say to take them back.

His caretaker, Anna, was there, a Dominican woman with ebony skin who came in a few times a week to do whatever needed doing. I had arranged for her through the county. Now she was dumping half-eaten Meals On Wheels cartons into the garbage.

"Say hello to my little West Indian bombshell," Dad said. "She's been trying to get me into bed."

Anna rolled her eyes. "Your father he say anything," she said. "He no listen to me, I no listen to him anymore."

"That's not true. I do listen to her. She has told me, using what she calls English, that I should switch to Pall Malls. And what am I smoking?" He held up a machine-made cigarette.

"I could never get him to smoke tailor-mades," I said to Anna admiringly as I swept junk mail and clothes off the couch and sat down.

Dad leaned toward me, his face bristly with white stubble. "She wants to marry me," he confided.

"Come again?" I reached out and brushed some fallen ash from his shirt, already sporting several burn holes. Was he still looney tunes?

"For her green card. She wants me to marry her so she'll have American citizenship."

"That's great, Dad. I'll have a new mommy."

"Joke all you want. You're the one who left me alone with her all these weeks."

"You were pissed at me."

"Yeah."

"Does she do a good job cleaning?" I asked.

"Worst I ever saw, outside of myself."

I looked around the room, which was indeed, as dirty and cluttered as ever, though the top surfaces seemed marginally cleaner. The green chair in the corner that usually held a stack of clothes had a single T-shirt on it.

"I have your getaway money here," I said, getting the old lamp he kept his stash in out of my bag and handing it to him.

"Put it on the couch," he said, indicating the place with a glance.

"I'm sorry I threw out your clothes, Dad," I forced myself to say. "I'll take you shopping." Here he was, healthy again, his green eyes bright. I remembered with shame that day in his apartment, throwing out the few things he had.

"What's a few pairs of boxer shorts?" he said, to my surprise. "That Tranzene was turning me into a statue. You and your sister saved my life."

"Well, thanks, Dad," I said, surprised again. I wanted to reach over and touch his dry old hand.

"I will repay that debt in my own time, in my own way."

"You don't owe us, Dad," I said. "We're your family."

"That's right, you are," he said, with his old crafty look. "It was nothing more than your filial duty." He moved his hand away, as if sensing my impulse.

He rolled a cigarette on his knee, settling in for a long talk. "Anna's been shopping for me. Last time I went myself, I got a package of diabetic pancake mix, thinking it was cookies, and a little plastic bag I thought was toffee, but turned out to be bubble gum."

I was laughing.

"Know what?" he added.

"What?"

"I'm gonna turn over a new leaf. For one, I am gonna work at mingling more than I have–might even smile at my neighbors," he said. He smiled now at me, his lips pressed together, his face creasing around them. Dad's smiles were enough to scare you out of a year's growth, but I didn't tell him that.

"How is your hellion?"

"Pretty good." I saw no reason to tell him about the abortion or the drugs. That was in the past. "She's stopped sneaking out and is doing well in school. I'm starting to feel like a good mom again."

"Not enough voting precincts have called in, so there's no way for you to know yet what kind of mom you are," Dad retorted. He lit a Pall Mall, though he already had one smoldering in the ashtray.

I was sorting through his mail, stuffing the bills in my purse. "You know," he said, "somehow, in the course of the last ten years or so, I've made restitution for the wrongs I did you–nobody else, just you. You know it and I know it, simply because it's unlike me, for all my faults, to take credit for what I haven't done." '

"How do you mean, Dad?" I asked. The birds were screeching in their cage, and I could hardly hear him. I leaned toward him.

"You wanted some kind of father, I fulfilled that contract. You now have some kind of father."

I sat looking at him. Anna was noisily sloshing a mop back and forth on the kitchen floor. Dad sat there, covered with ashes, gazing at me. He was only some kind of father, true enough, but that was more than I had expected to get. "Yes, Dad," I said. "I do."

"Maybe you needed exactly the kind of father I am to hone your own natural skills," he went on. "Sort of like the speck of sand that irritates the oyster–and produces the pearl."

"Are you saying I'm a pearl?"

"If I say yes, will you take these fucking birds home with you?"

chapter 19

AFTER the abortion, Morgan lay around with her pain pills and the sanitary pads she made her dad buy her, complaining that her ovaries hurt. Zack came over and drew pictures on her Macintosh while she watched TV. I left them alone. I felt shy around them, removed. They had been through something together.

"I want to switch to Zack's school," she insisted one day as she banged through the cupboards looking for something to eat.

"He goes to continuation school," I pointed out. My stomach clenched. Here we go again. "It's for kids who got kicked out of regular school. You're doing fine in yours."

"I hate it there, and I don't have any friends," she yelled at me. "I'm going to change to Zack's school."

"Okay. I'll just ring the principal there and tell him what school district we live in." A San Francisco resident can't enroll in a Marin school.

"I want to be with Zack."

"Why? Why would you want to be with someone like him?"

That night I couldn't sleep. She was going to get older and older, but she was never going to grow up. She wouldn't be anybody special. She would just be Morgan.

THE next day was Saturday. On our early morning walk, I bought her a fish-eye mirror in the shape of a sunburst at a garage sale, though her room was already crammed with junk I had brought home for her from our Saturday walks.

When we got home, the dog pausing expectantly as always on the second step to have his leash removed, there was a sign taped to our door.

HAVE YOU HEARD ABOUT THIS GREAT LITTLE PLACE CALLED MORGAN'S DINING ROOM? UPSTAIRS! GOOD SERVICE!

Though we'd had bagels at the coffee place, Bill and I dropped our backpack on the couch and hurried upstairs. The dining room was laid with place mats, silverware, napkins, and there was fresh-squeezed orange juice. Morgan was lighting candles in the middle of the table. She wore several things--a creamy dress, a filmy half-slip over it, and a pretty blue napkin wound around her head that picked up the intense blue of Jim's dining room walls.

We took our places at the table. Jim was already sitting down, quietly pushing his white china plates back from the edge of the table. Patrick sat in a chair, looking sleepy. I hoped he'd order off the menu, and tried to catch his eye, but he had already got himself a bowl of Cheerios. "I can't eat Morgan's cooking," he said.

"You're just mad because Mom loves me more," Morgan informed him. "Isn't that right, Mom?"

"Yes, that's right," I said. I looked at Patrick. "I love her more."

"She only puts up with you because the law says she has to," Morgan put in.

"Whatever," Patrick said, eating his cereal. "At least I'm not fat."

I threw him a pleading look, and he stopped. We consulted our handwritten menus–which offered fresh fruit, apple cinnamon muffins, toast, and eggs.

"Oh, miss?" Bill said.

"Yes?" Morgan waited with her pad.

"I'm leaning toward the scrambled eggs. But I'm wondering if I can get some salsa with that?"

"Of course," our waitress said, writing it down with a purple marker.

"Mom, I mean, ma'am? What would you like?"

"I'll take two eggs–"

"Poached, and on top of the toast, with blackberry jam."

"Perfect," I said.

We all read the paper for a while while Morgan banged pots around in the kitchen. Jim cast longing glances in that direction, but I shook my head at him. "Let her do it," I whispered.

When she came back, I leaned up to say quietly in her ear, "I'm sorry about yesterday."

"That's all right, Mom," she said, and then to my surprise, added, "You're right. Zack is a loser. I don't know why I was saying all that stuff anyway. I was just in a bad mood. Maybe I'm getting my period."

She moved off to hand some toast to Bill, while I followed her with my eyes, too surprised to chew. The Morgan we'd been living with did not take responsibility for her moods. If she felt cranky, she'd tell us she hated her life, or that her allowance was too small.

As we talked, Zack stomped around overhead–he and Morgan had slept in Jim's attic after staying up late to watch movies up there. Morgan set the plate of toast down and left the room. "Come on down, honey!" we heard her calling from the bottom of the stairs. "Everybody's waiting for you!" Zack mumbled something we couldn't hear.

"I'd just as soon throw the little fucker out the window," Bill said. He buttered a piece of toast so hard that it broke. "Tell me again why we let him be here, after he gave her drugs?"

"To keep her from going to Marin to be with him," I said, though it was something I often wondered about myself.

"He never says a word to me," Jim said. "He sat there yesterday with his cereal in front of him and did without milk until Morgan came in and got it for him."

When Zack came down, he was wearing a white shirt and a skinny tie knotted all wrong. "He has a job at Baskin-Robbins," Morgan announced for him. Then off he went without breakfast to catch the bus, a newly minted captain of industry, while we all looked at each other.

"I give him one day," Bill said.

"Till Wednesday," Jim said.

"He borrowed thirty dollars from his dad so he could buy a special kit to beat their drug test," Morgan commented.

"Did he tell his dad what it was for?"

"No. He said it was to buy shoes for his new job."

As much as I wanted to like Zack, as much as I genuinely did like his mother, I couldn't help feeling it all over again practically every few minutes: the relief at not being shackled to him for life by a baby. But I put down my napkin and hurried downstairs, catching up with him on the steps outside. "Let me help you with that tie," I said, and tied it for him. "Good luck," I said, meaning it.

On a Tuesday in early October, I knocked on her door. "Morgan! Time for school!"

"Okay, Mom!" came a cheerful voice.

Okay, Mom!?

I opened the door. She smiled at me. "Morning, Mom."

Morning, Mom?

On Wednesday she asked if she could watch *Melrose Place* with somebody named Javier. "No, sweetie," I said. "It's a school night."

"Okay, Mom."

Huh? A year ago she would have raged at me until my eardrums bled. Two years ago she would simply have gone anyway, thrusting one leg then another through her bedroom window and walking off into the night.

"It's amazing," I said to Bill. "She's like her old self." I remembered what I had read, that teenage girls often "go into it" on about March of the seventh grade, and "come out of it" in their senior year of high school.

"She's off drugs," he said. "That's got to make a big difference." Then, seeing my face, he hugged me. "What a relief," he said. Then he added, "You know, I think the abortion changed her."

"What do you mean?"

"Even I could see how hard that was for her. Yet she went through it like an adult, taking care of everything herself, making decisions that had to be made. I think it helped her grow up."

As Morgan began to handle problems more maturely, I did, too. One day she said, "Do you want me to clean my room up a little better, Mom?"

"No, it's fine," I said. And, surprisingly, it was. That soft mass of squashed articles washing over the floor used to scare me–it seemed to reflect her inner turmoil and depression. Now I just moved the bowl of SpaghettiOs with the half-eaten bagel in it aside with my foot so no one would trip over it, then looked up at the little paper stars hanging from her light fixture, and batted at them in a friendly way. I found the SpaghettiOs bowl in the sink later and smiled to myself.

I felt as if my real self, like hers, was beginning to come back from wherever it had gone. When she was late to school because she overslept, I said nothing. Getting to school on time was her problem. I remembered to hug her.

I became the way I'd been when she was a child–easygoing, humorous. I found her and a new boyfriend from school in my bathroom, coloring each other's hair and the sink an unearthly crimson hue out of a jar labeled Manic Panic Red. One of them would lean over the sink while the other dug into the jar with a piece of Saran

Wrap and then scrape it along a strand of hair. I just observed, "Hey, Morgan-Porgan. You dyed your hair to match your personality!"

Unfortunately, I had slid back to being my casual, I-can-wing-this kind of mom self where carrying out rules was concerned, too. We never did arrange therapist appointments, and Morgan never went back to AA. I gave her vitamins and waited outside the bathroom while she peed into the plastic drug-test cups I got from Koffman and dropped off at Kaiser once a week. They all came back negative.

I realized she might still have problems down the road, but so might we all. For now she seemed fine, and when she seemed fine I relaxed, like an alarmed mother bear who sinks back into her snooze in the warm clearing, convinced her cubs are all right after all. Maybe that wasn't the thing to do, but that's what I did. I had lived most of my life as an easygoing person, and given the least chance, that's what I came back to. Motherhood had changed my life, but not my nature.

She didn't stop hating her new school, but she dragged herself there from eight to two, never missing a day. At the end of October, she got four A's on her quarter grades–in math, English, creative writing, and government. I wrote "Wow!" across her grade report in yellow highlighter and slipped her $100.

As the days passed, and the shouting, the lying, the sneaking out failed to come back, I realized the moody, loud teenage hellchild I had harbored for four long years was gone. In her place was a cheerful, funny, likable creature who still walked around in the hellchild's ripped clothes. I found myself constantly looking for her, making excuses to talk to her or to hug her. She seemed to seek me out constantly, too, asking me not to go out Sunday night, or to see a movie with her. She called me from school asking me to come over and go to her classes with her. It was like a reunion between two people who hadn't seen each other for a long time.

Bill still watched her nervously one night when she was cooking us a vegetarian casserole, using four saucepans and splattering sauce all over the stove. I could see him trying not to say anything. Then I watched him give in: "Sweetie, you can't use that metal spatula on the nonstick pan, it'll scratch it." She stiffened and kept her eyes on the pan, taking the new spatula without looking at him. As always, he went to her room an hour later, too late, to apologize, tapping softly on her door. She steeled herself to the apology as she had to the original remark. But there were hopeful signs there, too. When he wanted to give her a message, he asked her to come to the phone, instead of relaying the message through me.

They were polite to each other and sometimes joked around, and that was going to have to be enough. It was one of the things I had learned: this wasn't my own personal Magic Kingdom. I couldn't control everything. They would have to work it out between themselves, how to be with each other despite the difference in their temperaments.

One Thursday I drove Morgan back for another Norplant appointment. I took the kit from my dresser drawer to take with us.

"I'm not sure I want to do this," she said all the way there, with the kit on her lap.

I ignored that as standard mother torturing. We were back in the same waiting room and once again I waited with her, reading my papers, until the nurse came for her. I couldn't concentrate, and watched the clock on the wall jerk forward in three-minute increments.

She came out with a huge white bandage around her arm. When it came off, I pressed them in wonder, the five little bulges on her upper arm that would keep babies at bay for five years.

One Saturday she and I went out for breakfast at Spaghetti Western down on lower Haight Street. As she studied the menu I regarded her. She wore a thrift-store ball gown and red bowling shoes. She was talking about going to College of Marin the next year, then transferring to UC Berkeley as a junior. She was a product of public schools and so had almost no concept of spelling or grammar.

"I have just two words for you: Bonehead English," I said.

She said, "That's three words."

"I rest my case."

One of my friends had started having some problems with her daughter, who was turning fourteen and already having sex with her boyfriend at his house while his mother worked. I knew Morgan had talked to my friend at a softball game we had all attended–I had seen them whispering together in the stands, Morgan talking a mile a minute. "What did you say?" I asked her.

"I said, you're not going to stop her from having sex. You don't have that much power."

"Are you saying that nothing would have worked with you?"

"I'm saying some mistakes kids have to make. Parents can't prevent you from making the mistakes–they can only make sure you learn from them. You couldn't have stopped me from going out. But your trying to stop me showed me how much you loved me, even though you were irrational."

I felt myself bristling at that. Irrational? Me? I opened my mouth to protest, then instead took a sip of coffee. The lessons had been hard, but I had learned a thing or two.

"So what should my friend say to her daughter?" I leaned forward, moving my plate away, intent on Morgan's face.

"She should do what you did–say I'm worried about this, and I wish you could talk to me about it, but I understand that you're a teenager and that you don't feel comfortable talking to me about everything."

"She shouldn't ground her?"

"No. It won't change her behavior. It'll just keep her around the house for a while."

"I made a few mistakes with you," I said.

Morgan was ladling sugar into her coffee, teaspoon after teaspoon. The din of conversation from the other tables made me have to lean toward her to hear. "Parents get to make them, too," she said. Our food had arrived, and she stuck half of a pancake in her mouth. "It's trying that sends the message. I knew a lot of kids whose parents had given up on them. When you grounded me, and did all the other

things you did, like those stupid locks on the doors, I figured if someone loved me that much, I must be worth something, so I should
make some effort to preserve myself."

Eight months later, when I heard "Pomp and Circumstance" start
playing at the McAteer High School graduation, I burst into tears. I
couldn't make out my own daughter among the students in black
gowns and caps down there, but I knew she was there. I sat at the
Civic Auditorium between Bill and Jim. Patrick sat beside Bill. Jim
held a bouquet of flowers through the whole ceremony, and had in
his pocket a gas credit card for her. I had already given her a car, an
old red Nissan Z I had bought from my friend Donna.

I watched from the balcony as she tripped across the stage when
they called her name. She had written something on her cap in yellow chalk. I couldn't make it out, but later I saw it up close: "Hi
Mom!"

That kid.

ONCE during her freshman year at College of Marin, Morgan was
coming home across the bay on the ferry, exulting in the feel of the
spray on her face, when she ducked inside to write me a note on her
napkin.

> Dear Mom,
> I am finding myself overwhelmed with many opportunities. I
> feel completely empowered to pursue any end I choose and young
> enough to enjoy the chase. Mom, I can do anything I want and
> finally I want the right things. I can't tell you how good that feels.
> Thank you for seeing me through it. I couldn't have done it with-
> out you.
> I love you, Mom.

epilogue

*In June 2000, at age twenty-one, Morgan graduated
with a degree in philosophy from the University
of California, Santa Cruz.*

ADAIR LARA is an award-winning newspaper columnist whose col-
umn appears twice weekly in the *San Francisco Chronicle*. She is
the author of five books, including *Welcome to Earth, Mom; Slowing
Down in a Speeded-Up World*; and her latest, *The Best of Adair Lara*.
Her articles and essays have appeared in *Redbook, Ladies' Home
Journal, Parenting, Good Housekeeping, Reader's Digest*, and other
national publications. She lives in San Francisco; her daughter
Morgan has just graduated from the University of California at
Santa Cruz.